BRUCE
CONVERSATIONS
THE LIFE AND LEGACY OF A LEGEND

BY FIAZ RAFIQ

BRUCE LEE
CONVERSATIONS
THE LIFE AND LEGACY OF A LEGEND

BY FIAZ RAFIQ

DEDICATION

This book is dedicated to the one and only Bruce Lee, who continues to
inspire people from all walks of life. Secondly, I would like to dedicate
this book to John Little, who did more than anyone to propagate the life
and philosophy of Bruce Lee, and opened the eyes of many people by
promoting the late legend as a multifaceted individual.

First published in hardback in November 2009
First published in paperback in November 2010

ISBN: 978-0-9562586-3-2

Designer: Martin Jennings
Editors: John O'Regan and Fiaz Rafiq
Published by: HNL Publishing Ltd
A division of HNL Media Group
Suite 185, 6 Wilmslow Road, Manchester, M14 5TP,
United Kingdom

Distributed by:

USA/CANADA	UK
Midpoint Trade Books	PGUK 8 The Arena,
27 West 20th Street, Suite 1102,	Mollison Avenue, Enfield,
NEW YORK NY 10011	LONDON EN3 7NJ

ACKNOWLEDGMENTS

I would like to thank the various individuals who have played an integral role in the success I enjoy today.

A big thank you must go to the following for their friendship and support: Diana Lee Inosanto, Bob Sykes, Royce Gracie, Michael Bisping, Dorian Yates, Seyfi Shevket, Abdul J. Tarafdar, Ron Balicki, Ronnie Green, Tony Sykes, John Dawson, Kevin Morris, Sandy Holt, Karl Tanswell, Peter Consterdine, Andy Farrell, Darron Chadwick and Jamie Clubb.

A big thank you to all the staff at *M.A.I.* and *Impact* magazines: Moira, Martin, Vicky, Neal, John, Roy, and especially *M.A.I.* editor and friend Bob Sykes. *M.A.I.* and *Impact* have played a key role in my success, without them I would have never accomplished everything I set out to. A big thank you to the editor of this book John O'Regan. Also thanks to Jesse Glover, Lamar Davis, Kevin Seaman, Mike Cogan, Rorion Gracie, Andy Staton, Mike Ellis, Joe Egan, Mike Leeder and Bey Logan.

A special thank you to Carla Seaton for arranging the Sugar Ray Leonard interview.

Thanks to Joel Snape at *Men's Fitness*, Steven Beale at *FHM*, Tris Dixon at *Boxing News/Fighting Fit*, Kevin Francis at *The Daily Star*, Mark Gilbert at *The Sun*, Alastair Good at *The Daily Telegraph*, Paolo Bandini at *The Guardian*, Elliot Worsell and Anthony Evans of the UFC. I must also take this opportunity to thank some of the agents and managers who made things happen. Last but not least, thank you to all those personalities I have had the pleasure of interviewing, not only those pertinent to my books, but for the magazines and the documentary. All those I've interviewed over the years, from Bruce Lee's co-stars, friends and students, professional Boxers and bodybuilders, MMA fighters, Hollywood actors and directors; you inspire me to continue to pursue what I always desired. This has enriched my life. Thank you!

CONTENTS

THE LEGACY

CHAPTER FOUR: THE BOXING LEGACY

CHAPTER FIVE: THE BODYBUILDING LEGACY

CHAPTER SIX: THE MMA LEGACY

CHAPTER SEVEN: THE MOVIE LEGACY

FOREWORD

When Fiaz first approached me about writing a foreword about a man I grew up calling 'Uncle' Bruce, an honorary relative in the family that I was named after at birth - Diana Lee - I wasn't sure what to expect. This man I only knew through the eyes of a small child. In my youth, I was oblivious to the fact that Uncle Bruce was becoming a famous star, had numerous martial arts students and associates, traveled around the world and was passionate about philosophy. I did know that he and Linda had the coolest kids to play with, Brandon and Shannon. The bliss of youth!

Then life took a different direction in my family. What became apparent to me at the tender age of seven was that Uncle Bruce was an important figure in my father's (Dan Inosanto) life and that upon his death, he would forever change the course of my father's future. What little did I know how Uncle Bruce would also change the lives of millions of people around the world!

That's what Fiaz Rafiq's book gives us (the reader) an insight to - a chronological 'train ride' into the life journey of a very special man, and how the world's journey continues without him but his spirit is ever so present. Through Bruce Lee: Conversations, we witness the memories of this intelligent, persuasive, muscular, small-framed man - with a great Chinese accent I might add - who created a vision for the future that would change modern martial arts history. We learn how this man broke down the barriers of racism, kicked his way through the walls of Hollywood discrimination and bridged the worlds of 'East meets West'. Even today, his influence, popularity and fan base still continues to grow.

After reading the diverse collection of interviews that Fiaz managed to put together (no small feat), I must say I was absorbed. There were people I heard about as my father raised me. They were people that I personally knew growing up but I didn't completely have 'all the dots connected' to their relationship with Uncle Bruce. They were people I read about and even worked with in the entertainment industry. And then, there were the tremendous athletes I have admired from a far but had no idea how a man I called 'Uncle' Bruce would leave his inspirational 'fingerprints' on the minds, bodies and souls of so many people. Some of the people highlighted may be controversial; some may be from unrelated fields, yet there is a common thread that flows through the fabric of what these people share together about one of world's most influential icons, and they call him 'Bruce Lee'.

- Diana Lee Inosanto

PREFACE

Bruce Lee belongs among the top echelon of influential stars and iconic figures in the world. More than 35 years after his death, he remains a perennial bestseller in video stores, comic bookshops, on T-shirts and posters. When speaking of someone's place in history, the terms 'icon' and 'legend' are too often thrown about by tongues eager to confer praise. These designations would more properly be reserved for individuals whose profound impact on the globe around them seems too great to measure. With that in mind, the terms 'icon' and 'legend' could be no more aptly applied to anyone in the last half-century than Bruce Lee.

To describe Lee as a cultural phenomenon is an understatement. He influenced pop culture more than anyone before or ever since. On 31st March 2007, he was named as one of history's 100 most influential people by Time magazine. It is a testament to his legacy that more than three-and-a-half decades after his passing he continues to have an enormous impact on the world. After Bruce Lee's untimely death on 20th July 1973, Enter the Dragon - Lee's first and only Hollywood motion picture - smashed box office records around the globe, catapulting him to worldwide superstardom. This film stands as the lynchpin of the Little Dragon's legacy. Lee had achieved the iconic status of cultural legends such as Elvis Presley, Marilyn Monroe and James Dean. Furthermore, he has had a greater impact on more people worldwide than that of Presley, Monroe and Dean combined.

Majoring in philosophy at the University of Washington, Lee developed a deep, profound ideology that encouraged him to combine Eastern and Western schools of thought to express himself. This eclectic personal philosophy mirrored his fighting beliefs. His energy fired the creativeness of his entire being, which paved the way for the creation of the innovative, personal form of martial art he labeled Jeet Kune Do (The Way of the Intercepting Fist).Over the years, journalists have tried to define the elements that make Bruce Lee an enduring and iconic cultural figure, one whose achievements have never been surpassed. Lee's humble beginnings have been chronicled and were at the root of his determination and drive to become the best and most famous martial artist in the world. But fulfilling his major goal of popularizing the martial arts worldwide via the medium of film proved an arduous task. Racism was the key element in his struggles, preventing him from attaining the kind of success he hoped for in his early years in America.

Long thought of as simply the pinnacle of martial arts, and the person who single-handedly propelled the martial arts into the worldwide cinematic mainstream, there were in fact a number of facets and much deeper layers to Bruce Lee, which totally defined his true potential. He was a fighter, film star, martial arts innovator, fitness aficionado, teacher and philosopher. He not only succeeded in popularizing the martial arts on a global scale - before Lee's death there were around 500 martial arts schools in the United States, by the late 1990s there were 20 million martial arts students in the United States alone - but also in redefining the action film genre. These various facets have been key to attracting Bruce Lee aficionados over the years. As far back as I can remember, I have always been intrigued by how people and athletes from other disciplines view Bruce Lee. Not just as an action star and martial artist but beyond that, as a philosophical genius, a supremely talented athlete and a source of inspiration. For a long time, Lee has mesmerized elite individuals from the worlds of film, Boxing, bodybuilding and sports of all kinds.

There is one more breed of athlete who certainly belongs on this list. Having interviewed a plethora of UFC fighters and champions - who are no doubt the toughest athletes in the world - I found the magnitude of influence Lee had on these athletes was immense. It is refreshing to see how these individuals have been enlightened by such an incredible human being, although perhaps unsurprising given their interest in the martial arts. Of course, I was still always curious of how A-list Hollywood actors and directors viewed the late martial arts star who epitomized the action hero.

This piqued my interest in finding the answers to the questions I always wanted to ask. Above all, I sincerely wanted to make a statement - or rather I wanted my subjects being interviewed to make a statement - that the late Bruce Lee had such an indelible impact on elite personalities beyond the confines of the martial arts fraternity. In spring 2006, I came up with the concept of producing a documentary film which I would pursue with all my might. Bruce Lee: The Life and Legacy of a Master would pay the ultimate tribute to Lee, and allow me to showcase his influence on a much grander scale.

In autumn of that same year, I embarked on a journey to Los Angeles to conduct some rare and groundbreaking interviews. Two years passed, and because of certain obstacles and hurdles the project had to be shelved. The passion, drive and determination firmly ingrained in me helped me to stand my ground and not give up. After much heartache and thought, I decided to channel my focus and energy in a slightly different direction, which would still allow me to propagate the same message via the medium of print. There are a lot of books on Bruce Lee, but none had been based around exclusive interviews with those who knew and worked with Lee alongside interviews with public figures we are all familiar with, such as athletes and actors. As a side note, by December 2008, I happened to come across another company who were producing a Bruce Lee documentary, with a similar theme to what I had been pursuing two years earlier. The footage I had obtained for my own documentary project was too good to waste and be buried forever. So I made a contribution to the film. However, I vehemently felt a tome with a compilation of interviews of the highest caliber would do Bruce Lee the justice he rightly deserves.

This one-of-a-kind publication will appeal not only to Bruce Lee enthusiasts - hardcore and casual alike - but to those beyond the confines of the martial arts fraternity. There is no doubt these revealing interviews will further elevate Lee's status as a symbol of inspiration, whose feats of strength and achievement are still looked upon as benchmarks by great athletes and fighters. In this unique and intriguing landmark book, you will discover a compilation of exclusive interviews with Bruce Lee's original students, friends, co-stars and colleagues. Those who knew him best give their candid views on the great martial arts master and action movie star adored by millions around the globe. Their memories and stories capture him in a way no straightforward narrative ever could. Furthermore, for the first time ever, you will discover exclusive interviews with some of the best professional Boxers, bodybuilders, UFC fighters and personalities from the motion picture industry paying homage to the legend who continues to have an impact on athletes and people from all walks of life.

In part one, personal students recall moments of sheer amazement at their teacher's feats. Some of Lee's closest friends and training partners offer an intimate and touching look at this charismatic figure and complex character. While co-stars and colleagues reminisce on Lee's burning desire to reach his ultimate goal of becoming the first major Chinese star in the world. In part two, we look at the enduring legacy of the Dragon. Some of the elite names from the Boxing, bodybuilding, MMA and movie industry fraternity share their personal thoughts pertinent to Lee's legacy. They offer a testimony to what Bruce Lee accomplished and explain why the status achieved by the late legend is unlikely to be replicated.

Bruce Lee's legacy lives on and he continues to reach us even though his light was extinguished more than 35 years ago. This is a unique and fresh insight into a man whose mysterious life proved one of the most startling enigmas of the century. This is the ultimate tribute to the man whose legacy continues to grow worldwide. Bruce Lee continues to capture the hearts and minds of people from all walks of life. In closing, I sincerely hope you enjoy this book as much as I took pleasure in compiling it. You will discover Bruce Lee from a rather different perspective: a man who is a legend to legends.

THE LIFE

CHAPTER ONE

ORIGINAL STUDENTS

During his lifetime, Bruce Lee taught very few people, mostly in small groups and on a private basis. He started teaching martial arts shortly after his arrival in the United States in 1959. He taught a modified version of the Wing Chun system, which he later named Jun Fan Gung Fu. Initially he taught some friends in Seattle and later opened his first branch of the Jun Fan Gung Fu Institute. Although when he later moved to California, his mantra of efficiency would lead him to form his own personal style, with the focus on the most expedient solution to any possible encounter, the Seattle period is an integral part of Lee's time in the United States.

Some of the more prominent original students of Bruce Lee from this era included Jesse Glover, Taky Kimura, James Demile, Patrick Strong, Doug Palmer, Skip Elsworth, Leroy Garcia and Jo Cowles to name but a few. According to Demile, Lee surrounded himself with street fighters; most of his inner circle students had some street fighting experience.

Whilst studying philosophy at the University of Washington, he also worked at Ruby Chow's restaurant to support himself. Lee's style was ever-evolving but its foundation took place here in Seattle. Jesse Glover was his first student and became a very close friend. Taky Kimura, his closest friend and his assistant instructor, was his confidant toward the end, when Lee finally got the fame he craved and became the biggest box office draw in Asia.

In 1964, Bruce moved to Oakland, California, and opened up his second branch of the Jun Fan Gung Fu Institute. This period - commonly known as 'The Oakland Years' - had a substantial impact on Bruce's evolution as a creative martial artist. This was the period when noticeable changes could be seen in his approach to and development of his art and his training methods. He changed his focus from being a follower to being a creator, a thinking martial artist in pursuit of finding the truth in martial arts. James Yimm Lee was Bruce's closest friend, comrade, mentor and the assistant instructor in Oakland. George Lee, Allen Joe, Leo Fong, Bob Baker and Howard Williams were also part of the core group which trained extensively with Bruce in Oakland.

In 1966, shortly after moving to the Los Angeles area, Bruce decided to open up his third and final branch of the Jun Fan Gung Fu Institute and did so in February of the following year. Located on 628 College Street in the Chinatown district, this secluded, anonymous-looking building had no signs outside to identify the gym. It was far from a commercial martial arts school; the individuals who were fortunate enough to train with the master were there on a trial basis. Unless the prospective student proved himself, showing continued dedication along with reasonable improvement in the first six months, he would not be accepted as a full member of the Jun Fan Gung Fu Institute.

Some of the most prominent and close-knit cadre of devotees from this period included Dan Inosanto, Ted Wong, Dan Lee, Jerry Poteet, Bob Bremer, Larry Hartsell, Richard Bustillo, Steve Golden, Pete Jacobs and Herb Jackson (who spent most of his time fixing his Sifu's unique specialized training equipment). Lee's students were carefully chosen. Bruce preferred to have students with some previous martial arts training because it was easier for the student to appreciate more deeply what Bruce was trying to convey. "I don't want too many students in my organization. The fewer students I have and the harder it is for anyone to join will give my club more prestige and importance. Like anything else, if it's too popular and too easy to join people won't think too highly of it," Bruce said.

Bruce's most important prerequisites when selecting a student were a person's sincerity in learning and willingness to train hard. In addition to these qualities, persistent training and the student's potential to extend himself in strenuous martial arts activity, which was fundamental to his Jeet Kune Do philosophy, was also imperative. Bruce was aware that many martial arts students did not achieve their potential because they lacked true understanding of what is required to achieve their genetic potential. Therefore he focussed on quality and not quantity.

With its exclusive closed-door Jeet Kune Do sessions, the Los Angeles Chinatown gym was one of a kind. The criteria did not include fancy uniforms or belts, rather the focus was on cultivating athletic attributes and technical precision. Lee was interested in the most efficient way to use the human body for street-effective combat. This is the wisdom that Bruce Lee compelled his students to follow. Bruce's teaching method was always individualized according to his students, and he definitely didn't like teaching large groups. His teaching method required a constant alert observation of the student, and he even specifically prescribed supplementary training programs tailored to each individual's needs. He was a hands-on coach, parallel to what you might see in a Boxing coach. According to one of his premier disciples, he once said, "If you are lacking in your physical ability and conditioning, then you have no business in the martial arts."

It wasn't long before Lee transferred the teaching responsibilities at the Los Angeles Chinatown school to his assistant instructor Dan Inosanto. In 1969, Lee ordered his assistant instructors to dismantle his schools. Both Taky Kimura - who was teaching in Seattle - and Dan Inosanto were allowed to teach handpicked students in small private classes thereafter, with a guideline to keep the numbers low, but the quality high. It is no secret that Lee's art was not meant for mass distribution. Lee believed it was dependent on its precepts being passed down in a very personal way. He had no interest in commercializing his newly found art of Jeet Kune Do, and he vehemently made this clear on more than one occasion to his disciples. The only three people to have ever been certified by Lee to teach his art are Taky Kimura, from the Seattle period, James Lee, deceased, from the Oakland period, and Dan Inosanto, from the Los Angeles Chinatown period, who is widely known as Lee's protégé.

Lee's core group of students were more than mere passing acquaintances, they were close friends. His ideals, his philosophy and his insights remain fresh and alive in the minds of his personal students. In the following exclusive interviews, some of the most prominent personal students of the master from all three periods ruminate on their relationship with the greatest martial arts exponent of the century.

JESSE GLOVER

Jesse R. Glover was Bruce Lee's first ever student in the United States and his assistant in the early years when Lee was based in Seattle. Both men attended Edison High School and became close friends, going beyond the typical student-teacher relationship. Today, Jesse teaches his unique style of Non-Classical Gung Fu privately and is known worldwide as being one of Lee's top students from the Seattle period, as well as being one of the most gifted students Lee ever had.

Q: Jesse, you were the first person in the United States to be accepted as Bruce Lee's student, can you recall how and when you first met Bruce?
Jesse Glover: The first time I saw Bruce was at a demonstration in Chinatown. He did a form from the Southern Praying Mantis and an exhibition of dancing. Later, I discovered that we went to the same school, so I used to walk in front of him and kick telephone poles thinking he would be curious and ask me something, but he didn't. So one day I decided to walk up to him. I knew his name from the demonstration but I asked him if he was Bruce Lee, and he said yes. I asked him if he did Gung Fu, and he said yes. I said to him would he teach me, and he thought for a while and asked if I had a place where we could train where no one else is around. I said yes. So we walked to school, we talked about Gung Fu and he showed me some stuff that day. We walked back that night, he asked me where I lived and I told him. He came down to my house that evening and started teaching me.

Q: Where did the personal lessons take place before he opened the school to the general public?
Jesse Glover: They took place in my apartment, on the street and at school.

When he opened the gym there were only ten people and they paid ten bucks towards the rent. Any money that came in after that was going to go to Bruce. Some of the guys had to leave town to go to work so we couldn't afford it anymore. So then we trained outside. Most people we got came from word by mouth.

Q: How would you describe his personality?
Jesse Glover: He was like this: if he liked you, he liked you and if he didn't like you, he just wouldn't talk to you. He liked to joke around. Even Ed Hart, who was his second student, they both had a sense of humor, they told a lot of jokes. He was a fun guy to be around. Like I said, if he liked you, he liked you. He liked to go to the movies, Jerry Lewis was his favorite actor. He liked to dance and draw. During the intermission we would practice a little, during the movie he would be engrossed in the movie.

Q: Did he have a temper or was he a calm person?
Jesse Glover: Well, he was both, if you made him mad he'd get mad. But when I knew him and the people that were there, most of them really liked Bruce. Even the guys who didn't care about Gung Fu liked Bruce as a personality.

Q: Were there any specific rudimentary guidelines which the students had to follow when he taught?
Jesse Glover: When I met Bruce he was pretty open, later on he became more and more traditional so a lot of the guys dropped out. It became more and more a traditional Chinese Gung Fu class.

Q: Bruce studied philosophy; just how much was he engrossed in philosophy when he was residing in Seattle? Can you elaborate on Bruce's philosophical goals?
Jesse Glover: He studied philosophy and related it to the martial arts. He practiced all the time and got pretty philosophical about it. He was interested in philosophy - Chinese philosophy mostly. He liked to talk about it. There was a guy named John Jackson who had studied Asian philosophy who was much better steeped in it than Bruce. Bruce would misquote people sometimes and John would correct it. I guess his thoughts about philosophy were all tied up with his Gung Fu. He thought somewhere in the philosophy he was going to find the keys to Gung Fu. And he loved to say certain things. He loved words, so he would play with words and stuff like that. Most of the guys who were in the first group were pretty intelligent and well-read. They weren't all that concerned about what Bruce said about philosophy unless he talked about fighting.

When he started talking about fighting my ears were wide open. Now all of the stuff, such as his quotes and sayings, later on I found that a lot of it came from Wong Shun Leung, who was his primary teacher.

Bruce was like a young guy who discovers literature and likes to put words together. He liked to read philosophy, Gung Fu and a lot of Boxing books. He had paperback Gung Fu books from China. There's a place in Seattle that's out of business now where he used to go two or three times a week looking for books. And he spent a lot of time in the library looking at books. It was research combined with outrageous amount of practice. People think that you can just sit back and philosophize and become a super martial artist - that's not possible. You have to train, train, train, get disgusted and train, train and train more.

Q: Did he ever talk to you about what career path he wanted to pursue after finishing his studies?
Jesse Glover: He wanted to make a lot of money. He wanted to be famous.

Q: Before meeting and training with Bruce, you practiced Boxing and did Judo. Because of the typical full contact training used in these two arts, did you not find these two arts to be more effective than the Wing Chun system which Bruce was teaching?
Jesse Glover: I found Bruce to be more effective! He modified the system. I did Boxing a little bit and studied Judo and won a lot of tournaments, totally different thing. I thought what he was teaching was a lot more effective and that's why I started practicing it. And it had unique qualities about it which Boxing didn't have. I always liked Judo because of its underlying philosophy, which was maximum effectiveness with minimum effort. It was to cultivate yourself in terms of speed, power, when you're going in close and just training (in general). I demonstrated with Bruce in Seattle and several times on television in Canada. Bruce had studied Boxing a little bit in Hong Kong. His primary teacher Wong Shun Leung had studied Boxing. One of the last things he said to Bruce when he left Hong Kong was to watch out for the Boxers.

Bruce didn't know much about Judo, but I took him to the Seattle Judo Club and I showed him some stuff and introduced him to a guy named Fred Sato, who was a black belt. They both became pretty good friends. Actually, I think Fred is the one who introduced him to the five ways of attack. He liked Judo but the only problem he said was, "How do you get hold of the guy?" When he was going to the University of Washington, he also took a Judo class from one of my teachers, Kato, who was a US 180-pound champion. Bruce definitely would not go to the ground if he had the opportunity to get you standing up. When he was here, in Seattle, he had a lot of books on martial arts and there were some Chinese books on Jiu

Jitsu. He showed them to me and did a few of those things, but I don't think Bruce was really a grappler at that time.

Q: Bruce utilized the wooden dummy to perfect his phenomenal skills, did you often witness him work his 'magic' on this unique piece of training equipment?

Jesse Glover: Bruce had a dummy set up behind Ruby Chow's (restaurant) and he worked on it in the afternoon before the restaurant people came in. He would practice entries and different stuff. He showed me stuff on the dummy. He didn't know all the dummy - later on I talked to a guy who knew Wong (Shun Leung) and he said Bruce knew 60 percent of the dummy. But the dummy taught him how to close the distance and engage the opponent and to punch over and in between the guy's structure.

Q: What unique or unusual training methods did Bruce implement into his workouts? Am I right in saying you witnessed him do a barbell exercise where he would hold it out in front of the chest to cultivate his forearms?

Jesse Glover: He used to hold a barbell across his forearms - 70 pounds - to work his forearms, his shoulders and his wrist. And he used to do sil lam tao. He would do sil lam tao 50 times with his muscles contracted, kind of following Charles Atlas' program for development, which is stuff you do with your muscles tensed. He did a lot of exercises right out of the basic Wing Chun. He did a lot with hand weights and pulleys. He used to have these pulleys attached to the wall and he could pull them overhand or underhand, and actually punch outwards. He did a lot of push ups with various weights, like he would have you sitting on his shoulders and stuff like that.

Q: Was Bruce starting to integrate these exercises and specialized equipment at an early stage of his arrival in America, or was it much later in his development when he moved down to Southern California?

Jesse Glover: Even in Hong Kong he was using some strength training stuff, and he just experimented when he came to the US. Things like forearms and gymnast push ups, he would sit on a table and push up on the table, in a movie theater he would push up against the seat; the whole time he was exercising.

Q: Why do you think Bruce broke tradition by investigating other arts? At the time a lot of martial arts instructors did not want to teach foreigners.

Jesse Glover: He started modifying stuff when he came to the US. He got into trouble with an older man who did not like the fact that he was teaching foreigners. He broke (tradition) in Seattle for sure. Ruby Chow - who owned the restaurant where he worked and lived - didn't like the fact he was teaching foreigners. She said, "You're teaching black guys this and that, they're going to beat up on Chinese." He said, "Well, they can beat up on Chinese anyway, so if I teach them they're going to have some respect for Chinese." Yeah, he was the first Chinese who was teaching non-Chinese - this was, of course, in Seattle, I don't know what was going on in California, Hawaii or other places. I heard later that there were some guys in the military who had been in China before the Second World War who actually studied Gung Fu. So it wasn't like I was the first non-Chinese to do so.

Q: Did you ever witness Bruce in an actual incident?
Jesse Glover: We were doing a demonstration at a school and a guy in the audience had a problem. Bruce said Gung Fu is a soft style and Karate is a hard style. He challenged Bruce. Bruce asked us if he should do something about the challenge, but we told him to forget it and that it isn't worth the time. The guy was a Judo player but also a black belt in Karate. I used to play Judo against the guy and I could throw him but he had a hard time throwing me. He saw Bruce doing a demonstration of another style and thought that's how Bruce would fight.

So he kept challenging him until one day he sent this stupid guy over and issued a challenge. Bruce and I were at school, when I came out of the door he told me to go tell the guys to meet him on the third floor. I told him, "We can't fight here in the school," so he said at the Y Club. So the fight was set up. We got the bus and went to the Y. The guy put on his gi, Bruce took off his shirt, I was the referee and Ed was the timer. The fight was supposed to stop after three rounds. The guy got in a cat stance, the guy threw a kick, Bruce blocked the kick, got the guy on the floor, bounced him off the wall and kept hitting him and chased him. I hollered, "Stop!" The fight lasted 11 seconds.

Q: He didn't like the format of competition fighting, did he?
Jesse Glover: He didn't like competition but he did have some fights where there were no referees and no judges. People talk about competitions - when they've got people to stop you, it's not really competition. Competition is two guys going in a room and one of them walks out.

Q: When Bruce became famous and a global name after his movies were released, did you keep in touch with him?

Jesse Glover: No, last time I saw Bruce was at a birthday party when he and Linda were staying at Linda's mother's house. I hadn't seen him for a while. We spent the whole time in the basement talking while they were having a party upstairs. Then I saw him when Brandon was born, he brought him over to my house. Then after that I didn't see him anymore.

I had a conversation after his fight with Wong Jackman. Bruce, James Lee and Linda were training in his gym and some guys showed up wearing Gung Fu uniforms. He said at first he thought he was going to fight all these guys but it turned out it was just him against Wong Jackman. So they squared off and he attacked the guy and the guy almost turned and almost ran away. But as he was going back, Bruce was hitting him in the back of his head and the punches were going in the same direction as he was going in, so it wasn't having a very good effect. Bruce was running out of gas, but he knocked him down and pinned him. The guy agreed that it was over. And that started his roadwork training; he never thought he'd run out of gas but he did. Then after that incident a lot of people said he started studying Boxing, but he was studying Boxing long before this incident. Boxing wouldn't have made him chase this guy any quicker.

Q: What are your thoughts on his movies, and was he trying to express and propagate some sort of philosophical message using this medium?
Jesse Glover: Yes, there was a message. In fact, I'm surprised martial arts guys haven't followed his patterns because Bruce got his patterns using Samurai movies. We practiced and after that we went to Ruby Chow's, then went to the movies where we watched Samurai and Chinese movies. And in Chinatown we did different stuff. Yeah, I thought (his movies) were pretty cool. Bruce was a movie star when he was a kid long before he was a movie star as an adult. So I wasn't surprised.

Q: Bruce remains a pop culture icon to this day, how much of an impact do you think he has had on the world?
Jesse Glover: Bruce has had a lot of impact on the world. Time Magazine picked him for their top 100 influential people. He's had a tremendous impact. Some guys have a positive impact on people.

Q: After Bruce's death what path did you take and what have you been pursuing since?
Jesse Glover: In 1961, I went to Bruce and said, "James Demile and I would like to start teaching," and Bruce said, "That's fine, as long as you don't call it Jun Fan or Wing Chun." Later, Jeet Kune Do came from a guy in Seattle who said they used to call it 'Intercepting Fist', and before he went to California, he was toying with the idea. The only

reason he modified his stuff was because he was always looking for ways to catch up with his seniors back in Hong Kong. He would have kept on changing stuff.

Q: In Bruce's book Chinese Gung Fu: The Philosophical Art of Self Defense you are seen demonstrating a few Judo moves. What was he trying to achieve with the publication of the book?
Jesse Glover: He was trying to make money. James Lee told him if he wrote a book he could probably make money. At the time Bruce didn't have any money when he was working at Ruby Chow's, that's why he did it. The book was OK, a lot of the stuff in there was staged, like the throwing which I did myself. At the time I didn't think I wanted to spend five dollars on the book. He did trapping and striking so he wanted to know what else I did and I told him Judo. He was exchanging information with this other guy too.

Q: Can you recall any funny incident taking place during your close friendship with Bruce?
Jesse Glover: Well, the funny incident was where I couldn't hit him (Laughs).

Q: Anything you would like to add, Jesse, about your friendship with Bruce and how he has enriched your life?
Jesse Glover: He influenced everybody who studied with him. And even today many, many years later, those people who are still alive are strongly influenced by Bruce. Some of the guys are gone. The latest guy to die is Skip Ellsworth, I think he was probably Bruce's third or fourth student; he died in the Philippines. Charlie Woo died, Pat Hooks, I don't know what happened to him, he disappeared and I don't know if he's still alive. John Jackson died from heart attack, Taky Kimura is still around, Leroy Garcia is still around and James Demile is still around but is crippled. That's about it. Ed Hart recently died. Howard Hall disappeared, nobody heard from him. Doug Palmer was the one guy who went to Hong Kong with Bruce. Bruce enriched my life. When Bruce said he could do something he'd do it. A lot of people say they can do stuff but really can't do it. Anything that Bruce said he could do, he could do it! So that impressed me.

JAMES DEMILE

James W. Demile was part of the inner circle of Bruce Lee's students from the Seattle period who had trained with him privately. Demile had an impressive Boxing background before meeting and training with Lee. After Lee's death, he continued to spread the word globally, basing his system - which he refers to 'Tao of Wing Chun Do' - on the teachings and principles of Lee's original system. He is no doubt one of the more well-known original students of Bruce Lee. This is his perspective of the Bruce Lee he knew.

Q: James, please tell me your introduction to Bruce Lee?
James Demile: In late 1959, I was attending a public school for adults who had not finished high school. Bruce had been expelled from a Catholic private high school in Hong Kong and needed to earn make-up credits in order to get into the University of Washington. I had quit school in order to go into the Air Force and also needed additional credits. One day, during a free period, I noticed that there was a lot of activity in the auditorium and stopped to look at the bulletin board to see what was going on. It was a special event for the different Asian countries to demonstrate aspects of their culture. It sounded interesting, so I went in and sat in the back.

There was a young Chinese kid leaping around the stage making weird noises, kicking and punching into the air. He was extremely agile, graceful and his movements flowed from one to another without any interruption. His final burst of energy was a high spinning kick where he reached forward and slapped his foot and then landed in an odd looking stance that reminded me of a tiger getting ready to attack. He paused and then went on to explain that there were many forms in Chinese Gung Fu and this one was called Jeet Kune and that they were all very effective methods of self defense. I thought that this was amusing, since I had been an undefeated heavyweight Boxer in the military and had been brought up in an orphanage where fighting was an everyday event. To me, fighting was a lot more involved than leaping around as if you were fighting butterflies. This kid had a lot to learn about what fighting was really like. After his demonstration I went up to join a small group that was talking to the kid. The kid was pawing and poking at the air while bobbing and weaving like a drunken monkey. I must have shown my disbelief because the kid stopped and looked at me with a curious smile. He asked if I had any questions. I quickly told him that here in America fighting was not a game and that all his fancy moves would not work against a fast street fighter. His smile vanished and he moved in front of me and asked if I would take a punch at him.

For a moment I was speechless. I couldn't believe he was serious. He was 5ft 7 and about 135 pounds. I was 5ft 10 and 225 pounds. But I suddenly realized he was serious and that everyone was looking at me for a response. Feeling totally confident, I said OK and dropped back into a loose Boxer's stance. He stood there, relaxed, with both arms hanging by his side. I thought I would tap him lightly on the forehead with my jab, which should impress him with my speed and control. I fired a quick jab with my left.

The next few moments were my first steps to learning humility. In a blink, the kid exploded into action, not only blocking my punch but yanked my body towards the floor, engaging my right arm and interlocking it with my left, so I felt like a pretzel. It was an odd feeling. I could not move. He had trapped both my arms and grounded me so I could not kick or even take a step. He smiled, tapped me on the forehead as if to ask 'is anyone home' and then he released his pressure and stepped back. This was my introduction to Bruce Lee. I immediately joined a small group he was training with.

Q: Why did Bruce modify his Wing Chun?
James Demile: There were two reasons Bruce modified his Wing Chun. First, was to be able to beat his seniors in Wing Chun. After training a while in the States, Bruce returned to Hong Kong and found he had made no progress in his Wing Chun skills. Frustrated, he decided he would train harder. So he focused on his students getting better so they would force him to get better. After a while, he once again returned to Hong Kong and the results were the same. Bruce finally realized that the problem was not in his training, but what he was training in. No matter how hard he trained, his seniors were also training and therefore would always stay ahead of him. The only way he could beat them, he decided, was to improve what he was doing. He needed to take his Wing Chun to another level. The second reason for

modifying his Wing Chun was the Westerners were bigger and stronger than him and once they learned the basics of Wing Chun they could become a real threat to him. Bruce became very selfish in his personal training. He would explore efficient fighting concepts with different students, never really teaching everyone the same thing. He said, "If you want to learn, you must take it," because he was not going to give it to you.

He admitted he was not interested in us getting good, as much as using us to get good himself. This is why there is such a big difference in the original Seattle group, the Jun Fan group and the JKD group. The original group was during Bruce's fighting and creative period, the second group was during Bruce's need to become independent and earn some money so he created a style to teach, Jun Fan. The third group was his Hollywood period where he wanted to become a movie star so his emphasis was on more visual techniques, such a as kicks and more graphic motion.

Q: How did Bruce conduct his early classes with the original group?
James Demile: Bruce's initial teaching was without structure or any set goals. We were not a club nor did we have specific training times. We did meet after school and train, but we also trained during school, after going to Chinatown and eating or after going to a movie at the KoKasai theater where we would watch Asian martial art films. Bruce would go to my apartment and we would talk and train. Actually, the reason he went to my apartment was to use my phone to make long-distance calls. But the training there was invaluable to me since we talked a lot about principles and concepts that were later to become the basis for Wing Chun Do. He would also go to Jesse Glover's or LeRoy Garcia's and train. Each of us had something different to challenge him with and he would squeeze anything of value from us.

The main focus to Bruce's training was what interested him at the moment. We never knew what we were going to train in, or how long we would train on any one technique. Bruce was always exploring and experimenting. You had to pay close attention to what he said or did since he was really talking to himself. Once he discovered an effective technique he would train in it till he was confident in his application and regardless of our skill level he would never teach it again.

Q: Did Bruce ever do any Wrestling when he was in Seattle?
James Demile: I do not remember Bruce doing any Wrestling in the early years, at least up to 1963. He believed Judo was essential for good coordination training. But he was very adamant about not going to the ground. He felt that ground fighting was very dangerous and difficult to be

in total control. He did not believe in 'luck' as an element of fighting. He always wanted to be in total control of each situation.

Q: You were an undefeated heavyweight Boxer. There is a world of difference between applying movements with an obedient partner who cooperates and an actual opponent who is bent on destroying you with full contact blows. Did you not find Bruce's style to be inferior to a full contact fighting form such as Boxing?

James Demile: I boxed in the Air Force and Bruce boxed in high school. He was very good as a natural Boxer with no training. Yet, oddly enough, when it came down to what to keep and what to remove from Boxing, Bruce said throw it all out. After thinking about it, it made sense. Springy footwork, jabbing, combinations, bobbing and weaving and even slipping were all inefficient when it came down to Bruce's rules of simplicity, efficiency and practicality. All Boxing principles were in conflict with the solid stability of the closed bai jong, footwork, the constant offensive/defensive potential of both arms, at the same time when using the centerline concept and the awesome power of the power line concept for use of energy in trapping and striking.

Once I understood his meaning, I threw out all my Boxing knowledge and have not regretted it for a moment. Also, he was a natural athlete and was good at any sport he tried. He explored many styles of fighting, yet remained loyal to certain underlying principle from Wing Chun. He felt that although the overall Wing Chun principles needed to be changed the root of the principle was still valid. His movements and applied chi sao and trapping became more refined and efficient, yet you could see a strong Wing Chun influence.

Q: Bruce Lee's contribution to humankind far exceeds the simple confines of the martial arts world. Was Bruce Lee a philosopher or a warrior?

James Demile: I believe that Bruce's early years were focused on the physical rather than on the philosophical. He quoted many philosophers, but I think it was for the effect it had on us rather than some interest in philosophy. He was amused at how Americans were so impressed with profound statements, even when no one understood what the statement meant. Bruce was young and had dreams of becoming famous. He also realized that in order to achieve his goal of becoming an actor, director and producer, he must be unique and different from any other Chinese kid. He had no skills, other than martial arts, so he decided to commit 100 percent of his energy to becoming the best. This would be his pathway to stardom. I think he became more serious about the philosophical side as he got older and saw the need to balance out his image as a martial artist. The TV program Kung Fu influenced him as far as how people reacted to the internal as well as the external aspects of martial arts, so a lot more philosophical sayings appeared in his writings.

Q: Could you recall any street incidents you witnessed Bruce in during the time you knew and trained with him?
James Demile: Bruce used to take Sherry Garcia, Leroy's wife, dancing. Bruce had won a Cha Cha contest in Hong Kong and loved to dance. This was told to me by Sherry. One evening Bruce was in Chinatown with Sherry and four guys approached them and made racist remarks about the Chinaman with the blonde chick. Bruce went ballistic and was going to kill all four of them. Sherry grabbed him and made him walk away. Those guys were unaware of having death visit them and then walk away.

At school there was a Karate guy from Japan who did not like Bruce and felt Bruce was all talk and no action. He would always bug Bruce with mean looks and snide statements. Bruce would ask us if he should fight him and we would always say no. However, one day Bruce snapped and told the guy, "OK, let's fight." They agreed to go downtown to the YMCA handball court and see who would walk out first. Jesse was the referee and Ed was the timekeeper. I was not there, but Ed told me the next day how the guy started out with a kick to Bruce's groin. Bruce swept the kick aside and double-punched the guy in the face and drove him across the court, bounced him off the wall and then smashed him with both fists. The guy crumpled to the floor. Ed thought he was dead. Finally the guy moved. It lasted 11 seconds. Bruce was not touched. Many of the incidents at that time were just moments in time. People would want to test Bruce, but Bruce would just trap and let them know he was in control.

I personally experienced the hard side of Bruce's fist a few times when he needed to demo his skills. Once in a while we would meet at Taky Kimura's grocery store, just prior to training. On this particular day, we were just hanging out doing loose practicing when one of the students walked in with his girlfriend. One thing about Bruce, he loved to demonstrate his skills. If a pretty girl was anywhere near, Bruce would perk up and start his spontaneous demo. In this case he would point at me and explain how fast and tough I was and then promptly knock me over, under and through all the vegetables in sight. Honestly, I tried to hit him. I would have loved to have knocked him out in front of everyone. He knew this, so enjoyed watching me disappear into the cabbage pile.

Q: Was Bruce using any specialized training equipment to elevate his skill in the Seattle area?
James Demile: Bruce really believed in using training aids. He felt that

training equipment was necessary in order to achieve high levels of skill. This is why I have developed so much training equipment, such as a variety of timers and spring-loaded dummies. Unfortunately, he had little access, in the early years, to any real useful equipment. By useful, I mean equipment for training technique. We did have access to a speed timer and Bruce had a mook jong dummy in back of the restaurant where he worked and lived. He did not workout with weights till later on when he was concerned about how he looked. In the early years he felt weight training tightened the muscles, which would slow him down and the bulk would restrict his flow. He changed his mind later on as he learned more about training properly with weights.

Q: What was the effect of power of the punch?
James Demile: The power of the punch for demo and the applied power are two different things. Bruce did what is called a 'push punch' when he did a demo. In other words, he pushed the punch through the target, knocking him (assistant) back. In reality, the person should not move, just drop in their tracks. The real punch is a concussion punch, where the energy explodes just inside the chest and affects the lungs and heart. You cannot get the concussion effect if the person moves back, since the energy dissipates through the whole body. But the punch has no value to a spectator if the person does not move. Actually, the power of the punch is secondary to the method of transferring the energy. People get all caught up in the power, where in reality it takes very little power to do a lot of damage. Bruce discovered the mechanics of the hand action that maximized the damage with a minimum of energy. Wing Chun has a power punch, but not the same as Bruce used it. He evolved their concept to a higher level. People are amazed at the short range effectiveness of the punch, but it is the short range that makes it work. Moving further back adds to the power potential, but is unnecessary.

Q: Can you tell me about the later stages of Bruce's evolution?
James Demile: Other than the stages I mentioned before, I think his evolution went in a different direction than martial arts. The first stage was critical since he needed the actual skills to beat anyone. Once he was satisfied in his fighting ability he could relax and use the martial arts for the next step in his plan: independence. Independence meant no more being a dishwasher, a waiter and a servant of the Dragon Lady, Ruby Chow. It gave him the freedom to explore the outside world and discover new ways to reach his dream. The only real 100 percent focus in training and skill development was in his early years. After that, the purpose of training was a means to a specific end: Hollywood. You can see it, not in what he did, but what he didn't do. Starting from Jun Fan he no longer

emphasized the closed bai jong stance, the centerline concept, the applied use of spring energy and even the most basic flow concepts for trapping. Later, in JKD he eliminated chi sao. Yet, each of these elements he left out were critical for applying his own skills.

Q: Can you shed some light on Bruce's reading habits in the early period you knew him?
James Demile: In the early years we used to go to the Chinatown in Vancouver, Canada, so Bruce could seek out books on Gung Fu written by past masters. He still believed that the ultimate fighting secrets were hidden in traditional training. This went on for a year or so. Then he began to change his perception as he started to recognize the impracticality of forms and blindly following the teaching of masters who had never really ever been in a fight. It was in reading and comparing what he read to the reality of the street that it soon became apparent that Gung Fu was a beautiful art, but basically impractical against an aggressive street fighter. Once Bruce began to expand his thinking, past tradition, he began to read and examine the modern day fighters of that period.

He was very impressed with Joe Louis, Rocky Marciano and Floyd Patterson, who was heavyweight world champ at that time. He also began reading about Fencing, since he liked their footwork. In other words, he began to expand his search for his personal answers. But it was all martial arts oriented, not philosophical. I think he became more internal as he got older and more involved in the insane world of Hollywood.

Q: Did you keep in touch with Bruce after he left Seattle?
James Demile: After 1963, I never spoke to Bruce again. He moved on into a different world that I was interested in and I went on to fulfill my own dreams.

Q: What would you say to people who ask the question if Bruce was really a fighter or just an actor?
James Demile: There is not really a satisfying answer for anyone who did not know Bruce personally and touch hands with him. However, I point out that I was known for being a very aggressive street fighter and at 225 pounds, with a Neanderthal mentality, feared no man. Jesse Glover held a black belt in Judo and was recognized as someone to avoid in a fight. Ed Hart was 6ft 3 and 240 pounds and quick as lighting and could knock you out in a blink with either hand. LeRoy Garcia, the mountain man, fought like a wild grizzly bear and would fight a gorilla and probably win. These were the people around Bruce in the early years. We were all lean and mean, yet Bruce could trap and control us like we were elementary school kids - unbelievable but true. Our training was an ongoing fight. We all

really tried to hit Bruce. So this is why I know Bruce was for real. Regardless of size or weight, Bruce could beat anyone I have ever met. I am happy to spar with anyone who says Bruce was not real. If they are that good then I should be easy to beat.

Q: How has Bruce enriched your life?

James Demile: First, by learning humility in my first introduction to Bruce it caused me to rethink who I was. Being brought up in an orphanage I always related to 'the survival of the fittest' mentality. Fighting was an important way of having respect and recognition. Until I met Bruce I had an attitude that I was unbeatable and therefore someone to respect. My chance meeting with Bruce made me step back and accept that my attitude had been an illusion and that it was time to seek new answers to who I was. My private time with Bruce laid the seed for many of my personal accomplishments. In creating Wing Chun Do I faithfully followed Bruce's rule of simplicity, efficiency and practicality when developing technique. He gave me the formula for speed, power, trapping, energy control and closing the gap. I just took these formulas and formed them into applied concepts and principles.

When I teach I always remember that Bruce said to teach what you know, not what you do. If you teach only what you do, the student will become a follower. If you give him the knowledge of how, what and why you do what you do, then he can mold that knowledge into his own creation. Bruce felt that what he did was unique to him and would not necessarily work for someone else, they had to find their own answers. This was an important point in my own evolution. Bruce opened the door to individual creativity. It was OK to do my own thing. Bruce was just a source of information. If I wanted to be the best I could be, then I had to take his as well as information from others, and restructure into something meaningful to me. This awareness has spread into every aspect of my learning evolution - and is all because of an accidental meeting with a kid in an auditorium who leaped around like a butterfly.

JAMES DEMILE: PART 2

Q: Bruce Lee never entered competitions. Can you elaborate on this?
James Demile: Well, the first thing and reason is that he felt if at any time you have rules, it automatically limited what you could do. In other words, the person fighting you knew something, therefore it wasn't like a street fight where you quickly as possible have to hurt the person and get it over with. Bruce never entered tournaments with rules versus street fighting, which is survival, and he was only interested in survival; he wasn't interested in competition because he felt that it didn't prove anything. He said that anytime you play by rules it automatically restricts you in what you can do; he didn't like that. Remember, this was back in the 60s when there weren't many tournaments going on, we had mainly Judo tournaments and few Karate tournaments. Bruce couldn't relate to those because they were just sport. So, it wasn't like he was relating to martial arts as we think of it today. It's really different if you look back at the 60s because there were only Judo and Karate tournaments you could enter as far as how good you were; so it wasn't like MMA.

Q: Muhammad Ali and Bruce Lee are both iconic figures, did he talk to you about Ali and what was his thoughts on the Boxing legend?
James Demile: Bruce really admired Muhammad Ali, Floyd Patterson, Jack Dempsey, he really thought their techniques were really good. He felt in the ring they would beat him but in the street he would beat them, because of what he could do in the street. In other words, he could do trapping, the kind of techniques that are on a street level, whereas in Boxing you have rules and it's really just different type of martial art. Bruce felt that if he went into a sports situation there was a good chance he would get beat. He felt really confident in his street abilities and no one could beat him in the street. A lot of people think what you do in the ring is what you would do in the street; that's not true at all. In competition the mentality is different and it's a sport - people just don't understand the difference between sport and street fighting. But Bruce did and he didn't want to waste his time.

Q: Later, when Bruce pursued a career in the motion picture industry did he ask any of the former Seattle students to be in any of the movies?

James Demile: He only asked Taky. Taky was always in the background and wanted to stay in the background, he didn't want to be in the movies. But Bruce really felt obligated to try and help Taky to get him some kind of recognition because he felt Taky was such a good person. But Taky just didn't want to do it. So the truth is he did ask Taky but he didn't want to do it.

Q: What was your reaction to the sensationalized Hollywood biopic Dragon: The Bruce Lee Story which seem to have deviated from Bruce's life?

James Demile: To me, it really looked bad. The story was totally inaccurate, it was done in a bad way. It was just commercialism, it gave no insight into who Bruce Lee was as a person and it didn't really expose the fears he had and how he overcame the fears. He never has a fight that shows with the guy he got injured, Linda Lee didn't write the book Tao of Jeet Kune Do. Almost 99 percent of the movie was inaccurate. I was extremely disappointed that they had an opportunity to really do something that would perpetuate Bruce's name (but didn't).

Q: Since Bruce's death, have you had any intriguing conversations with any well-known personality about Bruce?

James Demile: I've come across a lot of athletes who were inspired with his focus in training, his intensity, his dedication to becoming the best. That inspired them. Just because of the uniqueness of his abilities such as speed and power, their goal wasn't to be the best martial artists but they felt that the way he did what he did showed them the way to achieve their goals - hard training and being persistent. So in that sense, yes, I talked to people.

Q: In the Los Angeles area a lot of Karate champions worked out with Bruce. One of them has gone on to say Bruce never really sparred. What is your opinion on this?

James Demile: They didn't spar with Bruce but played around, you know how people go out and play around, sparring if you were serious. Again, Bruce would take you out if he thought you were a threat. You have to remember back in those days people like Bob Wall and Chuck Norris were champions of non-contact Karate. Now, that's a big difference, because that was even before Joe Lewis got into full contact. So, most of those guys what they did was non-contact or very light contact so you can't even compare that with the likes of today's type of full contact sparring. So, when we hear about Joe Lewis sparring , Chuck Norris sparring, it was just playing, there was no sparring. It was like I'd show him and he shows me, what we could do and then that's all. It was never of anything of any intensity or seriousness, because they couldn't compete against Bruce, they weren't in his league at all!

Q: Am I right in saying you had a fall out with Bruce at one time?
James Demile: It happened when Jesse and I broke away from Bruce because he was changing on what he was doing; he was starting his Jun Fan. Jesse and I didn't particularly care for the changes because we felt he was leaving out some of the key principles that worked. And Bruce told me that he was changing it because he didn't want to teach people to beat him. But one day I was down at the King Street club in Chinatown, and I was talking to some of his students and they asked me why Jesse and I didn't train with him and I told them we didn't like what they were doing. Well, I looked at Bruce and Bruce was very upset and said that I didn't have the right to say that to the students. So I apologized to him and said that he was correct and I was wrong in saying what I said.

But he was really upset with me, he thought I wanted to challenge him and he got really upset. The bottom line is back in those days I used to carry a gun. I always carried it after the service. And I had the gun on me and thought to myself: if this kid even flinches at me I'm going to shoot him (Laughs). This is a true story. I just walked out. Bruce was really upset. I was wrong. I shouldn't have said anything but I was at the mindset that if he was going to force me into a fight he would bust me up, and I wasn't going to go for that.

Q: Do you feel because you and some of the other students Bruce taught in Seattle had a street fighting background this helped Bruce in his development?
James Demile: I think that Bruce was extremely lucky to have us guys who were street fighters, bigger and meaner than him, because it challenged him and always forced him to get better. All of us would have liked to punch him out, and no matter how we tried it didn't work because he was always getting better than us. He was always working on how to overcome my Boxing background and his Boxing background, street background, or Jesse's Karate and Judo background. He was always examining all the different ways to overcome our skills. So, if he did not have that sort of challenge and threat of forcing him to get better, I don't think he would have got as good as he did, he would have just stayed a Wing Chun guy.

Q: Finally, what is the most significant or interesting conversation you ever had with Bruce which seem to define his uniqueness?
James Demile: The most fascinating part of my relationship with Bruce was just learning the way he thought about techniques and bringing things

down to a level where it's all practical. He was very selfish in the respect that he didn't want to waste time training in things that he himself could not do or believe, which wouldn't work for him. It wasn't that he taught and developed techniques for everybody in the martial arts, he was only interested in 'Bruce Lee'. For me, what was fascinating was the way he did it, the way he restructured and conceptionalized speed and power and trapping. He would think of ways of dealing with somebody who was a Boxer, Wrestler, Muay Thai or a Karate man, or who was bigger and stronger than him. So, the way he thought about this and how he would deal with it, how he developed the kind of techniques and concepts which would handle these kind of people, that to me was fascinating. This is what I try to do when I'm teaching.

People really don't realize Bruce was a scientist as far as martial arts goes, he didn't even know it. When I look back at all the things he did, it was like going back to a science program about speed, power, trapping, closing, spring energy and all these things. It was beautiful the way he thought about them and structured them as far as being able to use them in the street. To me, that was the most important thing, not that Bruce was top or Bruce was good, it was the things he gave me which I give my students and how to think. How to be able to look out there and see what techniques are out there, and how do you modify them or develop them for yourself? And that was where the real value was from Bruce's teachings. To me, it was the conceptualization and being creative in your own mind and how to do it.

PATRICK STRONG

Patrick Strong is a rare original student of Bruce Lee from the early period. His unique teaching approach, backed up with an intellectual insight into what he is teaching, is refreshing. Pat is one of the most down-to-earth instructors one can ever hope to meet and a true gentleman. Before meeting Bruce and signing up at the Seattle Jun Fan Gung Fu Institute, Mr. Strong had a Boxing background. He continues to teach in his garage privately.

Q: When did you first meet Bruce Lee and what was your impression of him?

Pat Strong: That would have been late 1960, or the beginning of 1961, when I first started training with him. I was Boxing at the time at the Church Street Gym in Seattle. I'd heard about Bruce, this young Chinese Boxer. I had no idea what Chinese Boxing was so I decided to go and have a look. At the Boxing gym I thought I'd seen some pretty tough guys who were professional fighters. Archie Moore used to come up all the way from San Diego and helped out some of the fighters in Seattle. I thought these guys were pretty tough, but I felt this Chinese Boxer was something I'd never seen anything like, so I immediately signed up.

Q: You have gone on record to explain just how quick Bruce was, can you expand on this?

Pat Strong: What made Bruce fast was his 'start speed'. What I mean by that is you see a lot of martial artists who appear to be fast, but what makes somebody really fast is how fast they start the movement. Bruce's big thing was in his 'start speed', and the 'start speed' starts instantly, there's no way to react to that. So, when somebody hits fast they have to contract their muscles to control the punch and the speed isn't instant; the speed has to follow the contraction of the muscle. What Bruce would do is that he would release his energy in a way that his muscles didn't contract. Consequently, the speed was instant, it was like a firecracker going off. It was more like an explosion.

Q: Can you disclose to me some of the speed drills Bruce utilized to increase this attribute?
Pat Strong: The thing about Bruce, which made him different from anybody else, is that he tied philosophy into his martial arts. His main philosophical sources were Zen and Taoism. And from the Tao you have two very powerful principles. One is the principle of Wu Wei, meaning the 'not doing' or 'letting it happen'. The other principle was the Wei Wu Wei, meaning the 'effortless doing' with the soft and invisible powers. He felt that these two principles were the very height of the martial arts, the highest level to attain. So the 'not doing, let it happen', the Wu Wei name he called it was the 'non-intentional'. He said in order to be fast you have to strike with non-intention. That means you strike without the aid of the consciousness itself. In his Tao of Jeet Kune Do he says, "The consciousness itself is the greatest hindrance to all physical action."

Bruce believed if at any time the conscious mind got involved in throwing a punch, it now became an effort, an effort which starts from the mind and signals to the body, to the muscles, to contract to throw the punch. Bruce believed in non-intention over the intention of throwing a punch. The non-intention would be to strike without the direct intention of striking. This sounds complicated but it's the simplest thing in the world. So, he used analogies to explain that. One of the analogies was bamboo. If you go to a bamboo in a forest you have to be careful. If you push bamboo and you let go, it will snap back and hit you. Bamboo doesn't have to think , doesn't have to stop and think or prepare to hit, it just hits. He was talking about physics - that would be the elastic potential energy, wouldn't it? You grab the bamboo and release it and it snaps. So plain. He also spoke about a set of keys on the edge of a table. When the table is jerked or moved the keys fall, they don't stop and think of falling, they just fall. What the keys and the bamboo have in common is that neither one has brains; they just act on physical forces.

In physics when you speak of energy, you have potential energy. When you think of potential energy, you have basically the elastic potential energy, which would be the bamboo. You have gravitational potential energy, which is gravity. So, Bruce used both of these two to describe his movements. Thereby he's using this to get his movement, so his movement could be absolutely instant without having to do a major physical contraction, which takes time. So Bruce's start speed was instant. Anything slower than instant wasn't fast enough.

Q: Can we talk about the period when Bruce was attending the University of Washington in Seattle?

Pat Strong: The thing about Bruce which made him different was...I've been around a long time now to know a lot of great masters, but what really, really made him unique was that his art was tied into his philosophy. His philosophy and his art were the one and the same, there was no separation. When Bruce talked about tan sao he would compare it to a tool of a carjack. He would say a tan sao has to be strong, it has to be like a Cadillac jack. To lift a Cadillac you don't lift it with a Volkswagen jack. So, the tools had to be very strong. Everything was tied to the philosophy. The greatest strength came from the soft invisible power. Instead of forcing something with great strength, he would make the same work with very little effort.

Q: Did he ever speak to you about some of the philosophers who influenced him such as Alan Watts or Krishnamurti? He voraciously read self help books...

Pat Strong: Yeah. Bruce collected a lot of books including Napoleon Hill's. When I was with him he didn't speak so much about the philosophers but he spoke a lot about Wu Wei. In his movies he says, "I don't hit, it hits itself." That's Wu Wei. In Enter the Dragon, when he's walking with the monk and describing to the monk in the garden, he uses this term. In Big Boss, when he's fighting in the ice factory, he hits this guy in the stomach and he grabs his fist as though suddenly it hit someone. He stares at it thinking he can't believe that this fist just went off and hit; the fist hits itself. That's all about the 'not doing, letting it all happen itself' (philosophy) and Bruce spoke a lot about that.

Q: How would you describe Bruce as a teacher? Did he accentuate the small groups structure when he was teaching in Seattle?

Pat Strong: Bruce didn't have any money at all in the beginning. He worked at Ruby Chow's restaurant, where he was a waiter. He posted newspapers for the Seattle Times. He didn't have any money at all. So he started teaching a very small group of pupils. Then, as he got more students, we would workout across the street from where he worked as a waiter, in an outdoor garage beneath the insurance building and early in the morning in parking places. There were no pads or hanging bags and no equipment of any kind, and it was cold. Later, when he was able to make just a little bit of money as his class grew, he was able to open up a school in Chinatown. Down in the basement he had two rooms, one of the rooms had water and the other was dry where we worked out. Bruce was always on a budget and he didn't charge much. Later on, as he made a little more money, he opened up a really nice school in a modern building near the University of Washington, where he lived and went to school. That was a large facility and very modern and he had a room at the back where he slept.

Q: He was very close to Taky Kimura...
Pat Strong: Taky was the oldest of the group. He had a grocery store and he was a businessman. Taky was Japanese and he had been in the concentration camps during the war. A very nice fellow. He and Bruce became very close. He would handle Bruce's financing, his business and help Bruce get around town. Bruce relied on Taky very much and when he went to San Francisco he left Taky in charge of the school. Taky would run the school and Bruce would come back up to Seattle and take over. But it was always Taky Bruce had trust in and he had him take care of things.

Q: He made a transition into Jeet Kune Do when he had moved to Los Angeles. Can you differentiate between the Seattle, Oakland and the Los Angeles Chinatown periods and why do you think he made this transition?
Pat Strong: It was a lot of reasons. I remember there was a very important Boxing match when a young fighter - then called Cassius Clay, now known as Muhammad Ali - fought Sonny Liston, who was a big heavyweight champion nobody in the world could possibly beat. Cassius Clay fought Liston and knocked him out. What happened was, there was some change in Bruce - he had an interest in Boxing. There were several of the guys at the school who had Boxing backgrounds. What Bruce liked about Boxing was the way it flowed from one movement to the other. What he didn't like about Sport Karate at the time was the point system, where one taps the other and the other taps the other. He really felt Boxing was alive, so he paid a lot of attention to Boxing.

Right after he started studying Muhammad Ali he changed something. He changed his footwork. What he saw in Cassius Clay was that Clay didn't have to step back to avoid an opponent's punch; he could move his body, he could snap his body back away from the punch. So when he did this he hadn't moved his feet back. When he planted his body forward he hadn't even moved. The other fighter, however, thought that he had taken a step backwards. And Clay hid his distance and concealed his distance. Bruce started training this ideal 'body snapping' of moving the upper body back without taking a step backwards. And he also used 'body snapping' which came lower to the midsections by simple pulling the stomach away. So he had changed his footwork. From his Wing Chun he also had what he called a 'snake step', where you slide from the heel to the ball of the foot. So, Bruce would slide in like that. If there's no step, there's no 'beat' in his movement. He was fluid, he could step in and out all the time. He appeared to be further away from you but he was there in front of you, all he had to do was lean forward and strike you. So, from Muhammad Ali he developed a new sense of timing - but that timing was related to his Wing Chun, it's the same timing used in chi sao. When two people are rolling their arms using this exercise, there's a 'beat, beat, beat' in chi sao, before you get to the next beat you're in a half-beat and you'd strike. Bruce was very conscious of the idea of the beat. What he saw in Muhammad Ali was that he'd strike on the half-beat. In other words, if I'm throwing a left jab at you and I hit you with a right cross, that's a beat. What Bruce would do, when I shoot a left jab at him, he'd snap his body back and counter-hit me in between my left jab and right cross. So he's hitting me in the half-beat.

This is where he came out with a whole new sense of timing and rhythm in his movement. That happened with him studying Muhammad Ali. What Bruce would do is use the mook jong, also known as the wooden dummy. He also had some little gizmos, something you hold onto and it was all mechanical. This developed Bruce's wrist and forearm power. Bruce really believed the power came from his forearms. Bruce's stance and everything on structural stance is something which is not taught so much   in no holds barred and mixed martial arts today. It's not taught in Jeet Kune Do but Bruce had it.

Q: When you think of Bruce, what is the most memorable conversation or incident that comes to mind?
Pat Strong: There were a lot of things. Back in the early 60s I was visiting a fellow who had just opened up a Karate school on Broadway. I was talking to him and he said he had a visitor coming over from Japan. I said, "OK, I'll leave." But he said, "No, you'll find this guy interesting, he's a friend." That visitor turned out to be Tohei of Aikido, who was a master at that time. He was very nice at showing tricks and when all three of us were together, he asked me to stoop down and tie my shoes on one knee. And he said, "Don't let me push you over." He came over and pushed me over. When Tohei kneeled down, he asked me to push him down with both hands and with all my strength. I was lifting weights and I was an athlete, a lifeguard and was in great shape. I couldn't push him over. And he showed some other tricks.

That very night in the Gung Fu class with Bruce, I went over to Bruce and told him about the master and some of the tricks he showed me. From that point on Bruce started showing me some tricks. What I didn't realize at the time is the secret to all the tricks was the same thing. When Bruce was demonstrating he would show little tricks - the same trick to do with the way pressures work - same as Tohei was showing. There was a time when a little girl, 14 years old, kneels down to tie her shoe and four grown men (try to) push her over but they can't do it. Or put a child in a wheelchair, hold out a tan sao, and four grown men cannot push the wheelchair back even if the brakes are off. It's the same thing with the soft and invisible power, it's really true with the magic of the martial arts. Bruce was experimenting with that at a very young age. Anytime he talked about these things, for me it was the most interesting conversation in the world.

Q: James Lee was one of Bruce's best friends who he often visited in Oakland from Seattle before even moving there. Can you tell us about him?
Pat Strong: Bruce had an awful lot of influence on James Lee. James Lee was a hard martial artist. Bruce told me a very funny story. He and James are parking a car in Chinatown. James pulls up and this other car pulls up right in the same parking spot, so this made James very angry. He jumped out of the car and this guy gets out and he's huge. So James Lee walks over and the guy yells back at him. James Lee lifts his hand and brings it back of his hood of the guy's car and smashes it, which dents the car. The guy couldn't believe what he was looking at (Laughs). Bruce said he was laughing himself so hard he could hardly stand up. The guy jumped back in his car and drove away.

Q: Today, we have mixed martial arts. You also evolved and have integrated grappling into your repertoire. In your own opinion, would Bruce have evolved and to what extent would this evolution have taken?
Pat Strong: Oh, yeah, he would have gone to the full extent. When Bruce was alive he was already interested in grappling. Even in the early Seattle period we had anti-grappling techniques. If a football player would attack you or tackle you, we had techniques for that type of attack which work against the opponent, down to the ground. Later on, when Bruce came out to California, he worked out with some Judo people. In Seattle we had some Judo people. He worked out with Gene LeBell and was training with him. He told Gene LeBell that he wanted to integrate Judo into his martial art. Later, when you see the movie Enter the Dragon, how does the movie open? He's fighting an opponent. How does the fight end? By taking the man down and putting on an armbar. So, Bruce was already planning strongly to incorporate the grappling into his martial art, it would have worked perfectly. If he would have met one of the Gracies or the Machados, they would have become best friends.

Q: When Bruce became famous what were you doing with your life?
Pat Strong: At the time he was living in California and so was I. We both were in Los Angeles. I had trained in Shorin Ryu Karate and wanted to

pursue Tae Kwon Do, and I was really kind of staying away from Bruce. He had opened up his LA Chinatown school. I stayed away because had I got in at the time I would have been teaching the beginners, and I had more interest in developing the kicking of Tae Kwon Do. I had planned to go back to train with Bruce but I wanted my black belt before I did. Actually, when I left Seattle Bruce gave me some names to look up in California, Ed Parker was one of them. Ed Parker and I became very close friends and I trained with his pupils for a very long time. I used to do demonstrations with Ed Parker. Consequently, the problem was that Bruce passed away before I could go back to him. Bruce had a couple of private students he was teaching such as Steve McQueen, Stirling Silliphant and Joe Hyams. When Bruce went over to Hong Kong, I took over teaching Joe Hyams, who recently passed away.

Q: In closing, would you agree that Bruce Lee's influence on the world continues to be felt, and is there anything you would like to add?
Pat Strong: I think what Bruce did was he researched martial arts, experimented and used his students as dummies. He was developing internally, always looking to the internal side. I think what's happened today is a lot of martial arts, mixed martial arts and fighters incorporate all types of training and fighting methods. It's become more sophisticated with weight training and core training, any kind of physical training, incorporating grappling into their arts, different ways of fighting. They're using Thai kicks, putting all of the information together and they're creating their own thing out of it. And this is pretty much what Bruce did and he was one of the first to do that.

The difference with fighters of today is they only go to the physical side, from the technical to the physical, and have no idea of the philosophical side. Bruce's true power and speed came from the philosophical side, there's a big difference.

DOUG PALMER

Doug Palmer, a Seattle attorney and original student of Bruce Lee from the Seattle period, was totally mesmerized the first time he saw Lee in a demonstration. He wasted no time in signing up. Palmer is one of the elite Seattle students who has kept a low profile ever since his instructor and friend passed away. He was fortunate enough to accompany Bruce to Hong Kong in the summer of 1963, where he spent time with his family. In this rare interview, Palmer sheds light on his Sifu and friend.

Q: Can we please talk about when you initially started training with Bruce?
Doug Palmer: Yeah, I started in the summer of 1961. It would have been midsummer in 1961. I saw a demonstration which Bruce did with some of his students at a street fair in Chinatown. I'd never seen anything like it before. Bruce did a Praying Mantis form and he did sticking hands with some of his students and showed some other things. I was just blown away by what I saw, the speed and the grace. I had a lot of friends in the Chinese-American community so I happened to find out the younger brother of one of my friends was taking lessons. So I let it be known that I was interested in meeting Bruce. That's how we got together and I started taking classes. The classes were held outside in the yard of one of the student's - Leroy Garcia - house.

Q: What essential elements did Bruce emphasize when teaching in the early period?
Doug Palmer: At that point, we would start a class with salutation and we would then do various stretching exercises. Exercises that were designed to stretch the tendons, both the arms and the legs, bunch of things that were

designed for stretching and warming up. Then we would do punches and kicks, usually pair up where one side would kick or do a pak sao or something and the other side would block, then we'd switch. We would do a bunch of basic punches and kicks and then he would usually give a lecture, introduce a new move or talk about some aspect of Gung Fu. Then we would spar.

Q: Would I be right in saying you had a Boxing background before joining Bruce Lee's Gung Fu class?
Doug Palmer: I did. I boxed from the fifth grade through high school. But when I took Gung Fu there was a one year period - senior year in high school - when my Boxing and Gung Fu was on the same night. So I had to make a choice. I chose Gung Fu because it was new and different and I also felt it had certain things the Boxing had, like certain punching and blocking, but it also had a lot more. (With) the kicking, it was more complete. I mean, I have a lot of respect for Boxing and I did it for a long time and continued to do it, and Bruce did too. Bruce used to watch the great Boxers and would adapt stuff from the Boxing moves into his repertoire.

Q: How would you describe Bruce's personality in those early days?
Doug Palmer: He was very outgoing, he was in his early 20s and he was fun-loving who liked to joke around and loved practical jokes. He was very informal, during class everyone had to address him as Sifu but outside the class he was one of the guys.

Q: You accompanied Bruce to Hong Kong in 1963. Can you please look back and tell me about your experiences meeting his family and so on?
Doug Palmer: It was in the summer of 1963, after my freshman year in college, when he asked me and another fellow to go with him. But the other fellow couldn't make it at the last minute, so instead of renting an apartment I stayed with his family. At that time his family was living on Nathan Road, on the second floor, which would be the first floor in British terms. There was his mother, father, older brother, sister Phoebe, younger brother Robert, his cousin Frank, an aunt and a maid.

Q: What was Bruce's relationship like with his family and did he ever mention to his family that one day he was going to be famous?
Doug Palmer: He may have, I never heard him saying anything like that. He was a child movie star in Hong Kong before he went to the States, so people he knew and introduced me to in Hong Kong were in the movie business. But I don't recall him saying he was going to be famous. Maybe

he thought he was going to be, he certainly had long-range vision and he certainly had the self-confidence in what he could do.

Q: When Bruce left for Oakland, California, did you keep in touch with him?

Doug Palmer: I lost touch with him when he was in Oakland and later when he moved to LA. But I was working in Japan for four-and-a-half years from mid-1969 to early 1974, and during that period I kind of lost touch with him. Then it must've been in 1973 or 72, about a year before he died, I went down to Hong Kong for business and I thought he was still in Los Angeles. But I thought I could see if I could find his family, so I went looking for his family thinking he was still in LA. I went to the old apartment on Nathan Road and they didn't live there anymore, and nobody knew where they were.

So I'd almost given up, but I was talking with an accountant who we were doing business with and I mentioned the name and that I was looking for a friend. I said it was a friend of mine called Bruce Lee whose father was Lee Hoi-Chuen. I didn't think this guy would know who Bruce was, but I thought he might know who his father was (Laughs).And this guy looked at me with this strange look and he said, "You're a friend of Bruce Lee?" and I said, "Yeah," he said, "You think he's still in Los Angeles?" And he grabbed a Chinese newspaper and opened it up in the movie section, and there was a full-page ad of Bruce's latest movie - I think it was his second or third one - and he said he's in Hong Kong! I said, "Oh, jeez!" So I had a friend call the movie studio in Chinese telling them a friend of Bruce Lee's was in town and would like to get hold of him. They told him, "Yes, sure," and took my name, and five minutes later the phone rang and it was Bruce! He said, "Hey, you son of a gun" (Laughs). So we hooked back up. We had kind of lost contact.

Q: So how did you spend your time now that you found a long-lost friend?

Doug Palmer: My wife was with me, and we went over to his house which he was having built in Kowloon Tong. It was not done yet so he gave us a tour of the town. We went to the movie studio where he was in the process of filming the Game of Death. I remember he was disappointed with one of the martial artists that he had down for that movie, who was from Korea. He had just filmed the fight scene with Kareem Abdul-Jabbar and he showed me some pictures. He was laughing, he told me that he and Kareem almost got into a real fight - it almost came to blows. He was laughing about that and telling me about the scene. And then we watched a movie in the studio, it was one of the earlier films, the first one he did called Big Boss. Then we went to dinner. I was with him for two days and then I had to go back to Tokyo. We were corresponding and I was actually thinking about going to Hong Kong and working with him after I left Japan, but suddenly he was gone.

Q: When Bruce was in Seattle did he ever want to commercialize his Gung Fu or was he selective in who he taught?
Doug Palmer: He was very selective. Actually, I shouldn't say 'very' selective but he was willing to teach anybody who was serious about learning Gung Fu. He didn't care about what ethnic background or what race you were, whether you were a Chinese or not, as long as you wanted to learn it. He was thinking about commercializing it (in the early days) and he had an idea of starting several schools. At one point I thought about not going back to college from Seattle to the East Coast but rather stay in Seattle and continue to learn, ultimately becoming an instructor in one of his schools. Instead he went down to Los Angeles.

Q: Do you feel Bruce was a well-educated individual because of the fact he was able to connect philosophy with a physical fighting art, which - to Westerners especially - would have been unusual in those days?
Doug Palmer: Yeah, I would call him intelligent. I mean, I'd call him a genius. By my definition of genius he was a genius. Education was part of that, but it was more than that. It was the way he looked at things, which was a new way of looking at things. Looking at a problem from a better angle like nobody had done before, that's what I call a genius. Somebody who looks at something and looking at it from a fresh perspective comes up with something completely new.

Q: Any last words on your Sifu and friend?
Doug Palmer: I miss the guy, it was a total shock when he passed away. I owe him a lot, he was a mentor and a friend and taught me a lot of things; not just Gung Fu but life in general. He was a major influence in my life.

JOSEPH COWLES

Joseph Cowles is one of the original Bruce Lee students - but one you rarely hear about. Since Lee's death, Cowles avoided commercializing his art, instead teaching a few students privately. He began training with Lee in 1960 and became part of Bruce Lee's first branch of the Jun Fan Gung Fu Institute. Cowles is one of the rare original students from the Seattle period and has intriguing insights to offer into his Sifu who achieved paramount success on the global stage.

Q: When did you first start training with Bruce Lee in Seattle?
Joseph Cowles: It was in 1960. I went to a meeting which he held with his first group of students in Seattle, Washington. A friend of mine and I watched his demonstration with his group, then we went to the locker room to congratulate them. Just before we went down to the locker room a Japanese man walked up to me and spoke to me, telling me how he just challenged Bruce to fight him. I didn't know who he was. He claimed to be a fifth degree black belt. I don't know who he was because I'd never met him before. I hadn't even met Bruce before. But anyway, we went down and we congratulated Bruce on his demonstration with his group.

About a week later I called him up - this was 1960 - and asked him if I could train with him. He told me to meet him in Chinatown, so I went down there at the appointed time. This young Chinese was walking around - of course, I didn't recognize him right away because he didn't have his Gung Fu outfit on - but he walked up to me and he said, "Are you Jo Cowles?" and I said yes. So we went to his car. Bruce accepted me into his group. In the first training session we were doing the arm-banging exercises, and I was going hard. I hadn't done that before but I was a mail handler, my arms were very hard and pretty tough at that age. The first student I tried it with quit before I did and it kind of surprised me. Bruce said, "How long could you go with me?" So I start banging forearms with him. We started going pretty hard and all of a sudden his fist flew up and struck me to the right temple, it was pretty hard so I stopped. He said, "You put your hand up there to protect." So I told him OK and we started again. Finally it dawned on me I better stop because he was the teacher and I better not keep this up, so I said it was enough. Bruce looked at me with a kind of cold stare. He said, "Don't try to be a hero. If it hurts, stop - or I'll break your arm" (Laughs).

But afterwards he took me to a Chinese restaurant and bought me dinner and he arm wrestled me - wrist wrestled me actually, because the arms weren't touching the table. All of a sudden it was very explosive, he had my wrist turned down on the table. There was no way I could stop it. It was just such overwhelming and explosive energy, it was kind of scary it happened so fast. Anyway, that was my introduction to Bruce Lee. I asked him how long it took to learn Gung Fu. He said, "You never quit learning until they lay you in a coffin." That statement reminded me of something when he died a few years later and they laid him in his coffin, he never quit training until then.

I really liked Bruce as a person, he was very gentlemanly type of person and always conducted himself in a very nice way. But he wouldn't backdown if someone challenged him. That Karate man who approached me in that first meeting, he did challenge Bruce. But Bruce didn't want to fight him because he didn't have anything to prove. Bruce wasn't afraid of him. Finally the Karate man met Bruce at the University of Washington and pushed him and walked by. Bruce said to him to hold on and he talked. He said he just let him talk first, but when he put his hands on him he said he accepted the challenge.

So they met at the YMCA handball court. The Karate man wanted to fight him in the main gymnasium, but Bruce refused and said, "Let's go down to the handball court." Bruce had Ed Hart and Jesse Glover with him. I didn't see the fight but Jesse Glover was the referee and Ed Hart was the timer. Anyway, they went in the handball court. Bruce told me the Karate man got all ready to fight - this is what Bruce told me which I'm relating to you - and Bruce said, "Wait a minute, you challenged me?" The Karate man said, "That's true!" So Bruce said OK! The Karate man tried to throw a kick at Bruce, which Bruce blocked and then got him so quick he was driving him backwards with straight punches from the Wing Chun style of Gung Fu, which Bruce had trained back in Hong Kong. When they got to the wall of the handball court the man tried to spin away, but Bruce caught him with a double-punch, which is another Wing Chun technique. The Karate man started to fall to the floor, and as he was falling Bruce kicked him in the face and knocked him flat.

And Bruce grabbed him and tried to turn him over to continue but

Jesse said stop, because Bruce would really hurt the Karate man really bad. So Bruce stopped. Bruce told us he walked up to this other man who was with the Karate man and he thought he was the one who tried to get it started in the first place. So he said to this guy, "Do you want to fight me?" and the guy said he didn't. Bruce said, "You see the blood on the floor?" and the man said yes. Bruce said, " Clean it up." The Karate man was still laying there on the floor but he was awake and asked how long the match took. Bruce told him 23 seconds, but Ed Hart didn't tell the man it was 11 seconds so he wouldn't feel bad. Ed Hart said it took 11 seconds because he kept the time on his watch. It ended that quickly.

Q: What were Bruce's thoughts on his education and what was he planning on doing after graduation?
Joseph Cowles: I don't know fully what he was studying but I knew one course which he was studying and that was philosophy. He did write an article on that in his first book - Chinese Gung Fu - he wrote which was published by James Lee's printing place down in Oakland, California. That book is pretty rare these days.

Q: Please tell me how many people were part of the Jun Fan Gung Fu school.
Joseph Cowles: It was a fairly small group compared to his group later. I never was acquainted with the Jeet Kune Do people down in California, but I would say there was about 20 to 25 students in the old basement school in Seattle's Chinatown. Later on I continued at the Seattle University district location, where I guess there were between 25 and 35 students.

Q: Taky Kimura was the assistant instructor?
Joseph Cowles: Taky Kimura was named Bruce's assistant instructor, I remember when he did that. Bruce said he respected Taky and he made him assistant instructor. Taky took over the class when Bruce would travel back to Hong Kong. Bruce was very thorough and you would have to give 110 percent in the class. If you didn't train hard then you were not part of the Jun Fan Gung Fu Institute - this is what he called it. And he said, "If you don't train hard you aren't part of the group even if you train here," that's how he put it. For myself, I tried to give 110 percent all the time, in fact so much so that I got sick and had to go down and lay down in my car a couple of times. I was working very hard as a mail handler, as a postman, lifting these heavy mail bags for eight hours. And then I was working out really hard, not just with sweat but like a Boxer in the ring. I worked that hard and I enjoyed working hard. So when I went to class afterwards, I was a little

bit down on my energy. Because the training in Bruce's class was difficult, he didn't put up with nonsense.

Q: What were Bruce's views on other martial art systems and also the Western-styles of fighting which he had now been exposed to?
Joseph Cowles: He felt the Americans were much bigger than he was. After he came to the US he felt he really needed to train hard because of his size. He did train with weightlifting after he arrived in California. In the early days he kind of looked at Boxing and at that time his theories probably changed. He considered Boxing to be grade school and Gung Fu to be university.

Q: Did you ever hear any rumors about Bruce being defeated?
Joseph Cowles: Yes, there were rumors. At one time, the rumor which was going around was someone had met Bruce in the park this day and choked him out. So Charlie Woo, an early Seattle student who was a third degree black belt in Judo, tried to follow that up and went up to a Judo meeting. He walked up to this Judo man, "I heard Bruce got choked out in the park," and the Judo man said, "I don't know anything about that." Charlie Woo said, "You should know because you're the one who supposed to have done it" (Laughs). The Judo man said, "No! I didn't do anything like that!" Someone was just trying to get something started between Bruce and someone else so they could see a fight, or just be troublemakers. The same thing happened with Al Dacascos. Bruce had confronted him, it was just the same type of false rumor. Bruce and him got along just fine. Someone was just trying to get something started in the audience.

Bruce was not the type of person who would go around looking for fights. There was one occasion in Seattle, one time two men started making fun of him on a ferry trip, made fun of his clothes, he was kind of dressed in a neat way. The two guys were making fun of him. He waited till the ferry stopped, and he followed them and he started mocking them. One of them attacked Bruce, and Bruce started punching and kicking him, knocking him across the sidewalk. The other guy suddenly didn't want anything to do with it when he saw what happened to the first guy. Bruce was just paying them back because what they did to him, but he didn't go around looking for fights. He was like a gentleman.

I'll give you one more example. One time Taky Kimura had him watch his parking lot, because some people would park there even though it was only for the grocery store customers. Taky got tired of it and asked Bruce to watch his parking lot, and he agreed. A guy pulled in there, parked his car and started to walk off. Bruce stopped him and said, "You can park here if you're shopping. If you want to shop somewhere else then you could park somewhere else." The guy didn't know who Bruce was, of course, since it was the early days. So he said, "Oh, is that so?" Bruce said, "Yes, that is so." When the guy saw that Bruce was so determined - Bruce didn't attack him or anything but just answered him - when the guy saw that, the guy lost courage and got back in the car and left. It was those kind of things that happened.

There was another thing which was kind of funny. There was a photographer I met in Idaho who told me he'd taken some pictures of Bruce when he was in Seattle. When Bruce saw the proofs of them he called the photographer up and let him know he didn't like those pictures. And the photographer got angry and Bruce got angry. They were both yelling and shouting, having a shouting match over the telephone about those pictures. The photographer didn't know who Bruce was, thinking he's just a Chinese guy. Bruce said, "I'll come there and punch your lights out!" The photographer said, "OK, I'll leave the door open for you." When the photographer found out who Bruce was, he told me, "When I found out who he was...Oh, man." That was kind of funny. It wasn't something Bruce was going to do (beat the guy up), he was just talking.

Q: Anything you would like to add pertaining to your training, friendship and your thoughts on the success he achieved ultimately?
Joseph Cowles: We all hoped that he would be seen by somebody, because he wanted to be in movies. Someone said if he could ever be seen he would really go places. He did and...you know the rest of the story. I would like to say that Jesse Glover was the first student in America, then Taky Kimura was Bruce's assistant instructor in the school. Both of them are really fine. Taky doesn't like to be in the limelight, Jesse has traveled to many different countries around the world holding seminars, and I guess he still does. We're glad (Bruce) made it as far as money is concerned, but the Hollywood scene I don't think is a very helpful scene to be in (Laughs). Anyway, Bruce was able to meet the needs of his family and do what he wanted to do the most, which was to showcase martial arts on the screen, and that's what he did. And a lot of movies showcase what he was doing. He wanted to show the public via the medium of the movies.

GEORGE LEE

George Lee was one of Bruce Lee's top Oakland students and a close friend. Although George was twice his age, both men got on like a house on fire. George (no relation to Bruce) was the man responsible for making Bruce most of the specialized training equipment which he used to cultivate himself and elevate his skill. George Lee's relationship with Bruce was special and both men continued to correspond right until the end. At age 93, George's memories of his Sifu and close friend are still fresh.

Q: Did you meet Bruce Lee at a nightclub?
George Lee: It wasn't a nightclub, it was a community center. It was way back when I first met him when he came over from San Francisco to teach our class the Hong Kong Cha Cha, which is a dance. During the intermission time, he went through some moves of kata and what he did was very impressive. So I asked him what type of martial arts it was and he told me it was Wing Chun. It was very impressive because of what I had learned for the last 15 years - I couldn't believe that he could move so fast, and he was very precise. So that's why I asked him when he would come back to Oakland; he could open up a school and I could get him some students. This was back in the early 60s. When he came back we opened up a school in Oakland and that's how we got started. From then on he did the TV series and he came back and forth to teach us.

Q: Could you please tell me more about Bruce teaching you, Allen Joe and James Lee private lessons?
George Lee: They were not private lessons, we had a class Monday, Wednesday and Friday. And he also had a class at Fremont, which is another city here. He was teaching three classes and as far as Allen, Jimmy

and I, we would pal up together and we got on pretty well. I had a few private lessons in his home in LA.

Q: You made Bruce a lot of the specialized equipment he later used to elevate his extraordinary skill and abilities. Can you please shed light on this?
George Lee: Bruce was always thinking about ideas. Back in those days we didn't have equipment like we have nowadays. So, most of the times when we went to lunch or dinner, he would pick up a napkin from the restaurant and start drawing. The first thing we started with was a nunchaku. We went through various designs because we had to improvise and finally cut it down to what he liked. We changed the pattern of the nunchaku many times and we finally got it down to what he wanted.

Then later on all the equipment I made for him was to build up his forearms, like the three-sectional staff and the gripping machine - which he just loved. Other punching bags and shields were all his ideas. He was very happy that I could do these things for him. If I can make a long story short, it all started in the beginning when he came to Oakland from Seattle to start up a school. He had all his loose change and receipts in a paper shoebox and I thought, "I've got to do something for him." So I built him a stainless steel metal box with a lock on it. That's what got the idea for the equipment going. He said, "You made that, what else can you make?" From then on we started making all kinds of stuff from the leg stand, punching bag, finger-jabbing ball, you name it.

Q: What was his favorite piece of equipment that you made for him?
George Lee: The nunchaku was the favorite. Then later on the tombstone I made for him which was for (reflecting) more of his philosophy. Also the gripping machine I made for building his forearms. He loved that too.

Q: Did he use the nunchaku in his movies only or did he use it in his personal training too?
George Lee: He practiced with it so he could perfect it without making a mistake. Then later he used it in his movies for fighting scenes.

Q: Did Allen Joe influence Bruce in bodybuilding?
George Lee: Well, he (Allen Joe) was doing all these push ups and doing a lot of weights because he was a bodybuilder. He did show him some weight exercises with barbells. When we moved from Broadway to Jimmy's house we trained in his garage.

Q: Being one of his close companions how did you spend time with Bruce outside of the Gung Fu gym?

George Lee: Oh, yeah, he did a lot of funny things like changing coins from one hand to another, and he'd tell a lot of jokes. He was a fun guy to be with. As far as friendship, he was particular who he palled around with and I'm very fortunate I was in on this. Like I said, we'd always go to each other's birthdays, he would come from LA down here and we'd go to LA. A lot of the times he was very interested in ancient swordwork. One time I went to Chinatown for him and bought one of these long ancient swords for him. That's what our lives were all about, in that we palled around together. We had a great time and a lot of the times he invited us to Hollywood to participate in Green Hornet. We had a ball just to be together.

Q: After Bruce moved to Los Angeles did you continue to see him?

George Lee: He used to send me a plane ticket to come over so that I could visit him, and he would teach me a few things. One time he wanted me to make him a Ying Yang, which I still have here. He didn't have the time to put it on his certificates at the time because he was already going to Hong Kong to do a movie. From then on he stayed there and I still have it here in my home. To make a long story short, Bruce Lee was quite a fellow and he was fun to be with. I was very fortunate that we stayed together that long and his son Brandon, his mother (Linda) and sister in Oakland. A great family.

Q: Writing letters was one of the avenues you both used to correspond with each other...

George Lee: He was constantly writing letters and drawing - things like helmets and punching bags - and telling me when he would be coming up and when he would like to see me coming over, that kind of thing. I have about 30 letters which are in my book. It really tells the story of the relationship of him and I. I'm 92 years old now. I was still playing tennis until the doctor stopped me when I turned 90. I'm very fortunate that I'm pretty active and I could talk to you (Laughs), because usually when you get to this age your memory fades.

Q: From someone who knew Bruce on a professional and personal level, how would you define Bruce's personality?

George Lee: Like I said, he was a great philosopher and he was so particular who he mingled with. To me, personally, he was a really down-to-earth fellow and we got on perfect like we were brothers.

Q: When you visited Bruce in later years in Los Angeles, did you witness any change in your friend's appearance in terms of having

improved dramatically in his body development?
George Lee: It was terrific! I mean, he was so dedicated to his body. He would build one part of his body to another, with his knuckles he'd punch on a pad day in and day out just to get the knuckles conditioned. The forearms gripping machine, he was constantly using it. I've never seen a man so dedicated to his body, when he decided to do something he would come out 100 percent. As far as the development, he had washboard stomach. From the Oakland period to the days in Hollywood when I went to see him, his body changed. He was much more developed and it was amazing he could develop a body as quick as he did. As far as his physical appearance, it was terrific. He didn't do drugs or anything like that, or smoke or drink; he was very conscious about his body.

Q: Do you think Bruce Lee was one of the first martial artists to implement equipment training?
George Lee: I think so. Like I say, it was all his ideas. Back in those days they didn't have all this equipment, all they had was a spring grip, which wasn't good enough. From then on he was doing a lot of push ups and chin ups, and on top of that all the equipment I made for him: the punching board, kicking board. These were all his ideas, he always drew a picture of what he wanted and we'd get it to the right specification.

Q: When Bruce went to Hong Kong to make the movies, which enthralled millions of people around the world, did you have any telephone conversations with him?
George Lee: Just one. At that time I think Hong Kong was getting a little bit too much for him. He came back for a physical. I noticed from listening to his voice he wasn't feeling too well. I don't know if it was jet lag or not, but he told me that Hong Kong was not right for him. I don't know but there must have been some problem for him in the movie studio or something. From then he said he'd get back to me but after that I never heard from him. I guess he went back to Hong Kong. He wrote me lots of letters when he was in Hollywood.

Q: What did you think of Fist of Fury (aka Chinese Connection) in which Bob Baker had a role in?
George Lee: Bob Baker was a good friend of mine. The movie was OK, not the best I've seen of him.

Q: Did Bruce talk to you about any of his movies?
George Lee: Green Hornet, Marlowe and Longstreet, the ones he made in the US.

Q: When was the last time you saw Bruce?

George Lee: He asked me to make that design for him, that was the last time I saw him; I could not deliver it. By that time the whole family went to Hong Kong and I had no contact with Linda, and Brandon was too young anyhow.

Q: Los Angeles Chinatown student Herb Jackson made equipment for Bruce too, were you both responsible for making Bruce the equipment?

George Lee: As far as I know it was bunch of stuff he bought for him, it wasn't made. Because the last picture I saw - which was in a magazine - with a bunch of stuff, it wasn't homemade things, as far as I know. I talked to Herb when he was alive, the poor guy, he was a really nice guy. A lot of times we talked about making the equipment. He said the only thing he made for him was a punching board. Also, he said a magazine made a mistake and took a picture and said the equipment was made by him, and he held it up (Laughs). He apologized for that. Herb Jackson did a lot of housework for him, he would always go to his house and repair the punching bag, the heavy bag and so on. That was the relationship between Bruce and Herb Jackson. He did a lot of repairing.

Q: Anything you would like to add pertaining to your friendship with the late great Bruce Lee and the impact he's had?

George Lee: I miss him. That's all I can tell you. I mean, he's somebody I worship, he's my Sifu, he's my master, and he taught me martial arts I never dreamed of.

LEO FONG

L eo T. Fong trained with Bruce Lee in Oakland and is one of the few original students from that period to have experienced direct instruction from Lee. Both men shared a mutual interest in the martial arts and fitness. Fong became a close friend of Lee's and continued to see him and correspond with him right until his untimely death. He has some intriguing stories which are refreshing and thought-provoking. He continues to train and teach martial arts and has also been involved in the motion picture industry.

Q: Can you please start off by telling me when you were first introduced to Bruce Lee?
Leo Fong: Yeah, I met Bruce in 1962. What happened was I was training with James Lee and he said there was a young guy who was going to come in and do a demonstration for Wallay Jay, who was putting on a fundraiser every year. So, he said this young kid was going to do a demonstration. (Bruce) started explaining the ineffectiveness of classical Kung Fu, which got some people upset I guess, and then he went on to say why it was ineffective. He got a couple of guys on the stage from the audience and he threw a front-hand jab and touched their forehead, they couldn't stop it. Jimmy said afterwards that we'll have a little meeting on Monday and get together to meet Bruce. On Monday evening there were about four of our people there. That's how I got to meet him in 1962.

Q: How would you describe his personality?
Leo Fong: Bruce was a very outgoing person, very cocky, very confident, and he would tell you what he was going to do and he would do it! And then on the other side, he was a very generous person, very giving; he did a lot of favors for me. He was able to cross-train and everything he read he related it to the martial arts.

Q: Can you describe some of the training in Jimmy's garage and how did Bruce's training methods differentiate to the traditionalists of that era?

Leo Fong: He was very incredible, sometimes he would workout and other times he would lecture, talking to us. It wasn't like when I used to train Japanese Karate, where they would line you up. He didn't like the organized teaching. He would line up six or seven of us and we would practice blocking, hitting or what they call lop sau, where you grab the arm and jerk and hit. Then we would do kicking and bag drills. Basically, we were working our first stage of developing of the tools. Then the second stage was when we are refining the tools and dissolving the tools. Then it was to learn to express the tools. Sometimes he got me hitting the bag, at other times he got me working on kicking form and my front-hand jab. At the time when I was there, he was doing the modified Wing Chun style. He did the typical bong sau from the Wing Chun on-guard position.

Later, when he got into the fight with the Chinese Kung Fu guy, he phoned me up one day and I said I couldn't make it because I was in Stockton, which was an hour and half from Oakland. He said to me to come down because they were to fight this afternoon. He told me afterwards how he chased the guy all over the place hitting him and finally got him in the corner, put his hand on his throat and knocked him out. The guy said, "I give up, I give up." Afterwards Jimmy called me saying the sucker kept running around and Bruce couldn't catch him. Bruce told me, "You know what? I just realized I need more angle. I just can't use the Wing Chun forward blast because the guy was ducking and running." I said, "Bruce, if you want more angles you've got to do uppercuts and crosses," and the blocking thing, which I used to do. And when I went back that week he had already changed his stance, which resembled a Boxing stance, and he was working with the right jab in a southpaw stance.

He was constantly evolving, every week you go there he would come out with something different than what he taught the week before. He started fooling around and I realized where his influence came from: Muhammad Ali. He used to collect films and watch Ali, who had a very strong influence on him.

Q: One time at the offices of Black Belt magazine Bruce lost his temper. Could you tell me what exactly caused this?

Leo Fong: What happened was at the magazine offices we met up with another guy who used to train with Ed Parker - in fact he was a dojo-mate of mine. Bruce and James Woo met for the first time at Black Belt offices and James Woo acted like he was some mysterious grandmaster. He said to Bruce, "You don't want me to fight you because if I touch you I'll knock you out." Bruce was fuming - he was mad! And he said, "I'll go and get that son of a bitch and kill him" (Laughs). Woo used to be in San Francisco and moved out to Southern California where he started training with Ed Parker. Later, Ed had thrown him out and Woo took some of his black belts with him, so he wasn't an honest person.

Bruce was a man of integrity. He had to be careful people didn't prostitute his art, because they're doing it right now. Everybody's going around saying Jeet Kune Do 'this' and 'that' and they don't know what the hell they're doing (Laughs). Actually, if you look at his art from a standpoint of technique, Bruce didn't have a lot of different techniques. Basically, his sparring skill - he was good - these were his inner skills; they weren't all physical. He could use techniques in many different situations and he was strong. Once he got inside in sparring you weren't able to get away. On the other hand, he was able to control the distance. I sparred with him and it was like fighting a shadow, he would move in on you before you realized it. He knew how to close that gap real quick. A lot of these people who teach Jeet Kune Do today, I don't think they can teach for more than half hour (Laughs). But Bruce could sit down and talk for eight hours doing a seminar and I'm sure he still wouldn't run out of stuff.

Q: Do you remember Bob Baker (who was part of the Oakland group)? How did he get the part of the Russian in Bruce's second movie Fist of Fury?
Leo Fong: I remember Bob Baker, he was a good guy and a student. As far as training when I was there, he was kind of awkward. I don't know what background he had before he came there. I had a Boxing background because I was training and working out every afternoon with the California State University Boxing Team. Bruce knew because he (Bob) had that look for the movie and Bob was very loyal to Bruce. I think he did a good job in the film. Bruce's ultimate goal was to show his stuff on the screen, he wasn't into competitions like all these other guys, he wanted to show his stuff on the movie screen. He was very good at that. All his films were successful. He was very conscious about a storyline, choreography and camera angles. He was amazing for a guy who never went to film school. He was the 'Jeet Kune Do' of filmmaking. And he picked Bob because Bob had the look of a Russian guy. Bruce told him what to do and directed him, and Bob followed directions and it looked great!

Q: As I understand, you were also partly responsible for introducing Bruce to weight training and muscle magazines?
Leo Fong: Yeah. What happened was at the time I met Bruce in 1962, I had been training with weights since 1955 where I was living. One day I

saw a big guy standing in front of this building. I got out of the car and I looked at him - a big muscular guy - and he said, "My name's Bill Pearl. I have the ultimate gym here." I thought wow. He was Mr. America and Mr. Universe. I was one of the first students to join and it was $19 a month. So I joined and he showed me everything about weight training. I didn't do weight training before 1955. I used to do nothing but push ups, sit ups, pull ups and squats. I ran track and boxed in college, I had never lifted weights before. I used to do three or four sets of pull ups every night and 150 push ups. Anyway, I started lifting weights and my arms got bigger and stronger. Most people think if you lift weights you can't fight.

I used to go lift for about two hours down in Sacramento University gym and workout. I found out I could hit harder. When I met Bruce he noticed my arms and my shoulders - which were pretty good in size - and so I told him about the training I did, and I gave him a copy of Strength and Health (magazine) by Bob Hoffman. And the next thing I knew he was collecting all these magazines. If you walked into his house in Southern California you'd see he had a stack of muscle magazines: Strength and Health, Muscle and Fitness - Joe Weider's magazines. Weider definitely started the whole nutrition and fitness industry. Bruce had his own program. He did a lot of high rep stuff, 25 repetitions. That's why he got so defined. He also worked out a training program for Dan Inosanto and some of the guys he trained. He would look at something and he was very innovative and would make it fit in with the martial arts. He told me that by lifting weights he didn't want to perform any exercises that didn't compliment his Jeet Kune Do. So everything was related, he didn't do it just because he just wanted a good-looking body but because it made him more fluid in his fighting. And he also studied nutrition.

If you notice his picture in the 1960s he wasn't defined - he had a big chest cage for his body, and if he took a deep breath the chest would expand four inches, which is unusual. His arm was kind of skinny, but later when he got into nutrition he started eating less fatty food and he started to look really defined, like you see him in Enter the Dragon. If you could see the difference between the Bruce Lee body of the 1960s and 1970s, you can see he had evolved more into nutrition and weight training.

Q: Which exercises with weights did he favor and did he perform any unusual methods which caught your eye?
Leo Fong: One thing he did was the way he performed the military press, where you have the barbell behind your back and you push it over your head. We push up in one and bring it back. He would push up and hold it there for a ten count before he brought it back down. With this method you can't use the heaviest weight but what it does is it works the body part. Now we call it the 'core development'. You push the weight up and you

hold it there for a few seconds then you lower it and you repeat. And he would tell me to do that. That developed a different dimension because if you push it up and down, up and down, you affect a certain muscle. But when you push it and hold it up and you pause, it developed a certain endurance in the muscle too.

Q: Which other exercises did he favor in his quest for cultivating a lethal body?
Leo Fong: What he did was an exercise which worked the lower back muscles, that's how he messed up his back. He wrote Tao of Jeet Kune Do when he injured his back because he couldn't move. He did what we call a 'good morning' exercise, bending forward and bending back whilst standing up. He did that with a 20-pound weight to develop lower back muscles. He moved a disc in his back. I know how he must have felt because in 2005 I moved my disc too, and I was out of commission for three months. I used to go over to his house and he told me he couldn't do anything. Then I went down two weeks later and he wasn't training too much because his back was hurting, but he was evolving his Jeet Kune Do. I didn't understand what he was saying, and finally what it was he had developed concepts for Jeet Kune Do while he was laying there because his mind was active whilst his body was at rest. He got over his back problem. It's amazing that it's not all physical; his art consists of both philosophical and also mental aspects of his martial arts journey.

Q: It is commonly known that Bruce had his own unique modified versions of performing sit ups and leg raises...
Leo Fong: One of his exercises was to raise up his legs, push up and slowly lower them back down. You arch your back and lower it down - it's a hard stomach exercise. What happened was he took a traditional exercise that he had seen and modified it the way it was performed. He always said to me you need totality in whatever you do. So if you do a regular punch and it doesn't always work, he'd think about how to make it work another way. One of his favorites was the leg raises. I tried it the way he did and I said, "That's pretty good." You get tremendous resistance in the middle abdominals. Then he would use a stick standing up and do alternate twists for the oblique muscles - the love handles on the side.

Basically, for the abdominals, leg raises worked the lower, sit ups for the upper, then he'd do the twists. The other thing he was big on was the forearms. I already kind of knew but people told me punching power comes from your back hip, etc. But I realized later it comes from your forearms. So he did a lot of forearm exercises. George (Lee) found out I was shooting my book Choy Lay Fut Kung Fu and Bruce found out too, so Bruce was down at the Black Belt studio for two days of the photo shoot. One day he came in and said, "Hey, grab my arm." Bruce started arm wrestling with me. Suddenly, I couldn't push his arm and he couldn't push my arm down, that bothered him all day. So he went back and trained all night. The next day he came in again and said, "Hey, Leo, let's try that arm wrestling again." So we did and he beat me! He did my shoulder in (Laughs). He said he'd developed this exercise which has a weight on the end of a bar and he lays down and lowers it in front of his chest. He would straighten his arms out and he would move it back like a windscreen wiper. He would do this with a 10- or 20-pound weight end of a bar. He really messed up my elbow. But he was doing that exercise.

Q: Which professional bodybuilders did he admire in the 60s...Dave Draper, Bill Pearl?
Leo Fong: I think guys that were short, such as (Roy) Hilligen, who was a short guy. Also Clancy Ross.

Q: What pertinent training were you accustomed to?
Leo Fong: Well, the thing I learned from Bruce changed my life. Like I said, I had a chance to be the champion of a Wrestling or Boxing team back in 1947 when I was a freshman in college. A friend of mine was a State Wrestling champion, so we were playing around one day and I said to him, "Why don't you try to take me down with your Wrestling?" Every time he'd move in I'd hit him with a jab and move, he couldn't touch me. Then I had a chance to cross with my right hand and knock him out. From there I decided not to join the Wrestling team because I thought Boxing was better than Wrestling. I trained in Boxing and had 25 fights, I developed a pretty good left hook and knocked out 23 people.

Anyway, when I came out of college my father used to talk to me about Kung Fu. He told me all about these Kung Fu masters who would come into the village with their begging bowl, and kids would come in and pick on them and tease them. The Kung Fu masters would kick the hell out of the kids (Laughs). He said these guys could do demonstrations where they would break boards with their fingers and bricks with their fists. I didn't doubt it. He saw Dim Mak where a master would touch someone and in a week the guy would be dead. That's all bullshit. My uncle and dad used to run a restaurant in Chicago in the ghetto. People would come in to eat and not pay, so my uncle would fight them and knock them out using Kung Fu on them. He would tell me these stories as I was growing up.

So when I moved up to California I started to look for Kung Fu schools. I was still working on my Boxing. I didn't think that Boxing was the ultimate so I found a Choy Lay Fut school and trained for three years in this style. Then I sought out other schools such as Chin Wu. I met

Jimmy (Lee) when I was training Choy Lay Fut and Sil Lum. I heard there was a Tae Kwon Do student at the Sacramento State University, so I looked him up. I found out that he was from Seoul in South Korea, so I asked him to teach me Tae Kwon Do. I had three friends and a pastor from the church, and every afternoon we would go to the church hall and train Tae Kwon Do. I would drive out to San Francisco to train Choy Lay Fut. I was training in everything (Laughs).

Q: Can you differentiate between the Oakland period and Bruce's style which evolved when he moved to Los Angeles and formed his own personal expression of the martial arts he labeled Jeet Kune Do?
Leo Fong: Bruce asked me, "Leo, what in the hell are you training in so many styles for?" I said, "Bruce, I'm looking for the ultimate, man," and he put his finger on my chest and pushed it and said, "Man, there is no ultimate, the ultimate is right in there." Boxing trains different ranges. I asked him what he meant. He said, "I train how to trap, how to kick - we integrate all that. You don't need all those guys." So that was a pivotal point in my life. I started thinking and little by little gave up all those different styles and then I started to integrate Boxing in relationship to martial arts, including my kicks and how I could counter that with my Boxing, Wrestling and trapping, etc.

In Oakland, basically his training was a modified version of Wing Chun and Jun Fan. Then after the fight with Wong Jackman, his art emerged into Jeet Kune Do. This was more like Kickboxing which he was starting and then, when he moved to LA, he developed the five ways of attack along with a bunch of other stuff that he talks about. In the meantime, his footwork was more like Muhammad Ali and he would use a modified form of Boxing - that's what he was doing. His skill...not so much physical, he had inner skills, his mind, his emotions, his spirit were all incredible. A lot of Jeet Kune Do guys go out saying they teach Jeet Kune Do but don't understand that the internal emotional structure is being screwed up in function. I've done seminars in different places where they claim Jeet Kune Do by fake - what I call 'winning by deception'. Bruce developed and he had a lot of influence by developing techniques and his regimens. He used to say you've got to hit the guy from the initial movement. Sometimes technique is there, but then you've got to duck, slip or bob. Once he's there you can hit or if he grabs you then you have to deal with that. It's too late, so it's better to hit him on the initial move. Bruce was able to hit you on your intention, when you were thinking about it he'd already get you. He said, "OK, try to get away from my front-hand jab," and he would do something like he had hypnotized you. He was in there and you were too late .

Q: What did you think of Bruce's performance in the Green Hornet TV series?

Leo Fong: Yeah, I remember Green Hornet. He also did a movie called Marlowe with James Garner later. He told me he was going to be in a series called Green Hornet. I remember in the show he did different stuff in the fighting he orchestrated   and choreographed stuff, what we may call 'worked out sparring'. He had such inner skills and he was very fast, his timing was right on and he really made it look good. That was when the door opened but Hollywood didn't really embrace him open-handedly, so he was little bit frustrated by that.

Q: Did you keep in touch with him when he was in Hong Kong pursuing his movie career?

Leo Fong: I lost contact with him after he went to Hong Kong. But when he was shooting the first movie I got letters from him and he told me about it. I have the last letter he wrote me when he got the opportunity to write to me. He says he had to be in Hong Kong and signed a three-movie deal so wouldn't be able to come over and see me for a while. I have that last letter. He said these things are coming his way because he tried to open the door in Hollywood for so many years and they weren't ready, they were discriminating against Asian actors. If you want to play a chauffeur or a cook...he said he won't do that (Laughs). Anyway, I lost contact with him but Jimmy Lee kept up to date. He would call Jimmy and they would talk on the phone. Jimmy would tell us what Bruce was doing. Bruce would correspond with me via letters. Then in 1973, when I was watching the news on TV, they said Bruce Lee had died. I thought it was a joke! By that time Jimmy had died already too. So I've lost two good martial arts friends.

Q: Tell me more about Jimmy's relationship with Bruce, they were really close friends?

Leo Fong: They were not related but they were close. Jimmy was the type of guy who was always in contact with different martial arts people. He would build a working relationship with them and then analyze how effective they were. Jimmy's big thing was, "Sure, this thing looks good but does it work on the street?" That was his thing. If it didn't work on the street and on him then he didn't wholeheartedly embrace it. So, when he met Bruce - and Bruce was really skilful - he was really smiling and he said to me, "I think I've found something that really works, something which is not bullshit, it really is the real deal." When I first met Bruce on that Monday night after the charity demonstration, he picked one guy out of the crowd and told him to place a phone book on his chest - which was the Oakland telephone book about three inches thick. Then Jimmy had a couch and behind the couch was a big window. Bruce hit the guy with an inch punch - I hadn't figured out what he was going to do - he just flicked his wrist and the guy fell back onto the couch and hit the window. I realized why he had to have the telephone book on his chest because he would have really hurt the guy (Laughs).

Jimmy was a bodybuilder. He used to hang out with the bodybuilders, the ones which lived in the Oakland area. He worked out with weights all the time, even when he was dying. I was at his house when he had lung cancer, he had lost weight and he was doing military press and upright rowing with light dumbbells. For weight training in those days you'd do bench press, military press, upright rowing, side laterals, then you'd do tricep presses. There weren't the state-of-the-art machines like you see today. They had couple of homemade machines but mostly it was all barbells and dumbbells. Nowadays you've got all this hi-tech stuff and exercise balls to the point it confuses you.

Q: Do you find it ironic that many professional bodybuilders are influenced by Bruce Lee's physique?
Leo Fong: A lot of them are impressed that he didn't have bulk but he had definition. His training basically was high repetitions.

Q: Bruce kept his classes small, similar to a Boxing class. Do you feel it was imperative for him to maintain quality over quantity?
Leo Fong: Bruce wanted to keep it small and he knew what they were going to do and what they're doing now. He said, "I don't want people to prostitute my art." He had an offer after Green Hornet and would have made millions, and in those days a million dollars was a lot of money. They wanted him to open up a whole chain of Bruce Lee's Green Hornet schools. But he said no and turned it down, even though there was a time he only had $50 in the bank and couldn't make his car payment. Steve McQueen offered to help pay but he said no. Then he developed the idea of doing private lessons. He printed a bunch of business cards and I came down to see him and he said, "Take one of these cards." I said to him, "What's this, ten lessons for $1,000? Is anybody buying this stuff, Bruce?" He said, "Yes, in fact (Roman) Polanski already called me to book ten lessons." So he flew over to film director Roman Polanski and came back and got $10,000 (Laughs). That's how he got started with giving private lessons. I wish I'd taken all of the business cards, they must be worth $1,000 a piece now. I just took a couple of them.

He had charisma, very good personality, very confident. Some may think he was cocky but he wasn't, he could back up what he said. He could just look at something and improve on it. When he was training us he had a small group, he closed down the school in LA because he didn't want people...mainly Bruce wasn't much interested in teaching, we all knew that. Bruce wanted to teach somebody different things so he could practice his stuff. He wasn't really interested in teaching. He did give us certificates but he wasn't...he gave certain people certificates such as Kareem (Abdul-Jabbar), the basketball player. I remember the day he had him come over to train. He said he wanted to learn how to deal with a tall guy.

I came down to LA one day and he said, "Guess who I've got training with me?" I asked him if it was the basketball player, and he said yes. He had a picture taken with Kareem holding Brandon and putting him on the roof of the house. He said, "You know why I'm getting him to train with me? I want to train to learn how to beat a tall guy." He said the best way to deal with this would be to cut his knees down, kick him in the knee. Kareem got into couple of movies, Aeroplane and others after Bruce's movie. But Kareem doesn't talk much about Bruce now, he's working with the Lakers. Bruce would go to different people and he would try his stuff out, that's why in the process those who hung out with him learned. Basically, everybody that was close to him and worked with him were his sparring partners. He developed with his sparring partners to train himself. He didn't care about whether you learned a thing well or not, he wanted you to go out and spar.

Q: Finally, how do you remember Bruce Lee and the impact he's had on the world, which to this day is a constant source of inspiration?
Leo Fong: He had a strong impact on the world, which helped him with the movies. The movies were a great medium to showcase his skills. Then out of that, the people who had the privilege to train with him were able to spread the message too. I think he was way light years ahead of his time. He was a very well-read, very smart kid, and was able to innovate in order to make his art better and more effective. In the modern analysis it wasn't so much 'I'm doing it because I want to beat up everybody'. One time in an interview in Black Belt magazine, he said, "The reason I'm training is to knock the hell out of my own insecurities and all my emotional problems."

Self-improvement was his main reason for developing and on what he was doing. He had goals. He said he didn't want to fight in the ring like Chuck Norris or Joe Lewis and these guys, but wanted to showcase his stuff, and the best way to do it is on the screen. He became very good at that, he was a very good filmmaker and good actor. Every time you see him on the screen you can't take your eyes of him. You know why? When you look at someone else imitate his movement, you couldn't care less, but Bruce had emotional content. A lot of Jeet Kune Do guys are imitators. I train at the park and I had a guy come up three weeks ago who trained with

Tim Tackett. God, he was so bad! I told him I'd been training since I was 12 years old, and I'm 80 years old.

Q: Anything you would like to add?

Leo Fong: What Bruce taught me was you have to have your own identity, you can't go ride on his tail and say, "Hey, my style of Jeet Kune Do." Therefore, you think you're good as Bruce Lee, that's what everybody says and it's really disappointing. If Bruce came back to life today he'd be really disappointed the way people treated Jeet Kune Do. I think you have to remember him really as a man who had a lot of influence, and I know he changed my life as far as telling me to seek my own truth and be my own person. He said, "Teachers open the door and you have to discover for yourself" - that's not what everybody's doing, they're imitating his movements. I know a few people who are still searching and are dissatisfied because they haven't come to the point where they have the mentality of 'I need to seek the truth for myself' and 'how can I be perfect like Bruce Lee?' You'll never be perfect like Bruce Lee, just like you'll never be perfect and do all the things your instructor tells you.

There's a weakness in being an instructor, an instructor has the tendencies to want you to punch the same as he does, but you'll never be like him. You have to take the stuff and figure out how you can make it your own. I do the technique and I become the technique, but if you imitate Bruce Lee you may look like him but you're not the technique.

BOB BREMER

Bob Bremer was one of Bruce Lee's original students who trained at the Los Angeles Chinatown gym as well as Sunday afternoons at Bruce's house. A down-to-earth individual, Bremer became part of a tight-knit backyard group who were fortunate enough to train with Lee privately. Always ready to throw humor into a conversation, Bob Bremer has some very interesting insights into Bruce Lee. Mr. Bremer was fortunate to know the Little Dragon socially as well as within the confines of the gym.

Q: When did you first meet Bruce Lee and how often did you go to the Chinatown school?
Bob Bremer: I met Bruce Lee in 1967. It was a couple times a week. He'd pick out what you could use and places you were weak in and he'd concentrate on that and bring you up. We covered everything. In five or ten minutes he could have you do twice as good than you normally could, because he could put a finger on what needed working on. He was a very interesting guy. I can't believe that some people quit coming. I think he demanded so much which scared some to put that much in. I figured I was too lazy, but I would bluff it and fake it. Sometimes when I left him on a Sunday afternoon, I'd feel like Superman (Laughs). I was learning things nobody had seen, it was very interesting. I thought he was real good (as an instructor) and he was capable of giving you the whole thing on a plate. He was really phenomenal. As far as philosophy, we probably got more than we realized because he would sneak it in (Laughs). You didn't realize how much influence you picked up till you went away from there.

Q: Can you tell me about when you would go to the beach with Bruce? Was his mind on the martial arts when you all were enjoying yourself?

Bob Bremer: Yeah, there were some juvenile delinquents who got up on a cliff and they were throwing eggs. We were all stretched out on the sands. Jerry Poteet says, "I wish I had one of them eggs and I'd hit Bruce" (Laughs). He said he'd be right there to help. Poteet said, "I'll be right behind him," and I said, "Are you going up there to help him?" and he says, "No, I'm going out there to watch" (Laughs). Bruce had a little mean streak a lot of people don't know about, his eyes would flash and he'd be mad! I was sure he was going to get mad at me but I had an excuse all worked up in advance. But he never did get mad at me. Bruce was pro-Chinese, he liked Herb Jackson to come around and said he always wanted a Caucasian houseboy (Laughs).

Q: How did he condition his body and integrate unique training equipment into his regime?
Bob Bremer: He was a fanatic about working out. While he was driving his car he would be doing stomach exercises, when he was watching television he would be squeezing tennis balls - he had something to do. He said, "When I'm putting on my pants I'm doing a balancing act." He just made everything into martial arts play. I used to drive home from the class and used to think this wasn't different to a Boxing gym, and I was aware of that. Bruce could show you a lot of stuff about punching and hitting hard. He said the easiest way to win a fight is to just reach out and knock him out. We were packing big punches and we had the explosion right in the face like a wet towel - 'SNAP'!!

Q: What would you say to people who may think Bruce wasn't a fighter?
Bob Bremer: I noticed nobody said that when he was sticking around. I would put him against anybody I have ever seen to this day! You've got to try to get pass his finger jab, if you can't deal with that then you're going out! It's like a blur. Most people could never believe if they could really see what he did, it was awesome. I don't care who he steps out in the parking lot with - 'boom'! The guy's gotta fight him with a Braille system, because he could stick a finger in your eye really quick. I mean, he could do it coming in from across the room. I've seen that physical part of him few people will ever see. It was to win at any cost, there was no substitution to winning. When you saw him workout you realized that a fight with him would only last a few minutes. He had such power in his fingers that if he'd hit you in the eyes...he was powerful for the small guy he was. I'd seen him hit the top and bottom bag, which had elastics at both ends, and he's hitting like this (demonstrates) with the bag going back six feet, and I'm thinking, "Why don't his fingers bend?"

Q: Can you tell me about some of the celebrity students he taught?
Bob Bremer: Well, they were in and out and I didn't meet a lot of them. I met Chuck Norris two or three times at Bruce's house. I was always thinking I may get to spar with Steve McQueen but it never happened. Bruce said Steve McQueen really put everything into it, so I thought, "Wow, I'll get to spar with him."

Q: You witnessed the depth of Bruce's intuition and brilliance, did this inspire you to work harder?
Bob Bremer: I was all excited right back when I met him. He would remind me of a little kid sometimes, he'd learn something new and he'd want to try it out and see how good it worked. He usually had it figured right. Sometimes he would teach it. Dan Inosanto said it had taken him a month to learn a form but Bruce had it mastered in 20 minutes. He said you can time it and go in; and he could do it. Bruce didn't just say something but he would be able to do it. I tried the nunchaku and hit something in the room and that damn thing came back and hit me right in the groin. I'm on the ground crawling around, nobody's home and I'm wondering how bad...(Laughs).

Q: The impact of the martial arts in the Western world would not be what it is today had it not been for Bruce. When and how did you find out your teacher had passed away?
Bob Bremer: I found out about Bruce's death on the television. I didn't believe it. I thought they'd made a terrible mistake, he was too healthy. But it was sure right. He would have never stopped, he would have kept going. He might have come out with new ways to fight we didn't know about. Even I didn't know a whole lot about his affairs of earning money, at the time I was working with him he barely had income. His only main income was playing Kato. I didn't realize he was behind with the money thing. He wanted to spread the word of Kung Fu and he knew he could be a star too. He looked at other guys and said he could do that.

I spoke to him when he was filming in Asia and he told me how he bites the guy in the film. Then when I saw the film Enter the Dragon I thought I know that (Laughs). I've been biting people for a long time. He was a childhood star anyway so it was easier for him, Just think about the movies he could have made had he lived. You know what, he offered me a part in a movie and I thought that would be neat. I could see what I look like on the big screen, but it didn't happen. The financing fell out, it was to go to India. I'm often wondering about the people who pulled the financing, later they sure knew they screwed up because they could've had nothing but money if he had been discovered back then.

JERRY POTEET

One of the few original Bruce Lee students propagating the original teachings, training methods and fighting methods of the founder of Jeet Kune Do is Jerry Poteet. Like most of Lee's Los Angeles Chinatown students, Poteet made a switch from Ed Parker's Kenpo school when Lee opened his third and final branch of the Jun Fan Gung Fu Institute. Poteet was one of the few selected students who had the privilege training at Lee's house in addition to attending the formal classes.

Q: Jerry, when did you first come into contact with Bruce Lee?
Jerry Poteet: I met Bruce at James Lee's house in Oakland, back in 1964.Ed Parker and I, plus one of his top black belts, were organizing the first International Karate Championships. We were at one of Ed's student's house. Ed was talking on the phone and suddenly he became very excited. "Bruce is at James Lee's house in Oakland! Who wants to go?" Some of the people had met Bruce before and said, "Yeah, yeah, let's go." So we dashed to James' house. My first impression was, here's this small, lean young man who did not look very imposing. Some of the guys started to ask him questions, and then somebody mentioned the wooden dummy.

Bruce stopped talking and went downstairs. The dummy was down in the garage under James' house. This dummy was sitting in the corner on a concrete base. It was very rigid and it looked like a section of a telephone pole with three arms sticking out of it and wooden leg. Bruce walked over and said, "This is the classical way to use the wooden dummy," and he moved to one side of the dummy and then the other side. Then he said, "But this is how I use it," and he literally exploded on the dummy. The way the dummy's arms rattled and sounded upon impact, it sounded like somebody was shooting a machine gun. Bruce was making the dummy bounce all over the place against the wall, and James yelled, "Bruce!

Bruce!" And Bruce stopped and said, "What?" James said, "You are going to tear my house down." Bruce was literally shaking the house foundation while working the dummy! Bruce just smiled and turned around and walked back upstairs. Everybody followed him. I went over and put my hand on the dummy and tried to push it, but it wouldn't budge. Then I put two hands on the dummy and tried to push it, and still it wouldn't move! I put all my weight behind it and finally it moved a little. I thought to myself, "My God, where did all that power come from?" I could hardly move it. I caught up with the group and asked if I missed anything.

Q: What kind of personality did Bruce have and what was it like to be around him?
Jerry Poteet: What most people don't understand is he was a practical joker. He giggled a lot, he was like somebody you went to high school with. On the other hand, he was very philosophical. He compelled you to be in his presence, and want to learn more.

Q: What was the typical training session like at the Los Angeles Chinatown school?
Jerry Poteet: Well, we did a lot of footwork. He emphasized footwork, footwork, footwork and more footwork. He was trying to get us to be more mobile. We also trained in his modified Boxing drills and also the modified trapping drills from Wing Chun. He was a hands-on teacher; he walked around and made sure we were doing everything correctly. Everything had to be precise!

Q: Did Bruce ever give you a personalized training schedule and what did this consist of?
Jerry Poteet: Yes, he did. If he saw that someone was working hard, and training away from class, he rewarded your progress. My supplemental training program included weight training and flexibility training. He was working on every part of the body. One of the flexibility exercises he had for me was the splits between two chairs! When I looked at it and read it, I said, "Splits between two chairs?" And he just shot me a look and said, "It's something to shoot for." Needless to say, I didn't press the issue!

Q: Bruce had a select group of students who worked out at his house, and you were one of them. Can you tell me about these legendary private sessions?
Jerry Poteet: They consisted mostly of what he called the 'core of Jeet Kune Do'. That was the energy training, the chi sau, all the energy drills, the reference point training and all of the philosophy that went with it.

Q: What did Bruce have to say on conditioning and equipment training, which was obviously essential to the development of a Jeet Kune Do student?

Jerry Poteet: Bruce's training philosophy was, when you're working with equipment, any kind of exercise you do should parallel the actual application as closely as possible. So, for example, he had us do vertical fist push ups, because it tied the arm and body together in the same way that you would be delivering a punch.

Q: On the subject of technical training in Jeet Kune Do, what elements did he emphasize in his classes?

Jerry Poteet: It was mostly over at the house. As I said, we covered reference points, closing the gap, broken rhythm training, etc. We had naval Boxing headgear - which was all you could get at the time. It was terrible, since you couldn't see a hook coming! We used 16 ounce gloves and everybody had to have a mouthpiece and a cup. At one time, we had chest protectors and shin guards on, and you could wear as much equipment you wanted to. I didn't like the equipment because I thought it was cumbersome. Along with Daniel Lee, I tore everything off and just stuck with these three pieces of equipment because everything else restricted our movements. All I used was a cup, mouthpiece and gloves, so I had freedom of mobility. We went full contact, all-out fighting: low-line kicks, punches, strikes, elbows, knees, etc.

But Bruce said that it was still restrictive, because once you put on the gloves, it took away much of the trapping he used to close down an opponent on contact. In fact, I would say that is why some Jeet Kune Do people claim it does not work. If you are wearing huge pillows on your hands, of course, it eliminates many of the strikes, slices, eye jabs and so forth. So, when you go to so-called 'anything goes' sparring with Boxing gloves, you have just taken away your most lethal weapons.

Q: When you saw him training on equipment, what impressed you the most?

Jerry Poteet: He spent a lot of time on the heavy bag, but he also had a double-end ball where he could hit with broken rhythm and make it 'talk'. It's also called a top and bottom ball, with elastic on the top and a rope on the bottom. The air shield he was using for kicking was used in football and it didn't hold up well for a kick; most of them were flat and there was no air in them. Not too many of us volunteered to hold it for Bruce's kicks! And we had focus mitts. Bruce was the one who invented the focus mitt use for martial artists. I was the one who came up with the idea of the dot in the middle for focus and made some for him. If only I had patented the idea! And once again, after holding them once, nobody wanted to hold the mitts for him because he hit and kicked too hard.

Q: How does Bruce Lee's method of Jeet Kune Do combine physical conditioning, technical training and tactics, full contact sparring, and the mental and philosophical components to bind together?
Jerry Poteet: First of all, Bruce's Jeet Kune Do is an 'art', not a mere method. The physical tools and elements have underlying 'principles', which are always true no matter what the combat scenario. He never proposed or taught something people call 'concepts', which may or may not be true for any given situation. But regardless, the physical is just a stepping stone to what he called the 'open end' of Jeet Kune Do. The art is a process of self-discovery, not only on the physical level but also the psychological and philosophical level as well.

Q: Do you believe Bruce advocated one-on-one coaching as opposed to a large class?
Jerry Poteet: I asked Bruce one time what was the perfect size of the class and he said, "Two students and one instructor." And he explained that when he's working with one student, the other can watch from the outside.

Q: Would you say it is almost essential in Jeet Kune Do if someone wants to develop himself to a maximum level then one-on-one instruction should be pursued?
Jerry Poteet: Bruce was a hands-on teacher, he wouldn't just sit back and watch a class. He was in the middle of the class making sure everything was done the way he wanted it to be done. He was a perfectionist. But of course, Jeet Kune Do can be learned in a classroom. It is only necessary that the instructor has to genuinely care about each student.

Q: Can you recall any interesting stories when you spent time socializing with Bruce?
Jerry Poteet: Too many! I'll go back to the practical jokes. He pulled a practical joke on me. I was over at the house one day and Bruce was in the other room doing sit ups. I took off into the library and there was a sign saying 'Do Not Touch'. I'm leaning over looking at the different books, and my hands are behind my back so I won't be tempted to touch anything. Suddenly, Bruce opened the door and said, "Jerry!" Just as I turned a three-sectional staff hit me right in the face and I fell to the floor. I'm waiting for the pain to kick in, and then I realize he hit me with a rubber weapon. Bruce started laughing and said, "Gotcha!"

Q: Bruce was an avid philosopher. How philosophical was he and who influenced him in this area?

Jerry Poteet: Well, he was very philosophical. He gave me a reading list which included Sun Tzu and The Book of Five Rings by Musashi. His library had volumes of books on philosophy, both Eastern and Western.

Q: Bruce believed in weight training and regularly made this a core part of his overall training regime. Can you shed some light on this subject?
Jerry Poteet: In regards to weight training, much of it was to develop a look for TV and film. And judging by the reaction to his physique after all these years, I'd say he accomplished his goal! He also performed isometric and isotonic exercises. And he used the wooden dummy to develop explosive close-range power. I have put out a DVD of Bruce's dummy training, available on my website.

Q: When Bruce became famous, just after the release of his movies worldwide, did you keep in touch?
Jerry Poteet: I talked to him when he came back from Hong Kong. He was packing up his books and his belongings to ship to Hong Kong.

Q: Can you tell me more about his library and the kind of books he read and absorbed knowledge from?
Jerry Poteet: He had everything in it: philosophy, Fencing and old Boxing books. I went one time with Bruce to search for some books to an old bookstore, and there was maybe only two or three books on martial arts, a few on Boxing and a few on Fencing. Bruce just bought all of them. I asked, "Why all of them?" and he said, "I don't want to look through them here because I don't have enough time. I'll buy them all, then take them home and sort through them at the house." The books he kept were very special to him, his library was an essential part of his life.

Q: Why is Bruce Lee still so popular to this day compared to some of the other stars?
Jerry Poteet: There is something about Bruce on or off film, he has the charisma, he has the ability to capture it. He was always for the underdog, he gives people hope and he's saying if I can do it you can do it.

Q: At the height of his fame, back in early 70s what was the public's reaction when the movies came out?
Jerry Poteet: People couldn't get enough. Large crowds tried to get in the theaters to see the films.

Q: Do you think Bruce would have gone on to doing even bigger things pertaining to the movie and martial arts worlds had he lived?

Jerry Poteet: He was always feeling there was never an end to his training. He was always maturing but never matured, development was something that never came to an end. So I believe that he would have taken the film to levels that have never been seen as far as the action and emotion. But film was just one vehicle for him. On the personal level, there was no end to his self-discovery and personal growth.

Q: Since Bruce died what is the biggest misconception about Bruce Lee's art?

Jerry Poteet: That it is many arts thrown into one, or an endless 'adding on'. Nothing could be further from the truth. But it's much easier to be a beginner in dozens of arts than to focus on one. The art of Jeet Kune Do requires a tremendous skill level. As you progress, you utilize less and less, refining it down to the essence.

Q: Had Bruce lived do you think he would have evolved and modified his art to fit in today's environment?

Jerry Poteet: Jeet Kune Do already fits into every environment. This is because the principles he taught applied to every martial art. The principles of simplicity, economy, longest weapon to nearest target, etc, there's no where else you need to go because Bruce simplified everything.

Q: As far as Jeet Kune Do is concerned with competition, some people will say Jeet Kune Do is for strictly street fighting and not for competition!

Jerry Poteet: As far as I am concerned, whenever you have a ring, a judge, a bell that signals a 'start', right away, this is a sport. Surprise is the biggest element the street fighter uses to his advantage. And then there are rules against certain strikes, gouges, bites, etc. For Bruce, there were no rules of engagement. And certainly none of us were using the types of drugs and steroids required to sustain blow after blow in order to entertain the audience.

Q: Finally, how would you describe your friendship with Bruce and just how much of an impact did he have on you as a human being?

Jerry Poteet: First of all, we were very good friends and we talked frequently and in depth. He imparted so much to me and changed my life completely. I have been asked at seminars if meeting Bruce Lee changed my life. And I say I've been all over the world. I've done movies. I've choreographed fight scenes for movies. I did the movie Dragon. Yes, I'd say he changed my life completely.

LARRY HARTSELL

The late Larry Hartsell was widely known as the premier Jeet Kune Do fighter and a grappling authority. Hartsell, one of Lee's original Los Angeles Chinatown and backyard students, became one of the most in-demand Jeet Kune Do instructors on the seminar circuit. After Lee died, the grappling supremo taught at the Inosanto Academy and privately in his garage. He also worked as a bodyguard for Mr. T and Larry Flint. In this interview Hartsell culminates on Bruce Lee's training methods.

Q: Bruce Lee is well known to have placed emphasis on supplementary training, just how essential was this component to him?
Larry Hartsell: It was very important to Bruce to train, sometimes he trained four to five hours a day. Sometimes just stretching, kicking, such as using air shields, dummies, sometimes weightlifting for certain parts of his body. He was constantly experimenting to improve his conditioning, his punching and his kicking. So, it was very important to him to come up with different segments for different part of his body.

Q: Do you think it was Bruce's approach to training which separated him from all the other martial artists of the time?
Larry Hartsell: Bruce was definitely ahead of his time in this area. He's probably one of the first people to do plyometrics and really put to use the isometrics for the muscles, as opposed to weightlifting, which at that time most Boxers and fighters didn't do because they thought it would tighten the muscles. He would experiment with different methods to increase his power, his speed, his overall cardio. And he did this by experimentation, adding and deleting.

Q: Bruce was a paragon of health and fitness and seems to have a large following from the iron pumping fraternity. Is it true you were responsible for introducing him to legendary professional bodybuilders Bill Pearl and Dave Draper?

Larry Hartsell: Well, Sigung Bruce Lee, Guro Dan Inosanto and myself... I took them to Muscle Beach, which at that time was on Third Street in Santa Monica, California. Bill Pearl happened to be there as well as Dave Draper and some of the other bodybuilders. Bruce was impressed by quite a few of them, but he said sometimes someone like that who had too much muscle mass probably could not move that much. After this meeting, Bruce had his own weightlifting gym in his garage up in Roscomore Road in Bel Air which he trained in. He had an isometric machine, squat rack, bench press, dumbbells, grip machine for forearms and he started training with weights, experimenting with weight programs.

Q: Bruce had many tomes and magazines on the subject of bodybuilding and exercise and read voraciously. Which bodybuilders did he admire?

Larry Hartsell: I think he admired Boxers as a lot of the Boxers had a good physique, along with bodybuilders. He voraciously also watched a lot of Boxing films. He particularly admired Muhammad Ali because of his footwork and Rocky Marciano for his power punching.

Q: It has been documented that Bruce never trained at a gym but preferred to workout at his home. Did he use a training partner for weight training?

Larry Hartsell: Sometimes, but not really on the weight training, mostly with air shield kicking. People like Kareem Abdul-Jabbar, the basketball player, would come up and especially Guro Dan Inosanto and myself on the punching and holding the air shield. When working the kicking and punching, mostly he'd use a partner. He didn't use a partner really on his weight training.

Q: Bruce devoted time and effort to his midsection. How did Bruce train his abdominals?

Larry Hartsell: Bruce trained his abdominals by different methods: leg extensions, sit ups, crunches, just a general routine. But he took it to extremes, not too many people can do what Bruce could do with his stomach routine; he would just do repetition, repetition, repetition (Laughs).

Q: What weight training principles did Bruce follow to cultivate his extremely defined physique. Did he use any Weider principles?

Larry Hartsell: He used a lot of isometrics. He trained isometrics quite a bit, supplemented by weight training such as bench press, squats and so on. He did use a Weider principle at one time, he researched so many bodybuilding magazines he probably took this and that and integrated into his own system.

Q: Many top bodybuilders such as Lou Ferrigno, Shawn Ray, Dorian Yates, Flex Wheeler, Sharon Bruneau to name a few were mesmerized by Bruce's trademark physique. What makes his physique stand out?
Larry Hartsell: Definitely his body definition and his six pack abs. What I really liked about Bruce's physique was his forearms, when he flexed his forearms it was just like they'd come out. When they were measured, they were 15-and-a-half inches whereas his bicep was only 13-and-a-half to 14. Bruce had phenomenal forearms because he worked the grips every day, worked his forearms all the time for the punching. He believed the forearm and the punching was in the wrist and forearm. That used to amaze me when he flexed his forearms.

Q: Isometric training and dynamic tension was another method he implemented into his schedule. We can see him displaying this concept in Way of the Dragon. Did he perform any of this in his private training?
Larry Hartsell: Yes, I watched him. He would do a time of 30 seconds to nine minutes on the isometric machine doing military press. Then he would do the biceps and would push for 30 seconds to a minute, then for the lower back he would do the deadlift. He also did the 'good morning' exercise with the weight over his shoulders for his lower back.

Q: How much emphasis did he place on stamina and endurance-building activities and what sort of exercises did he favor in his quest for achieving a high level of endurance?
Larry Hartsell: He put emphasis on all aspects of his physical training. He would run four to five miles in the morning, sometimes with Bo, his Great Dane (dog). Hitting the heavy bag, constantly kicking and punching, focus gloves - always working out for stamina, flexibility and strength.

Q: Did he have specific stretching exercises for his students that were the core flexibility exercises?
Larry Hartsell: Yes. When I was at the Chinatown school we used to stretch and condition our bodies, stretching legs, punching with half-pound weights to develop the straight blast, various stretching exercises such as the straddle stretch and hurdlers stretch.

Q: Do you feel to truly excel in Jeet Kune Do the student must follow a supplementary program and not merely rely on accumulating techniques?

Larry Hartsell: Yes, there is an old saying 'fatigue will make cowards of us all', so conditioning should be 70 percent (of a regime) and 30 percent technique. In other words, you have to have supplementary training within your program. For any type of contact sports especially, you have to have the strength, endurance and speed to excel and you should work on these. Maybe have a personal trainer give you a program, make you more effective in all of these areas.

Q: What kind of push ups did Bruce perform and did he modify the positions in any way to target specific areas?

Larry Hartsell: Yes, he did. He had a special pair of handles he used. I remember this was during the 60s, he used to use different positions. Sometimes he would do one-hand push ups with one hand slightly elevated, and he did quite a few with one hand each side. A lot of times when I was over at his house he would be watching TV and he would have a couple of dumbbells where he would do 10 to 15 repetitions with the dumbbells whilst watching TV. Whether he did this all day I don't know, but I guess he was trying to get everything in because he had a pretty busy schedule. He also researched and experimented with different type of exercises, and performed push ups to develop his overall fitness.

Q: I believe he conditioned his knuckles using some kind of straw pad, wall bag and sand...

Larry Hartsell: Yes, he had a specially made sandbag which he had up on the wall. They are sold now but back then no one had that. He would condition his last three knuckles. He said he'd developed his speed and power, now he wanted to put the armor on his knuckles. So he developed the last three knuckles of his hand by vertical punching all the time. I've seen his hands really callused up from the punching. And (he used) the straw makiwara, he would be sitting watching TV and he'd hit the straw pad - which I have in my possession.

Q: Some people and authorities say Bruce was the fittest man in the world. Do you feel he has influenced people from all walks of life as far as fitness, training and dedication?

Larry Hartsell: Yes, I do. I think Bruce was the first person to tell people to look within themselves and to find what they need and cross-train. And a lot of different classical martial arts today are cross-training in different arts to supplement their training; going to Boxing and Kickboxing to add to their own styles, going to grappling systems to add to their styles. But I think Bruce at that time was way ahead of his time on cross-training, utilizing different methods. For Jeet Kune Do, he borrowed from 26 different systems as far as I know, and put them together to develop his system and concept of fighting.

★ ★ ★ CHAPTER TWO ★ ★ ★

FRIENDS

Most if not all of Bruce Lee's close friends were involved in the martial arts or the film industry. Those who were close to the Little Dragon still remember him as the great innovator of martial arts and a loyal friend who would go out of his way to help his companions. During Bruce Lee's stay in the United States, there were just a handful of elite and dedicated martial artists with whom he associated, worked out and exchanged ideas. Impelled by an insatiable desire to learn everything he could about various martial arts styles, Lee's favorite pastime was trawling through books and putting his newly found knowledge to the test with his training partners. In 1966, Lee moved to the Western world's Mecca of martial arts: Los Angeles, California.

It was during this period that some of the greatest Karate champions came to Bruce for personal instruction. Chuck Norris, Bob Wall, Joe Lewis and Mike Stone had between them won every major Karate tournament in the United States. These champions realized Lee's genius. Bruce was also shrewd enough to realize that he had as much to gain from the relationship as anyone. Lee was both a maverick and a pragmatic. He researched and integrated elements from Karate, Tae Kwon Do, Judo, Western Boxing, Fencing and Northern-Style Gung Fu systems; if he found an effective way of doing something, he would absorb it into his personal fighting style. Throughout the 60s, Bruce had assimilated as much knowledge and experience as he could pertaining to the diverse aspects of fighting. In addition to working with the champions, he would study books on all forms of combat and styles intently, analyzing their fighting techniques and strategies and determining the effectiveness of such concepts by acting them out.

Victor Moore was a Karate black belt who demonstrated with

Bruce at the Long Beach Internationals in 1967. During this historic event, the audience witnessed Lee's lightning speed. In eight attempts, Moore blocked zero punches. In a rare interview with Moore, he rewinds the clock on the day he squared off with Bruce Lee.

"He had been questioned quite a bit. People wanted to know how good he was really, and how would he stand against the national champions, as he had not been competing in tournaments. But he was very famous and a very good martial artist. He made a challenge to the national champions. Dr. Robert Trias, who was the father of American Karate, was there. Bruce Lee wanted to prove his Jeet Kune Do was pretty much superior to any other style. And he wanted to challenge some of the national champions to a speed test. And Dr. Trias selected me. I wasn't that excited about really showing anything, but Dr. Trias selected me to test against him. And he pretty much said to Bruce, 'If your Jeet Kune Do could stand against one of my good students, I'll have more respect for it'.

I went reluctantly on and accepted the challenge. And we had a conversation on what we were going to do - trade punches, who could stop whose. And we demonstrated, it proved to be very well. Afterwards we talked for a little while and also did a little personal randori, where we traded techniques. It was a great honor being able to do this with a good martial artist and a famous movie star. He said that I was the fastest American he had ever met. Also, we had a good talk and I have a lot of respect for him. I can't take anything away from him, he did quite a bit for Karate. If it wasn't for his movies' popularity, Karate probably wouldn't be what it is today."

- Victor Moore

Apart from being the catalyst for really exploding the popularity of martial arts, there was a much deeper side to Bruce's personality. He had a special charismatic dominance; he was self-assured and some even found him to be a cocky, buoyant young man. He ruffled some feathers - but he also practiced what he preached. According to Chuck Norris, who appeared in Lee's third movie Way of the Dragon, "Working out with him, changing philosophies and so forth, I could see that he was always striving to learn. He was very creative. He was a genius at creating new ideas. This is what amazed me about him - his inventions, the new things he would create and develop."

In the following pages, you will discover Bruce Lee's deeper personality as a martial artist and a friend. From his boyhood companions back in Hong Kong, William Cheung and Hawkins Cheung, to world champion martial arts personalities in the United States like Jhoon Rhee and Joe Lewis. These men recall candidly their friendship with the Little Dragon. You will also discover the man behind the myth, before he was a heroic image to people all over the world.

Bruce expected a lot out of people because he demanded a lot of himself - he was a perfectionist. The seasoned champions who worked out with Bruce believe he did more for Karate and martial arts in general in the United States in a short time than all his martial arts contemporaries put together. Yet for all the success and excitement, the adulation which came Bruce's way, he continued to see and keep in constant touch with his friends and fellow martial artists. These individuals to this day practice and live the highest ideals of the martial arts.

WILLIAM CHEUNG

William Cheung was one of Bruce Lee's closest friends and a fellow student at Yip Man's Wing Chun school in Hong Kong. During Lee's early days growing up in the mean streets of Hong Kong, Cheung was his constant companion. Both men shared a close-knit friendship and mutual respect. When Bruce Lee left Hong Kong for the United States, he kept in touch with his friend, updating him of his development and his career in Hollywood. Master Cheung is one of the grandmasters of the Wing Chun system.

Q: Can you tell me about your early days training with Bruce Lee?
William Cheung: Actually, we met on his birthday in Kowloon, in Hong Kong. My uncle was also involved in Chinese opera and Bruce Lee's father Lee Hoi-Chuen was a very famous Chinese opera singer, so they knew each other. Me and Bruce were the same age, I was 47 days older than him. My uncle took me to his birthday party. In the Chinese system when you are born, you're already one year old. So when you're nine years old, it means you're ten. So it's a very important birthday at ten.

Bruce was especially superstitious. When Bruce was born his elder brother had died as a baby, so they believed that there was a curse on the family; the devil taking the child from the family. So they gave Bruce a name which is not very well known outside the family circle. Actually, Bruce Lee's Chinese name is Little Dragon, so they gave Bruce a female name, the opposite of the Dragon, Little Phoenix. In the family they called him Little Phoenix and he was often dressed in female clothes. On the tenth birthday - which is actually the ninth birthday - it's all about coming out of that. During that time the streets were not very safe, so young kids didn't go out on their own. I didn't meet him again until almost three years later. He was going to school and I was also. So, that's how I met Bruce again at Junction Street, in Kowloon.

At that time he was in a lot of trouble, his school was not very strict. Bruce was a quarter-German and three-quarters Chinese. At that time the Chinese people did not accept someone like that. He didn't belong to Caucasians or Chinese, he was in between as he was mixed blood. It was more or less quite open in school, so at school we had a group - not a gang as such, but just a few people together - and they called themselves The Junction Street which Bruce was part of, back in 1953. Bruce at that time was in between changing schools. The school he went to had a lot of Caucasians going there. There was one big Caucasian who threatened young kids and used to take their lunch money. Bruce one day armed himself with a pocketknife. Not to actually attack him - he took him to the lavatory and told him to take all his clothes off and locked him in the cubicles. After school the kid didn't arrive home and his parents were worried. They looked for him everywhere in school but the lavatory, the last place they looked was the lavatory. They heard some noises like somebody snoring. The kid actually went to sleep in the cubicle. Bruce got into a lot of trouble. They basically told his parents that they will take him away.

At the time I was already training in Wing Chun for a couple of years. Bruce remembered that we met at his birthday so we became good friends. I was also in a lot of trouble at home because my parents' half-brother was like a big bully in the family. So I actually ran away from home and stayed with Yip Man and trained full time. The Wing Chun school was right next to Bruce Lee's school, so at lunchtime I would go say hello to Yip Man and after, when the school finished, I would then pick Bruce up. He was already a famous child movie star and he was not very big in size, so some kids would pick on him and I would help him. After a few months, he decided he wanted to learn Wing Chun.

Q: Why did Bruce take up Kung Fu and did he always have a fascination for fighting?

William Cheung: No, he was more or less a victim of the police. Because in Hong Kong at that time there were a lot of serious gangs controlled by the Triads, and they recruited young people to do their dirty jobs. They would use 'good guy, bad guy' tactic. They would get the bad guy to bully you and the good guy would come along and say, "Look, I can take care of you, join the gang and you'll be OK." I would say 50 percent of the kids in Hong Kong joined the gangs. Real Triad gangs. They became victims of them. So, Bruce was the main target of this gang and I was at the Wing Chun school which just happened to be right next to St. Xavier. We knew each other and got on well. I was always helping him, making sure nothing happened to him when he came out of the school. He decided to learn Wing Chun, and this system was known to be effective. Everywhere Bruce went, his brother was always with him. Peter, who was his elder brother, was like a minder to him. Bruce was quite famous even back then, because he was a child movie star in Hong Kong.

Q: Bruce was introduced to Western Boxing when he was attending school in Hong Kong, can you shed light on the tournament he won?
William Cheung: We actually trained him for the tournament. What happened was, Bruce already started doing Wing Chun when he was attending St. Xavier. Bruce had a few little fights with the other students that were Caucasians. So the sports master said to him, "OK, you think you can fight, let's put on a pair of gloves and I'll spar you." The sports master, who had been a Boxing champion, decided to put him in the Boxing team. Every day after school we would go with Bruce to training sessions. There were two twin brothers who were hanging out with us and training. Because the twin brothers looked exactly the same, sometimes Bruce didn't know whether it was twin number one or two, so we were swapping them around in sparring to build up Bruce's confidence. That's how Bruce got involved with the school Boxing Championships.

On the night of the fights, I told Bruce to look calm. Boxing is five rounds, two minutes a round. Bruce was so pumped up and as soon as the bell rang he ran over to the other corner. His opponent Gary Elms was a three-time champion. Bruce got him in the corner on the ropes and threw Wing Chun punches, knocking his opponent out in five seconds. He won the Inter-School Boxing Championship.

Q: How would you describe Bruce's personality when he was growing up?
William Cheung: Bruce was very unusual when he was training. Most martial arts students when they learn the first lesson they want to learn the first form, but I think Bruce's reason for being so good at martial arts was he would never...I'll go back to tell you why Bruce would train hard. Less than a year after Bruce had been training at the school, Bruce had progressed so far that a lot of the seniors had trouble sparring or doing chi sau with Bruce. At that time everybody thought Bruce isn't even Chinese, he's quarter-German, and so they ganged up and put pressure on Yip Man to expel Bruce. So Yip Man told him to go, so he trained with Wong Shun Leung. If you were half-Chinese and half-Caucasian they wouldn't let you train Wing Chun. He would train hard for weeks and weeks, until he mastered it. He was so good. All the other things he incorporated later, like kicks, he would master the kicks before learning the variations. Most people would train half an hour on something and just follow the teachers movements. Another thing is Bruce was virtually so into Wing Chun that

he would be doing training methods, he would do row punching with dumbbells.

Q: Bruce integrated a lot training methods when he arrived in the United States, did he ever delve into sophisticated training methods in Hong Kong in his early Wing Chun days?
William Cheung: Yes, yes, he would be sitting and doing arm movements. Then when he's walking on Nathan Road in Hong Kong, which is so busy, he would have dumbbells in his hands and he would be throwing row punches. He virtually focused all his energy on training Wing Chun at that time. Even on the first day, I remember the first day, it took him an hour to get permission from his father Lee Hoi-Chuen to learn Kung Fu. His father probably told him if he wanted to learn Kung Fu then he better be the best, because there's no second best fighter in Kung Fu because it's useless. On the first day, after he did the lesson he said to me he's going to make Wing Chun or Chinese Kung Fu a common name in households. I said to him, "What? And how are you going to do that?" Because he had a vision and also he was experienced in movies and so on. When you have something good you can make it worldwide.

Q: When Bruce left for America did you keep in touch with him and did you write to each other and correspond?
William Cheung: Actually, I still have the letters Bruce wrote me from America. Bruce was very serious about success, he didn't have time for nonsense, although often he did practical jokes. One time we were on the rooftop training and there were workers working on the roof. And Bruce paints the railings red. In Hong Kong it's very congested, there's no space to do a lot of things on the roof. Next to the stairway there was a canopy so Bruce painted it red. Now everything's red, and Bruce starts yelling, "Fire!" And this guy woke up and sees everything's red. He thought it was fire, as he just woke up, and jumped up and started running but couldn't see anything properly. So we had to restrain this guy because he was three feet away from running off the roof (Laughs). Bruce liked to do practical jokes.

There was this other instructor who was doing a system called Chow Gar Chinese style, and he was a very high level in the ranking in this system. He wanted to find other masters. On weekends we would organize challenge matches; good fighters were in the Triads. The best fighter I remember who I fought was someone called Red Dragon, who was the best fighter in his Triad gang - big Triad gangs virtually controlled half of Kowloon - and they called him 'Very Fast Kicks'. I fought him and actually hit him twice. He was the highest rank in the Triads so they lost face because their best fighter got beaten up. So they started to play rough.

Bruce always hung around with me, and then he got involved. The gang cannot survive unless they have corrupted police with them, the police and politicians, so there's a vicious circle there. And we were set on so many goals. Things got out of hand and the gangs at the time, just like any gang these days, made money with drugs, prostitution and protection and so on. They lost face and lost all this business because people wouldn't pay. That was the basic theme of this very true story.

One friend who I knew was part of these gangs, the gang took her to Macau where they sold her into a sex place. Then we went to look for the gang and it got really serious. The gangs had a lot of contacts including the corrupt police. In the end a friend of ours was killed in a fight, then in the end we were told to leave Hong Kong. So I left Hong Kong on Christmas eve and Bruce left Hong Kong in 1959. Even on the boat they had paid workers who belonged to the gangs. They paid four guys to kill me in the boat and I had a big fight in front of the passengers. The ship's passengers reported it to the captain who came down with half a dozen men with guns and rifles.

Q: When Bruce was establishing himself as an actor in Los Angeles did he talk to you about his latest martial arts developments and his TV series?
William Cheung: Yeah, he wrote to me about the development of Jeet Kune Do. Bruce was a very fast learner. Basically, his Jeet Kune Do was based on Wing Chun and he investigated the other arts, he looked into a lot of arts. He was a very good dancer and he won the Cha Cha. He could look at some movement and copy it. When he first met Jhoon Rhee at the Long Beach tournament, Jhoon Rhee did three kicks - round kick, spinning back kick and another kick. The audience looked at these three kicks and it looked like ballet. Bruce locked himself in the garage and told his wife to just bring in the food, and he was training these three kicks. Bruce and Jhoon Rhee both were at the tournament again and Bruce came on to do the demonstration first, and among other things he did these three kicks. Jhoon Rhee came out to do the demonstration and remembered the part of the demonstration, and he never did those three kicks again. That's how fast of a learner Bruce was.

Same with the Jeet Kune Do. One of the best things about Wing Chun is you have to train in full contact reflexes. Bruce was very good at reflexes and when he mastered kicks and so on, he could do a lot of routines. He was very good at contact stages, that's why he became a very good fighter. By 1967, four of the world Karate champions were training with him. Bruce was teaching them and they became better. He was ultimately developing Jeet Kune Do. One thing that people don't know is Bruce never wanted to teach Wing Chun to his students. After Bruce Lee died, more than three years later, Dan Inosanto came to train with me and my students for three years. When he first came he knew nothing about Wing Chun, because when Bruce taught them he never taught them the form, Dan Inosanto only knew three techniques. Dan Inosanto actually trained with us whenever I came over to America. His knowledge of Wing Chun was limited. Bruce actually wrote to me stating Wing Chun was too good to teach to the general public, and actually advised me to teach to selected students only.

Q: When Bruce came back to Hong Kong to carve out a movie career in 1971, did you communicate with him?
William Cheung: I spoke to him on the phone on numerous occasions when he rang me. The problem with Bruce was he used a lot of wrong people when he was famous. The minders, the bodyguards. He had a lot of really loyal friends in Hong Kong and he ignored them, that's why probably this became his downfall. Nobody could really advise him in the right direction. Bruce became very difficult for the people around him. I'm not in the movie industry but I know a lot of people, and when they want something they come round and treat you like a king first, and when they get what they want then they don't need you. Raymond Chow originally worked with Run Run Shaw, he was the guy arranging young girls for Run Run Shaw.

Let me tell you something: my father was one of the top policemen in Hong Kong. The biggest gang in London, in 1956, was involved in a big riot and the head of this gang was the son of the informant for my father. I heard (Betty Ting Pei) was deported to Taiwan, linked with a political organization. Bruce Lee and I were one time surrounded by eight guys and they had weapons, in 1956. In 1986 the police raided the great Red Dragons and all the gang officers, and even all the computers were raided at the leader's house. And when they opened the files they discovered 32,000 gang officers listed all around the world - this is officers, not normal members. So they probably had over half a million members around the world. From negotiation officer, communication officer, warrior and so on. They sent the leader to jail. The reason I tell you this is after Bruce had died the gang had a contract to have Betty Ting Pei killed. So Betty had to marry the Grand Dragon's brother. She knew too much. People still don't know how Bruce died but I have a fair idea.

Q: When did you hear about Bruce's death?
William Cheung: People don't know half of the people involved. Betty and Raymond Chow's wife knew when Bruce died; he actually died two days before the newspapers published his death. The doctor who went to Betty's apartment, his son was training with me. And I went to talk to Dr.

Chew and he told me that when he went to the apartment Bruce was already dead. But in Hong Kong they need two doctors to write a death certificate. Raymond was also there and he was told to find another doctor. A doctor's not going to turn up and do a death certificate, so they called the ambulance and bribed the ambulance and the hospital. He was already dead. So it took hours for the ambulance to run around and eventually they negotiated and paid. So they let the hospital say he was dead on arrival, but he was already dead earlier that day.

Bruce was registered on the death register in the hospital as Lee Jun Fan, so nobody knew Bruce had died. And after almost 48 hours a journalist looked up in the hospital the name and time, and found this was Bruce Lee. Then people knew about his death. The autopsy was done after 48 hours. I didn't get to know about Bruce's death after one day. Betty Ting Pei is writing a memoir, but I think somebody already paid her so she's not going to write that memoir now.

HAWKINS CHEUNG

Grandmaster Hawkins Cheung, who now resides in Southern California, was one of Bruce Lee's childhood friends who trained under Yip Man alongside Bruce. He is one of the few grandmasters of the Wing Chun system. During the early period in Lee's life in Hong Kong, Cheung was one of his closest friends and training partners. Cheung was also present at the infamous rooftop fights and participated himself. He is a well-respected master all over the world and continues to spread the teachings of the Wing Chun system.

Q: When did you meet Bruce Lee?
Hawkins Cheung: We went to school together. We learned Wing Chun at different schools. When Bruce went to high school, then I found out he learned Wing Chun. Then we would train after school at about two o' clock in the afternoon. We trained together after class for almost about four years before he went to the United States. We were young, about 14 or 15, when we were learning Wing Chun and at that time we didn't really concentrate on the style, we just learned how to fight. Whenever we learned something new we would go out in the street and try it out, then we would compare. And if it didn't work, we would say to Yip Man, "Hey, this didn't work." He would say, "Why don't you try it this way?" So we would go out and try it again. We learned the applications before we knew the system, so that way we didn't really want to learn the stuff for teaching but just for survival. Then after that, when Bruce Lee went to America, he hadn't finished the second form. He only learned 20 to 40 wooden dummy techniques. After he left Hong Kong he returned back to Yip Man again.

I know the system. I'm a small guy, I don't use physical force against a big guy. When Bruce Lee was in the United States I researched his JKD system. His style is much better than the

Americans, the defense was not that good so he jumped into offense. In Wing Chun the structure and bong sau is strictly for defense. Against somebody who is a really big guy, when you're going to do a bong sau your whole body is going to get affected. So, when I came to the United States I found Bruce Lee was right - if you're a small guy, if you don't attack your defense won't be very good and you can't hold the pressure. I can use Wing Chun to punch you and I can use any other stuff. When you get older you don't have the physical attributes you had when you were younger, so defense will work for you.

Q: Did the older students give Bruce Lee any trouble in class?
Hawkins Cheung: He liked to work with me, if he went hard I went soft. Bruce Lee was very muscular and so powerful on his tan sao. He played the hard way, I played the soft way. So, it was a teamwork.

Q: You had a close-knit friendship with Bruce and spent countless hours at his house...
Hawkins Cheung: He was an actor and started doing movies when he was young. He had two brothers and two sisters. His family wasn't rich. When he went to America he told me he wanted to study to become a dentist. I did a joke on him, saying, "If you become a dentist you can pull the guy's whole tooth out." Because he was very muscular for a Chinese guy, he had very powerful forearms. When he attacked I had to play defense. When he did sticking hands (exercise) he was always on the offensive, I would start the defense. So, all the Jeet Kune Do he learned was based on the art, power and speed. I lived near his house, not too far. He was afraid of his father, when his father would come he would close the door. The only thing he was afraid of was his father. I would sometimes pick him up from his house, sometimes he would come pick me up from mine. We would do homework together at his house. His brother was a Fencer. Sometimes we'd go to dancing.

Q: Any interesting or humorous incidents when you were growing up and attending school together?
Hawkins Cheung: There were funny incidents, he was a performer in front of more people as he always wanted to joke around. One time in a Boxing match in the school, there were three guys - we all were Wing Chun guys - and we went to the match, and first Bruce Lee fought an Eurasian guy. Bruce's nickname was 'Chicken Legs'. In the Boxing ring, any Boxer starts from outside. Whenever the guy threw a left hook, Bruce would tan sau. Bruce Lee's tan sau was very powerful. We also liked fighting films, but (as for) normal movies, we didn't go to see them.

Q: There were a lot of notorious gangs in Hong Kong at the time and the city of Hong Kong was crime infested. Could you tell me about the rooftop fights which you and Bruce often took part in?
Hawkins Cheung: I was supposed to fight a guy but Bruce Lee fought him, and the referee was Wong Shun Leung. In the beginning Bruce Lee fought, but I did most of the fights. Bruce Lee needs his face for the movies, he doesn't want his face damaged. Usually it was me and William Cheung who fought for him a lot. A lot of people say Bruce Lee fought in the streets a lot. No! Because he needs his face for the films. How can you do movies when you've got cuts on your face?

Q: You stated Bruce Lee's nickname was 'Gorilla'. How did he get this label?
Hawkins Cheung: He had a big body. A bigger upper body and chicken legs underneath. When he came to the United States he had to work very hard. He was afraid of losing.

Q: What was Bruce like in school?
Hawkins Cheung: In school we were in the same class, and he would always make fun of his colleagues and sometimes we would compete with each other. Also at that time we liked Cha Cha. I had a whole bunch of Filipino style dancing, so we would compete in Cha Cha and Wing Chun. In school everybody knew we were troublemakers because we liked to fight, so nobody dare to touch us. Then when he went to the United States, everybody needed a good citizenship report from the police. Everybody in the police station had a report of all the troublemakers. At the time the Triads were all over and would pick people to join. Bruce Lee and I had bad records so he had to do a lot of explanation, because we were not part of the Triads, we just had fights and had been in trouble, that's all. He had to explain to the CID that we were not Triad people. So Yip Man cleared his name because he had a good citizenship record to show it to the Americans.

Q: Did you keep in touch with your childhood friend when he was in America?
Hawkins Cheung: Bruce Lee did his last movie (The Orphan) in Hong Kong before he left for America at 17. When he left for USA, he left on the ship and me and his other friends went to the shipyard to say good-bye, and I saw him cry. His family was not that rich. He told me he had to work part time and teach martial arts and make some money, he didn't need his family to help him. We did keep in touch, mostly he said he was teaching Wing Chun to all his friends, and he wanted to come back to learn the rest of Wing Chun. In 1964, he came back but he had not formed Jeet Kune

Do yet. He showed me some of his techniques, he was so fast in closing the gap. Then he did a television show, Yip Man and all of us heard about it and we said, "How come he uses Kung Fu rather than Wing Chun?" He did a demo in Hong Kong and called it Kung Fu, and it wasn't, it was Wing Chun. So all we Wing Chun people were kind of surprised why he called it that. Then he went back to the United States and did Green Hornet and he changed the name to Jeet Kune Do.

Q: When he came back to Hong Kong in early 1970, and later in 71 to work on the movies did you see him? There's a photo of Wong Shun Leung on-set of Enter the Dragon...

Hawkins Cheung: He came back in 1970 and did more TV shows. In Game of Death he wanted Wong Shun Leung as one of the masters of the pagoda, and they talked about it but then he passed away. He became a celebrity and we were old friends, young teenage friends. When a guy's rich and famous, I didn't want to say, "Hey, Bruce Lee, we are old buddies." I wouldn't do that. I only saw him once when he did the TV station. Before the show we talked to each other, when he saw me he showed me some new kicks. He was already a big star, he said to me you should do this or that. At the time that was way off from the Wing Chun style.

Q: Did the fame he achieved and the attention he was receiving affect him in anyway?

Hawkins Cheung: Totally different person. When I saw him he talked to the (TV) host like he had conquered the world. He still remembered me and knew we were real good friends, but now we couldn't talk like old times. He showed me his power from the hip, he wanted me to touch his hip and he swing his hip to demonstrate the power.

Q: The untimely death of Bruce Lee left the world stunned in disbelief. When did you hear about his death?

Hawkins Cheung: When he died, of course, I was really shocked. At that time they were showing it all over the television. He wanted to be the best, he was in the movies and also the Mafia and the mental pressure was mounting up.

GREGLON LEE

It's no secret James Lee was one of Bruce Lee's best friends. When Bruce Lee moved to Oakland, he and James opened up a school and later taught in James' garage. James' son Greglon was around when Bruce and his wife Linda moved in with them. Greglon was fortunate enough to know the 'real' Bruce Lee. And it was during the Oakland period that Bruce began to make a transition in his approach to fighting. Today, Greglon continues to spread the word and teachings of his father and Bruce Lee.

Q: Tell me about your dad's relationship with Bruce Lee, they were very close?
Greglon Lee: Well, they understood each other. They worked together, they lived together, they just understood each other really well because they both could speak English and Chinese and loved martial arts. They hit it off really well.

Q: What was Bruce's typical routine when he was staying at your house in Oakland?
Greglon Lee: When Bruce lived with us my dad was still working full time as a welder. My dad would leave for work before eight and get back home about four. Bruce did most of his training during the daytime on his own, a lot of running, stretching, a lot of calisthenics, punching and kicking. At night they would practice their Kung Fu together. But most of the time during the day Bruce would do his own training when dad was at work.

Q: Was Brandon already born when Bruce and Linda moved in with you?
Greglon Lee: They moved in right after they got married, and Brandon came around eight or nine months later. Brandon was born in the

Oakland Hospital, which is about two miles from the house. Linda helped take care of us. At the time our mother had just passed away, so in a sense Bruce and his wife helped take care of us. Linda would cook and do everything and Bruce was around during the day, my dad was at work. And my dad would run classes at night and train with Bruce a little bit. And during the day Bruce was on a pretty strict regimen, training six or seven hours every day.

Q: Your father made unique training equipment for Bruce, what kind of devices did he make for Bruce to sharpen his extraordinary skills?
Greglon Lee: My dad by trade was a welder, he used to make his own equipment for kicking and punching and Bruce would use it. And when Bruce moved to LA, he wanted his own equipment and said to James, "I want mine to look a little nicer." My dad's stuff was made out of rough metal and Bruce wanted something chrome-plated, which looked a little more nice. So my dad made special equipment for Bruce and we had to send it out to the place to get it chrome-plated. Bob Baker, one of my dad's top students who played the Russian in the Chinese Connection (aka Fist of Fury), would drive down to LA to deliver the equipment to Bruce on weekends when Bruce had moved to LA.

Q: What about the training dummies your father made for Bruce?
Greglon Lee: The training dummies were basically like this: they had a board base put into the base on the ground with shock absorbers on the bottom and a metal head with a little bit of rubber around it that flexed, so if you popped it, it would flex. Most of the stuff had shock absorbers, coil springs, and it was basically made out of metal. When you practice kicking at it, the dummy had a leg that stuck out so you could practice hitting the knee. Or if you hit the board, you practiced kicking the body and the resistance was a shock absorber, which was probably equivalent to a 150 to 200 pounds of pressure.

Q: Regarding Bruce's connection to bodybuilding, am I right in saying your father was one of the individuals responsible for getting him involved?
Greglon Lee: My dad had always been hand balancing, doing acrobatics and bodybuilding when he was young, and his buddy Allen Joe did the same. Allen Joe was actually Mr. Northern California in 1947 or 57, and he influenced Bruce a lot too. Allen Joe was a bodybuilder almost to the point of a professional. Bruce used to go and visit this gym. My dad did know Jack LaLane, the famous exercise person from the Bay area.

Q: Did Bruce begin to research bodybuilding more thoroughly and

absorb what was useful?

Greglon Lee: They would show him some basic stuff, Bruce used to always...his basic day was, if he wasn't training he was reading, researching and he used to like to go to Holmes Bookstore in Oakland - it's no longer around - where you can buy used books. And he would buy any book he could on martial arts, Boxing, weight training and exercise. He was always researching things.

Q: Did he use a grip exerciser to develop his forearms and did your father make one for him?

Greglon Lee: He made a machine where you could grip and you could put weights in it, you could also use the handle which has a weight on it, you put 30-pound weight and work your wrist. He worked on his grip a lot. He had a very strong grip. He also did a lot of pull ups so his grip got so strong. He did get into breaking boards later on with his kicks and punches and developed a callus on his knuckles.

Q: Your father ran a publishing company, how did Bruce's book Chinese Gung Fu: The Philosophical Art of Self Defense come to light?

Greglon Lee: My dad had been self-publishing his own books for about five or six years: Oriental Art of Self Defense, Kung Fu Karate with Al Novak on the cover. At the time he published those books, I think it cost him somewhere between 50 cents to a dollar, he sold them for five dollars. Then Bruce asked James to help him, and Bruce produced the book The Philosophical Art of Self Defense. A lot of those pictures were actually taken in Seattle when Bruce was there, with several of Bruce's students in Seattle. I don't think they published more than 1,000 copies initially.

Q: Can we talk about the birthday parties...

Greglon Lee: They would celebrate either my dad's birthday, Bruce's, Allen Joe's and George Lee's birthdays - these were the main people. It usually was at the Silver Dragon Restaurant or it would be at this other restaurant. So, you know, everyone has a birthday once every year, so it would be four times a year.

Q: There's a picture of you, your sister, Bruce and your father on the set of Green Hornet. What was his reason to move to Hollywood?

Greglon Lee: The main reason to move to LA was because when he was demonstrating at Ed Parker's Long Beach, he got an offer from Warner Brothers to play Charlie Chan's number one son. William Dozier was the producer, but that thing didn't pan out so the Kato role opened up for him in Green Hornet. The set of Green Hornet was right next to the Batman set, so when we visited the set of Green Hornet we got to visit the Batman set too. We got to eat there and see the odd famous actors and people dressed up in different characters.

Q: When did your father and Bruce start teaching in the privacy of the garage?
Greglon Lee: They actually started teaching on Broadway and Garnet Street, two blocks from Oakland Technical High School. They started teaching there for six months, but they only got enough students to pay for the rent, so they decided to train at 3039 Monticello in the garage because we don't have to pay rent. At the studio, which he had in Oakland, is where Bruce Lee had a challenge. The garage at the house was just a standard two car garage, probably 25 feet by 22 feet.

Q: You were growing up when Bruce Lee lived with your family, any stories you would like to share?
Greglon Lee: When he was living with us I was probably about 12 years old, he lived with us for two-and-a-half to three years. I just started junior high. He was very focused. He did like to joke around in a friendly way with me, he told me to train properly and study hard. He liked to make Halloween tapes. He would make funny noises, very scary, and we would play it out to kids who came to the house, they would hear these goblins, and he liked to do that. He was very organized, he used to take notes and he would draw. He was very focused and he had a routine; every day he did pretty much the same routine and his training and did a little bit of running. He loved it when we had the dog Bo the Boxer. Later, he got his own dog in LA called Bo the Great Dane.

Q: What is the most significant memory about Bruce that comes to mind?
Greglon Lee: He worked hard all the time. Little by little he progressed, layer by layer, a little progress here and a little progress there. He would work on his speed, power and flexibility. He kept reading and writing, taking information. He'd go visit different places with my dad, the other Kung Fu and Karate people they knew. They would visit Ralph Castro, Wallay Jay - who influenced him quite a bit. In San Francisco they would go visit tournaments. He constantly worked at his timing, footwork and the reality of combat.

Q: After he moved to Los Angeles, how often did he return to Oakland?
Greglon Lee: He'd come back at least four times a year, mainly when the birthday parties were coming up. When Bruce was coming down, the word on the telephone between James, Allen Joe, George Lee and some of

the other people was that Sifu was going to be in town. So, that was a common occurrence. He would usually come up on the weekends. Sometimes Allen Joe, George Lee and James would go down to see Bruce too. So, he kept in touch via the phone and writing letters.

Q: When he came back to visit did you see any changes in him as he was carving out a Hollywood career?
Greglon Lee: He started getting very developed and stronger, and he dressed really well. One time he came wearing white shoes and they were flexible. One time he came in a fur jacket.

Q: When he left Hong Kong for the movies what form of communication did he use to stay in touch?
Greglon Lee: His main method of keeping in touch with James was via letters, he probably wrote my dad at least 80 to a 120 letters - a whole bag. He was a letter-writing person, he wrote letters not just to James but everybody. I would say on average Bruce was writing one or two letters a day to different people, he's always writing to somebody, he's always taking notes. I mean, the man was organized.

Q: Is it true that he invited your dad to the movie premiere of Way of the Dragon in Hong Kong?
Greglon Lee: He sent...I think it was Herb Jackson and Ted Wong by the house in 1972 to give my dad a flight ticket to go to Hong Kong. But my dad already knew that he already had lung cancer, so he didn't want to go over there to become a burden in case he got real sick over there. The joke was Bruce always wanted James to be in the movie and said, "Hey, James, you could play a bartender." James' top student at the time, Bob Baker, did the Chinese Connection (aka Fist of Fury). He and another of my dad's top students Curtis Yee were invited to go to Hong Kong also. But Curtis was at Cal where he had one more year left, so he had to make a decision to finish Cal or go to Hong Kong. Curtis decided to stay in Cal.

Q: When Enter the Dragon was released, which made Bruce a worldwide phenomenon, what was the Oakland bunch's reaction?
Greglon Lee: We were, believe it or not, somewhat surprised. We had seen him in Green Hornet, but TV is one thing and the movies are another. Plus, Enter the Dragon and his other movies emphasized his fighting art more than in Green Hornet. In Green Hornet, where he wore the mask, he hated that, he wasn't that happy with it. He didn't like playing a servant. So that was kind of going backwards, you know. We were somewhat surprised. I could see his development of his body, especially in Enter the Dragon and

Way of the Dragon, you could see Bruce had been working out more . He got more and more developed and strong, more and more quick, working on his stuff.

Q: Did Bruce mention to your father anything pertaining to his future plans in the movie industry?
Greglon Lee: To some of his friends - such as Allen Joe, George Lee and James - he said that one day he would have a million-dollar home in Hollywood and that he would make it really big. But his motivation for making it was not ego, it was a natural process. If he could become good at something, it's just going to happen, all the other stuff is going to happen. Bruce wanted to find himself and develop himself to the best he could. That was his motive. It was not to become a movie star, it was to become a great martial artist. I could actually say that he reached that (goal), because it was a combination of a lot of thought and a lot of hard work.

Q: Who were Bruce's prominent students in the Oakland area?
Greglon Lee: The main students of Bruce were George Lee, Allen Joe and James Lee. Bob Baker became almost like Bruce's brother. Howard (Williams) trained a little with Bruce but not much, he trained mainly with James. Gary Cagnan, one of my dad's top students, trained a little bit with Bruce. But people who really trained the most with Bruce are Bob Baker, Allen Joe, George Lee and James Lee.

Q: In your opinion, what is the biggest misconception about Bruce Lee since he died?
Greglon Lee: Most people don't know Bruce. Until you really know Bruce it's just an idea of your imagination. I mean, obviously when you see him on screen you could see a lot about him. There's been a lot of books written on Bruce, a lot of different things. I would say if you read everything out there and look at all the films and all the articles, you'd have a pretty good understanding of what Bruce was like, but most people don't do that. He was very intelligent, and his focus on what he wanted to do is probably the most important thing that people miss. I mean, he didn't have anything, he had to earn everything he did, inch by inch, pound by pound, ounce by ounce. I mean, he had to really work for it. To this day, not many people have that dedication and that desire or the physical ability to pull that off.

Q: Am I right in saying you were initially interested in tennis? How did you make the transition into the martial arts?
Greglon Lee: I trained in high school with my father where he ran a class.

I was always athletic during my college days. When my dad died I didn't train much as I did before, or play sports on the weekends eight hours Saturday and eight hours Sunday. Then I got back into training with some of my dad's old students in the 70s, like Felix Macias and other people who trained with him and I started retraining and relearning. Then I went to LA in the early 80s where I trained with Ted Wong and Herb Jackson. And in the last 20 years I've been training and teaching, also monthly with a group of people under Wallay Jay.

Q: Anything you would like to add?
Greglon Lee: He listened to James for advice. My dad was 20 years older than Bruce, so in a sense James was more of a father or uncle figure. James lived most of his life in America and he understood the struggles of Asian-Americans in America. My dad supported Bruce and said to him go for it, we'll help you in any way we can. And that was the basic understanding.

WALLAY JAY

Bruce Lee exchanged ideas and martial arts philosophies with a number of elite martial artists in the Oakland area. Wallay Jay - of Small Circle Jiu Jitsu fame - was one of them. Master Jay is often credited with showing Lee the finer points of grappling and exposing him to various techniques which Bruce would later integrate into his method of fighting. Professor Jay and Bruce Lee shared a common interest in the martial arts and a close friendship. They continued to see each other and corresponded until the end.

Q: When and where did you meet Bruce?
Wallay Jay: A student's mother was teaching Cha Cha and Bruce was in her class, so she brought Bruce over. He was fabulous.

Q: What did you make of his fighting style?
Wallay Jay: He was more into Wing Chun at the time. Our team was the weakest team in Judo in California, and I never competed in Judo in my life. I took lessons but I wasn't good enough. I had to learn a lot of stuff. Ken Kwachi was my instructor, he was the Hawaii Judo champion. There was only one open division, he was only 135 pounds, he used to throw big guys around. He always emphasized the wrist action, so I finally got the secret.

Q: What kind of conversations would you and Bruce delve into regarding the martial arts?
Wallay Jay: Footwork and all kinds of stuff. We both had fancy footwork and we used to laugh at each other and shuffle. He believed footwork was very important, the angles and so on. He was only 23 and I was 44 years old. It was 1962-63, he wasn't famous then but around 1967 he got really well known.

Q: Where did Bruce pick up the power and the speed which he became famous for?
Wallay Jay: He has training for that, but he was born with speed. He had tremendous speed. Speed is power.

Q: Did Bruce emphasize sparring with gloves?
Wallay Jay: He did, when he was in high school he was the Boxing champion of Hong Kong. But he didn't have any lessons, it was the Wing Chun he was using.

Q: You once said Bruce could do Judo throws and even name them in Japanese. Just how did he manage to do this without any formal Judo training?
Wallay Jay: I think he had some training in Seattle. I never said he knew all the throws, but he could do some throws. I was fascinated by his punching power and his speed. I learned from his student James Demile, who became a friend later.

Q: What did Bruce think of grappling in general at the time when he was in Oakland?
Wallay Jay: Not much, he mostly did stuff standing up. He wasn't too good at it (groundwork). I think cross-training is important. I came from a traditional school and I cross-trained and really improved.

Q: Do you think Bruce was a complete fighter? Had he lived, do you think he would have absorbed more grappling into his fighting style?
Wallay Jay: Yes, he would. Everything he did he improved it. His mind was on it all the time. We would go to my dojo and practice with Jimmy Lee. Bruce stayed with Jimmy for two years and this is where his son was born, then he moved to Los Angeles.

Q: After Bruce died some people would make certain comments saying that he wasn't a real fighter. What have you got to say on this subject?
Wallay Jay: I think he was great. He had a fight with this Chinese Kung Fu guy in Oakland who told him to stop teaching non-Chinese. The Chinese guy said, "If I win, you don't teach to anybody else other than Chinese." Bruce just went inside and the guy started running. Bruce was fast, chasing the guy and punching the back of his head.

Q: When Bruce became famous did he still keep in touch with you?
Wallay Jay: Yes, he wrote me letters when he was in Hong Kong and we talked with each other.

Q: Your friend George Dillman knew Bruce. Can you recall any stories he's exchanged with you pertaining to Bruce Lee?
Wallay Jay: Yes, he asked Bruce Lee, "Who is the toughest guy in the Eastside?" Bruce said, "George Dillman," and then he asked who was the toughest guy in the West Coast, to which Bruce replied, "Wallay Jay." I'm not tough, but scientific.

Q: Did you ever witness Bruce working out on the heavy bag?
Wallay Jay: Oh, yeah, he had a big bag and I could hardly move it when I punched it. He said to me, "Watch this," and he stepped back and hit the bag and it went flying up in the air. I was amazed. He was about 135 pounds. So much power. He wasn't a Boxer, he did enter matches in Hong Kong but he used Wing Chun. He didn't care for Boxing. He hit so hard, you know, it was a sight to see. He had the mook jong, different sizes of punch bags, weights, etc.

Q: Are you close to the Lee family?
Wallay Jay: I met Brandon several times. Also at the Bruce Lee Anniversary Dinner I gave a talk. (Brandon) was sitting on the next table to me. It was Bruce's birthday so there was a crowd of very important people. Movie directors and so on.

Q: Just what kind of a person was Bruce?
Wallay Jay: He was good to me. He'd do anything. I had a Judo tournament here in Alameda and he'd come from Seattle and sign autographs in 1967.

Q: Which other high-class and elite martial artists of the era did Bruce exchange ideas with?
Wallay Jay: Gene LeBell, (George) Dillman, Jhoon Rhee. I don't know Chuck (Norris) too well but I've held a seminar for him in LA. He learned some stuff from Hayward Nishioka.

Q: In your opinion, what was the most intriguing attribute he possessed?
Wallay Jay: He was smart, very clever. The secret is 'repetition'.

Q: Do you still keep in touch with Bruce's students?
Wallay Jay: I have not been feeling well in the past couple of years. Greglon Lee - Jimmy Lee's son - visits me every week. Dan Inosanto and a whole bunch of guys come to my seminars. My son used to see Bruce waiting for me on a Saturday outside my house, and he used to call me at work saying don't go anywhere after work because Bruce is here.

Q: How did you hear about Bruce's death?
Wallay Jay: I read it in the paper, then people started calling me. I don't think people have that much drive now. Bruce was training 24/7 literally. I don't think there is anybody as big as him, he was the tops and a special person. He has appeared in more magazines than anyone else. The best part is the movies that are very popular and you can enjoy them in any era.

LEON JAY

L eon Jay, son of Master Wallay Jay, was fortunate enough to witness the extraordinary skills Bruce Lee possessed on countless occasions. Because of the close friendship between Bruce and Leon's father, Bruce would often visit the Jay household to workout and exchange concepts. Leon has an interesting perspective on the Bruce Lee he knew as a child growing up. Today, he continues to tour the world teaching his father's system of Small Circle Jiu Jitsu.

Q: Can we talk about your father's friendship with Bruce Lee and when they met, etc?
Leon Jay: Dad first met Bruce through one of his students, I think it was Dr. Jane Lee, because Bruce was into Cha Cha and so was she. Bruce was there and my father came there because she asked him to come see this guy. It was the first time they met. I think the next time they met was in Seattle. We went with dad, who took the Judo team up - because he used to take the Judo team and tour throughout the US, Mexico, Hawaii and Canada - and we went up to Seattle. We went to this basement of a church together as a whole team where we saw Bruce. We got to watch him do his demonstration and everything else and we were absolutely gobsmacked and stunned. We'd seen a lot of people but never anyone that dynamic. That's pretty much how it all started with dad long time ago.

Q: Can you tell me how Bruce would be waiting outside your house for your dad when you used to come home from school?
Leon Jay: Bruce and dad had a pretty good relationship, he met him in Oakland. There was a guy named Jimmy Lee who was an Iron Palm Kung Fu master, and he used to do breaking and stuff like that. He was really exceptional. Back then he had a book out on breaking. So, when Bruce

used to come over from Seattle he used to stay with Jimmy. James Lee used to bring Bruce over to our house all the time, and they'd come over and sit on the front porch waiting for dad to come home from work, because dad was a postman back in those days. He got a transfer from Hawaii to California. I would come home and there was Bruce. Dad would come home and they'd train. It was interesting times. Bruce used to hang out, dad always talked about him. I mean, ever since they met, they just clicked. Dad was twice his age.

I remember as a kid watching Jimmy Lee breaking the bricks. I remember he'd line up five bricks and he'd ask which one you'd want him to break and he'd break the one you picked. I remember seeing that as a kid and saying, "Jesus, that's amazing!" I saw Bruce demonstrating with Jimmy and he was pretty much controlling the issue, slapping him around a bit. I thought, "My God, this is pretty interesting. This guy's that tough."

Q: Did your dad have a gym in the basement and what elements of martial arts did they work on and discuss?

Leon Jay: It wasn't in the basement, the dojo was in the extension on the back of the house. It was quite large, but mostly they did a lot of stuff in the living room and sometimes they would go back in the dojo. Dad and Bruce both talked about the power in the wrist, and one of the things that came up was Bruce saying, "Wallay, when you do your finger locks and things like that, I notice that you're doing a lot of down movements with the wrist." And my dad said, "Yeah, Bruce, when I get hold of the guy and his fingers," and took him down and said, "Can you get out?" and he goes, "No, man, I can't get out." Then my dad says to Bruce, "I notice when you're doing your floating punch or one-inch punch you're snapping the wrist up when you're doing that," and Bruce goes, "Yeah , because it really lifts them up and sends them across the room, and is pretty impressive" (Laughs).

Q: Can you expand on Bruce's interest in grappling at the time when he was in Oakland? Your father was one of the main men who actually worked with Bruce on grappling!

Leon Jay: I was quite young, it wasn't until later on when we went to see Taky Kimura in Seattle when he used to tell dad, "Hey, Wallay, how is it seeing Bruce doing your techniques on the screen?" Because he (Wallay) used to show him armbars, joint manipulations and stuff like that, and how to perfect them. I think more than anything else, other than just techniques, they really clicked on the principles of martial arts. It was more about that than just how to do this or that; it was what made it work. How do you use the power of the wrist? Footwork - they loved going over footwork and how to trim it off and things like that.

Q: Bruce started delving into the arts by using the medium of research at a fairly young age...

Leon Jay: I was quite young back then but later listening to my father talking about Bruce, he really liked the idea of change. Sticking with traditional stuff, if it doesn't work change it, man, get rid of it, make it fit for you. Dad always said, "I don't care how many ways you teach a master how to run he'll never run like a greyhound." Bruce and dad had a lot of insight into the martial arts. Because dad was senior and he had so many people against him for a long time, my old man was a fighter. It didn't matter, the old man kept going, and Bruce really liked that part. I think it was the strength of character they liked about each other. There were lot of people who put Bruce down, and they'd go, "Hey, Wallay, why are you hanging out with that Bruce Lee guy? He's too cocky." Dad would say, "Well, he's not cocky, he's cocksure. He can just do it."

Q: Your father was a prominent name in the Judo and Jiu Jitsu world. Did Bruce often come over to his school and demonstrate Judo throws?

Leon Jay: He could do throws but mostly I really remember him do his floating punches, his trapping hands, his kicks. Dad had the top team in the country and guys there were really good at throwing. Mostly we remember him for his speed and things like that, we all talked about it a lot. Dad says it's all about training, it doesn't come just because you wish it to be there. He trained all the time and this is something dad always emphasized to us. He really gave us the boost to keep doing it and keep going. Their relationship was special. Bruce used to come over to the Hawaiian festivals for dad and dad would try to pay him, because there would be a couple of thousand people there. He was really spectacular in his demonstrations, slapping everybody around - kindly - but Bruce wouldn't accept any money from my father at all, he refused.

It's funny because later on down the line, dad actually found out from Linda Lee that they were actually broke at the time, but he still refused to accept any money. In the year 2000, I had a convention for dad, he wanted to dedicate it to Bruce. This was at the Marriot in Oakland and about 500 people from all over the world showed up. We invited Linda Lee as a guest of honor. I asked her to speak and she was there 15-20 minutes, speaking about the Oakland days and how much Bruce respected my father and how enthusiastic he was. Bruce wanted his son Brandon to start Judo first because he felt that was a good base to come from, the close contact and moving with each other. Dad made a huge impact on Bruce's ideas and training and things like that, and vice versa. I talked to my dad and he said, "He wasn't my student, we were friends and we shared." Bruce was half his age but was way ahead of his time.

Q: Your dad and Bruce shared a common interest in cross-training. Your dad was cross-training way back in the early 60s, which was very rare in the martial arts fraternity in those days, wasn't it?

Leon Jay: Late 40s and early 50s he was cross-training back then. People he trained and grew up with in the martial arts really didn't like it and they were on his case, saying, "No, that's not how Professor Okazaki did it." The answer is Professor Okazaki changed, he didn't do the same thing, but some people get stuck in one thing. Dad always promoted for us to learn and think outside of the box. He's always taught us to go learn other things and bring them back into what you're doing. Dad had been cross-training for quite a long time and he'd always taught like that. It wasn't until the late 50s, early 60s that it really started showing in his Judo. He said, "If I keep doing what the Kodakan guys are doing I'm always going to be behind them." So, that's when he really went outside of the system and came back. The next thing you know is his team started winning in the Nationals and pretty soon they were one of the top teams in the country.

That's what Bruce liked about it; Bruce really liked that part of it. James Demile actually said when he came that Bruce talked a lot about (cross-training) because dad was so successful at it. Because of the success dad had with it, he thought (it was) OK and he took it even further. When dad first met him, Bruce was pretty much just doing Wing Chun. He really liked the idea (of cross-training) and searching for everything.

Q: Bruce would visit your house often. What memories do you have of him from a perspective of a kid?

Leon Jay: I was just a kid and he'd say, "Hey, kid, how's it going?" It was like that. A lot of the guys used to come over all the time, we had hundreds of people come to the house and it was interesting to watch. I always saw dad finger-locking people and putting them on the ground, and Bruce was no exception (Laughs). My old man had him down all over the place, man. Bruce was really fast and we thought that was pretty damn cool! I've got to say this: part of the reason dad was so loved by so many people was because of his enthusiasm for martial arts, and Bruce loved that in my father as well. I think Bruce and dad had the same thing in common. Let me put it this way to you: there was one of our guys in High School Nationals, he threw another guy, won first place, he became the champion that year. My father went over to the other guy - from completely another organization - and he told him what he did wrong. It wasn't about his guy being the best, but about elevating the level of martial arts. I think that's where Bruce and dad had something in common

Q: When Bruce left Oakland and moved to Los Angeles did your father keep in touch with him?

Leon Jay: Yes. Bruce would come back up, like I said, he would come do demonstrations and dad would go down to see him. He would come back and tell me the stories about the big bag: when he hit the bag it hardly went anywhere and when Bruce hit it, it went flying. I remember one time we were in Oakland at the restaurant, and Bruce was sat on another table. He shouted, "Hey, Wallay!" and dad responded with, "Hey, Bruce!" So we had a chit chat, they were good buddies.

Q: Nowadays the UFC and MMA is popular. Bruce hadn't fully explored the grappling aspects of the martial arts. But Bruce did work with competent grapplers which included your dad and Hayward Nishioka, who were impressed with Bruce. Do you think it was only a matter of time before he would have become a competent grappler himself?
Leon Jay: I know Bruce's focus was to win a street fight. I don't think his goal was to jump in the ring with one person. I don't think that was it. I think he would be thinking not to go to the ground. The Brazilians and the Ultimate Fighting Championship...they're brilliant at it, man, absolutely brilliant at ground fighting. Personally, I don't want to go to the ground. I've been in fights before and if you're on the ground you'll get the boot in not by one guy but six. His goal was not to go to the ground.

Q: When he went to Hong Kong did your father continue to correspond with him?
Leon Jay: Yeah, dad has some letters that Bruce wrote. They still corresponded but not as much because he was too busy. It was a shocker when he went. You never think of that kind of thing, you know.

Q: When Bruce made it big in 1973 with the global success Enter the Dragon achieved, you were pretty much a teenager. How did you perceive your father's close friend?
Leon Jay: We were in California, we were so happy for him. Obviously, he was my idol when I was a kid and to see him on the big screen...I don't mean to be funny about it but back before Bruce hit it big we lived in Alameda, Oakland, where the Black Panthers came from. Before Enter the Dragon it was 'hey, chink' and after Bruce's movies came out it was like 'hey, brother' (Laughs). Wait a minute, last week I was a chink, this week I'm a brother? It was funny. He really made an impact for the Orientals and it really changed a lot of people's perspective.

Q: What's the most significant or unique element which was the backbone of the enormous success he achieved?
Leon Jay: What made him unique and special is his focus. When he made

his mind up to do something he would focus at it and constantly go at it till he got it. And it was through hard work and training that he did that, and versatility. He was able to be on the target but not so stuck that you're not willing to change your ways.

GEORGE DILLMAN

Many martial artists and Bruce Lee aficionados will no doubt be familiar with George Dillman and his relationship with the late Bruce Lee. Globally known as the master of pressure points, Dillman shared quality time with Bruce Lee during the mid-60s to early 70s. The pair first met in Washington DC in 1966 which would be the start of a long friendship. A fascinating character himself, Dillman has some intriguing stories which can only inspire those mere mortals who wish to know more about their idol Bruce Lee.

Q: When did you meet Bruce Lee?
George Dillman: I met Bruce Lee in Washington DC. A man named Ed Parker brought him out to my house. He called me up and said, "I want you to meet someone." At that time, Bruce Lee was not that quite famous, he got more famous after he died. For a lot of people, what happens is it takes death to become real famous. He was just an average guy like anybody else at that time. I came out of the house and shook hands and we just settled into the living room and started talking about the martial arts, the future of the martial arts and what he intended to do with martial arts. He held my son and sat on the couch with my children, and that was good, really beautiful. He asked if he could stop by the dojo and train and he did. He came down to my school three times and that's it, then he passed away. He stopped by the dojo and wanted to spar and fight with some of the students. People say Bruce didn't enter tournaments, but he did. He got discovered for the movies by winning kata - first place at Ed Parker's International Championships. People thought Bruce Lee didn't like kata. What he said was where he is at now (level), he doesn't need kata, but he needed the kata to get to where he got to. Otherwise that's like saying I can learn to write without ever learning to print or without learning the

alphabet; I just want to learn to write. He thought the kata was the alphabet, to learn to write. That's the way he described it to me at the time. He got discovered doing kata, but he didn't necessarily like entering tournaments because he didn't like the fact it was what he called a 'one touch and run game'. They go like this (demonstrates with hands) and someone goes 'point'. He liked to put on gloves and hit you, and he liked to be hit, that was the difference. He said, "If you hit me we'll give you a point, and if I hit you I get a point."

So he liked gloves, he liked to make contact and he didn't like the 'point and run' system, that's one of the reasons he never wanted to enter tournaments. What he was famous for - and this has been written up in a lot of things - he used to go round to different Karate schools and fight students. To him this was better than tournaments, and he would fight all the students. Some of the write-ups made it sound like he was aggressive, but he was not, he was always polite. When he went into someone's school he wouldn't ask the instructor to fight or beat up the instructor in front of the students, like some of the articles lead you to believe he did. When he sparred with students he did very well, beat them up most of the time. Not bad, but it was still point fighting, but he would hit them (properly).

Then you'd ask him to fight. I asked him to fight, he didn't ask, I asked him. I said let's fight and spar, and he said yes. After that he was the first man I'd seen who would use both hands equally, we all strive for that. He'd hit you with a left but you weren't sure if it was a right or a left , he'd hit you with either hand and they both had the same power. He could kick with either foot like 'Superfoot' (Bill)Wallace. Bruce Lee could do that with both legs, and he's the first man to kick me in the head. First time we sparred, I went into my fighting stance and all of a sudden 'whack'! I tried to get into my fighting stance and all of a sudden 'pow'! - I get hit in the side of the head. I actually thought a guy should be refereeing this! And I thought he can't be allowed to kick that way! At that time in the martial arts people didn't kick high till he did in the movies. He's the reason we have a Bill 'Superfoot' Wallace, he's the reason we have people kicking high, because he started it. He said hands and feet are equal so we're going to use them the same. So he would kick you and punch you.

Q: What kind of a personality did Bruce have?
George Dillman: If you knew him, fantastic, you loved him. If he didn't like you, he let it be known. Some people have said he was arrogant. If he didn't like you he didn't waste time, that's the way it was - see you later. He was polite and he'd leave. And if he liked you and thought you had intelligent answers...he's the one who introduced me to Professor Wallay Jay. We got talking and he said, "You gotta meet Professor Wallay Jay." At the time I hadn't heard of Wallay Jay (this was back in 1967). He said,

"There's a man out in California, and as far as I'm concerned he's one of the roughest guys on the mat. When he gets on the mat he means it." And he said, "You've got to train with him too, this guy's good."

He's really the one who introduced me to Wallay. And through Wallay and Bruce Lee I ended up meeting Leo Fong, who is a man to this day in tremendous shape. Leo Fong, who I guess is heading for 80, or is in his early 80s, trains every day like he has a professional fight. He does bag work, roadwork and he hits. I run three-day camps in Pennsylvania , and Leo Fong comes in and teaches and he wears the young guys out.

Q: He displayed an open-mindedness that most people didn't acclimatize to in those early years. What do you think Bruce was trying to achieve with his research into different arts?
George Dillman: Quickest, simplest way to get out of a self defense situation. He made that clear all the time. He would say, "If you have a better idea, better technique, show it to me! And if I like it I'm going to be doing it." Wallay Jay is the same way. He said to Wallay, "Jay, you changed that technique a little bit," he says, "A car in 1960 and a automobile in the year 2006 made a lot of changes." That's what Wallay told me.

Wallay and Bruce had the same philosophy, which was you've got to change and stay with times and if there's a quicker way to put somebody down then you've got to do it. Bruce was into simplicity, the people who are calling themselves Jeet Kune Do are making it too complicated. Bruce did not have it complicated. Bruce's philosophy was, he said, "You're gonna touch me and I'm gonna hit you, and hit you hard and fast and often, and you're going to go down." And today when they teach his art, they say you do this and touch this then grab here; but he never did that. Bruce liked to train with other people's students, and he made a little joke afterwards. He said, "If you're going to beat your students up they'll quit. They're going to think you're going to beat them next week. If I come in and beat them up, they won't quit, they'll just be glad I'm gone." So he could come in and beat the daylights of the students and I'd say, "He's gone, you won't have to see him again!" (Laughs). That was one of his things also, he used to like to spar with strange people.

He was into realistic training, realistic fighting and everything he had to train with had to be able to work in the street. You couldn't give him an idea which wasn't going to work in a real situation. And if you could give him an idea which worked faster and harder, he was in on it. So he was open-minded. That's what I liked about him. He once said some people are so set in their ways, in their styles, that they have tunnel vision and they can't see left and they can't see right, they just want 'their' way. He actually opened my mind that way, because he wasn't that way if you showed him a technique. Like when Wallay Jay in Jiu Jitu showed him some techniques that worked fast and quick, Bruce Lee did them.

Q: Do you think Bruce brought a whole new flavor to action films when he started making movies?
George Dillman: He actually not only brought a flavor to action films but everybody's martial arts schools picked up through the 1960s and 70s. I had one of the largest dojos in the United States. I had over 400 students, unheard of back then - everybody had clubs with 20 or 30. I had over 400 students and a lot of it I owe to Bruce Lee because people knew I was connected to Bruce Lee. It was a shame Bruce died at a young age because he was going to do more and more with martial arts in films in this country. He only went over to China (Hong Kong) to make movies because they were cheap and he could get his word out. Once the word was out and he had enough profit, he wanted to come back here and put it to play. He wanted to have a television show. There used to be an old television show called Charlie Chan where there was a Chinese detective and he had a number one and number two son. Bruce Lee wanted his own television show and to redo Charlie Chan. He wanted to be number one son, and when the father got into trouble Bruce was going to show up and clean them up (Laughs).

Q: Do you think Bruce expected too much of everyone around him?
George Dillman: Maybe some of the reason why he died - there's another reason behind that - was that he pushed himself to the limit. The human body can only take so much. He had a drive. And maybe he knew he was going to die, but he would constantly do push ups, sit ups, practice with piece of wood. And on the movie set when they would take a break, and everybody would sit down, people tell me Bruce went over and would do push ups, pumping up for the next scene so he looked strong. He would give the people problems on the movie set. On the TV show he gave people problems because he didn't want to do anything that didn't make the martial arts look good, and that's one thing I think all martial artists really respected Bruce Lee for. He wouldn't do anything in the movie or TV show that would make the martial arts look bad. He wouldn't use a springboard. They wanted him to use a springboard to jump up and kick a light in a TV show, and he wouldn't do it. He said, "If I can't jump up and kick that light then we're not breaking that light." And he worked on it and worked on it and finally he jumped up and kicked the light bulb out. He did not use a springboard.

Q: Any interesting conversations that you would be willing to share during your friendship with Bruce?

George Dillman: We had some telephone conversations, actually, and when we were together in restaurants I learned more from Bruce Lee just sitting there talking than in the dojo. In the dojo you're fighting and you don't hear anything other than 'put your hands up' and 'block'. But when you're sitting one-on-one…we talked about some things in the restaurant where you could learn and pick his brain and really learn something.

Q: Were there any incidents when he sparred with your students?
George Dillman: No, other than one time. I had an instructor called Daniel K. Pai, he was a very tough person and he wanted to spar Bruce, and it got a little rough and I had to separate them. I had to go between them which was hard to do, because I had Bruce Lee on one side and my instructor here. And what it mounted to was they started hitting each other harder and harder. If you pulled your punch against Danny Pai he'd pull his punch, if you hit him hard he'd hit you hard. If you were going to hit him harder he was going to hit you harder. I was at a tournament, which Jhoon Rhee was running one time, and Daniel Pai and a fighter got on the stage to fight and they had to get the police to pull them apart!

Q: For a guy who was 5ft 7, 135 pounds, how was Bruce Lee able to develop his body and fighting prowess?
George Dillman: He could hit you with every pound he had. His whole trick was he'd hit you four times faster. When I first met him he told me, "I could hit you four times before you can hit me once." And I doubted that, but he did. By the time I got in my stance he'd hit me, that's how fast he was.

Q: The emotional intensity and charisma he possessed makes him so watchable on the big screen. What was the reaction in the United States when he smashed his way to the box office?
George Dillman: Anytime anything came out relating to martial arts at the time, people would pack in to see it. It was the only thing we had as martial artists at the time. When there was television in the United States there were only three channels, now there's hundreds. It was different that time, the movies were the answer and you went to them. If you were a martial artist and heard somebody threw one kick in the movie you went to see it. Back then there weren't videos, DVDs or books. You couldn't even get a good book on the martial arts. There were one or two books and you'd get them just because they were on the martial arts, but there wasn't a lot of books. Today, there's books on every style by everybody, there's DVDs and everything you want. Now you can almost train at home. Stick a DVD and see all the big guys teaching. Back then this wasn't the case. You had to learn firsthand, and to learn you had to train with the big guys. And a lot

of people didn't like doing that, because it was like, "Oh, he might hit you," but that's what the learning was all about.

Q: You knew two men, Muhammad Ali and Bruce Lee, who are regarded by many as the greatest legends of our time. Can you compare Bruce Lee to Muhammad Ali?

George Dillman: Two different sizes. Muhammad Ali was 6ft 3 and Bruce Lee was 5ft 7. But I gotta tell you this, Muhammad Ali asked me to introduce him to Bruce Lee. And one time in a telephone conversation Bruce asked me to introduce him to Muhammad Ali. I was training with Muhammad Ali at the time and Bruce Lee said, "When I get back from China, I've got to meet Muhammad Ali." And what happened was Bruce never returned on that trip.

Q: Bruce Lee was a rare blend not likely to be duplicated. What has Bruce achieved on a worldwide basis compared to all these other movie stars?

George Dillman: Well, he got immortality. His name is known all over the world. I just returned from a trip in China, he's still as famous in China today as he was back in the 70s, you just mention his name. I had some pictures of me with Bruce Lee and the people just wanted them all over the place. So he's famous all over the world. I go out and do talks, and even little children today know Bruce, they don't know anyone else but you say Bruce Lee and they say, "Yeah, I know Bruce Lee."

Q: Bruce Lee is sorely missed by all and his legacy continues to blossom. How did you find out about his death?

George Dillman: I think it was caused. I'm going to say it was caused. I believe it was an acupuncture needle that went under the back of the skull. There's a pressure point under the skull, with one needle you can take somebody out. I believe it was caused. Even the wife now believes it, everybody now believes it. There was too much money involved. He went to make the movies in China and in the (contract) clause in small print, it said if anything happens to Bruce Lee the money goes to the movie company.

If you think about it, Hong Kong in those days was the number one crime city in the world, you think someone can't get it done? Yes, you can! They got all the money, Mrs. Bruce Lee never got any money until Enter the Dragon was released by Warner Brothers. She was threatening to sue and they gave her, as I understand, some money to shut her up so they could release the movie. I'm not sure of the figure but I think they gave her $2 million. She didn't get any of the money in Hong Kong. When Bruce Lee died $100 million came into the bank. $100 million back in 1973!

JHOON RHEE

Tae Kwon Do master Jhoon Rhee was one of the few elite martial arts masters with whom Bruce Lee traded techniques with in pursuit of accumulating knowledge and research. Lee and Master Rhee would often visit each other's houses and train in the basement until four in the morning. Bruce Lee was able to integrate various kicking techniques with the help of Jhoon Rhee and absorb elements which best suited his art and stature. Jhoon Rhee is a grandmaster of Tae Kwon Do who respected his friend's skill and cherishes the good memories.

Q: Could you please tell me how you got involved in the martial arts?
Jhoon Rhee: When I was six years old I was beaten up by a five-year-old girl in my hometown of Suwon, which is around 25 miles from Seoul in Korea. When I went to my mother crying - and as a six-year-old boy as honest as I can be - I told her what happened and she was so mad that she beat me even harder. There was really no place to train in Boxing or Tae Kwon Do in my small town so I began to lift weights and do push ups, etc. Then when I was 13, I went to Seoul to start my middle school. There I found a martial arts school behind my uncle's home where I lived when I was attending school. That was the beginning of my Tae Kwon Do. Then when I watched Marilyn Monroe's movies I fell in love. I was around 15 years old and I really decided I would go to America someday when I grew up. I thought to myself, "How am I going to make a living?" and then I thought with Tae Kwon Do. From that moment on I really put my effort into improving my English as well as Tae Kwon Do skills; I did nothing but Tae Kwon Do and English.

Q: You met Bruce Lee at the Long Beach Internationals in 1964, what was your impression of him and his demonstration?

Jhoon Rhee: Yes, I had never heard of him, but I met him for the very first time in 1964 at Ed Parker's International Karate Championships. I think it was a Saturday and Sunday in the month of August. In the evening, Bruce Lee was giving his own demonstration and I was doing my own. I think we really impressed each other, and ever since then we became friends. One day, in 1965, I saw him performing a demonstration on one of the Washington DC television stations - Channel Seven - and I called the station up. He didn't call me because he must have forgot. I called the producer and after the show we met and had lunch, then we became much closer friends from that point on. The following year, in 1966, at my annual championships I invited him as my guest and he really helped with gathering the crowds. So whenever he came to Washington, my home was his home and his home was my home.

Q: Can you tell me about some of the training sessions you both enjoyed in your garage and what extent did you both take these sessions to?
Jhoon Rhee: Yes, it was in the garage but sometimes it was in the basement, we would be breaking boards and fighting in the basement. He didn't really care much about forms, but I paid a lot of attention to forms which led me to invent musical forms. We were working out till three in the morning whenever he would come to my house. My wife would complain because we were making too much noise (Laughs). He really had a good idea about hand techniques and I had a good idea of foot techniques so we exchanged ideas. I watched him repeating the same technique over and over again. It was repetition.

Q: At one time you invited him to be a guest at one of your tournaments in the Dominican Republic!
Jhoon Rhee: That was in 1970, when I had black belt testing for my students. I asked him if he would like to come and he said yes. He gave several demonstrations in several cities, he was already very famous from the Kato character he played in the Green Hornet TV series. It's a shame I don't have any clippings, but in one of the demonstrations he did jump side kick breaking boards for the first time - in my garage he broke four boards using a jump side kick - he kicked and the boards flew and he broke the lamp of the TV show. It was one of the most spectacular scenes, I wish I had a clipping. We tried everything we could to find that clip but couldn't find it. That was in 1970, when not many people had video cameras back then. He made a really good impression on the Dominican Republic people.

Q: Bruce was devoted to his body development. What are your views of him implementing weight training into his martial arts?

Jhoon Rhee: He was an avid trainer, he really spent a lot of time and he didn't have a still moment. Even when he was reading he had a spring device for the forearms. Always lifting weights, I've never seen anybody so dedicated to training like him. He always did his own training without a trainer. Bob Wall, Mike Stone, Joe Lewis and Chuck Norris used to come over to his place to train with him. All the stars today trained under him. First they didn't like him because they thought Bruce Lee was very difficult to get along with, but once he becomes a friend he's very well liked by people.

Q: Bruce was an advocate of cutting edge supplements and nutrition. As I understand it, he gave you advice on the use of supplements?
Jhoon Rhee: He asked me to really try protein powder and even sent me cans of powder. I didn't really keep up with it depending on my daily diet. He was really dedicated to his training. He had a 300-pound heavy bag, a very, very heavy bag, and he'd practice his side kick on it. A very heavy bag is not too effective for punching but is more effective for kicking. Bruce Lee agreed with me that basics were everything. In the human mind basics are everything. There is only one good important basic which we should abide by in everyday life, which is 'honesty'. In Tae Kwon Do there are only three basics: good punching, a good side kick and round kick.

Q: What impressed you most about Bruce Lee and what was his strongest attribute?
Jhoon Rhee: His strength. I never saw anyone beat him in arm wrestling. As small as he was, less than 145 pounds, but no one beat him. And he was so quick! Very explosive in punching and kicking. He learned how to kick boards from me in my garage the first time in 1970. A few days later he broke more than I did.

Q: You became friends with Muhammad Ali, did you ever discuss Ali with Bruce?
Jhoon Rhee: Yes, Muhammad Ali really respected Bruce Lee. They are the same age, and Bruce Lee thought Muhammad Ali was the best and Muhammad Ali also thinks Bruce Lee is the best. They both didn't know just how good they were. They never met each other. I tried to arrange something but Bruce died too early.

Q: He had a very extensive library which encompassed books of all kinds pertaining to the martial arts, weight training, self help and philosophy...
Jhoon Rhee: He had his own room with two walls full of books, thousands

of books. Almost 50 percent was martial arts and the rest were other type of books from philosophy and other subjects which he was into. Even in his college time he was a philosophy major. I've always been very philosophical and religious, so we were really very close from a martial arts and philosophical point of view. He had a hobby of collecting all types of martial arts books and I found a dozen books in his library on Korean styles of Tae Kwon Do and Hapkido. He was really an avid reader and had a very beautiful handwriting. While he was alive, from our ten years of friendship I have 19 handwritten letters from Bruce Lee which I'm keeping in my safe, and I wrote a book called Bruce Lee and I. Reading these letters shows the true philosophy and thoughts and his personality.

When I did my movie in Hong Kong (When Tae Kwon Do Strikes) which was shown all over the world in 1973, I also did another movie. One day Bruce Lee called me and said my movie was all edited but the director tried to switch the leading role to an actress - a Chinese lady who happened to be the director's goddaughter - and Bruce Lee fought to reverse that. And finally I became the leading actor. After he congratulated me, the next day I heard he died. Then I called his wife Linda Lee and she confirmed it was true, and I was so sad.

Q: You stayed in touch with him right up till his death, can you talk about his success in the Orient and can you recall him talking to you about his movies?

Jhoon Rhee: When he had the contract with Warner Brothers for Enter the Dragon, that was really an exciting moment of his life. We talked intensively about that movie which became a big success. Enter the Dragon made his name all over the world. This was the beginning of his big life. I could not believe the popularity of Bruce Lee that time. He invited me to join the preview of Enter the Dragon. The place was packed, the reaction of the audience was really great and Bruce Lee was introduced after the movie. People could not believe it. Me and one of my lady students were present at this event.

Q: Millions are familiar with Bruce Lee's legendary image. Can you tell me just what type of a person he was from the perspective of a personal friend?

Jhoon Rhee: I think he was a great man. Not easy to approach at first to become friends with him, but once he trusted you he would go out of his way to help you. He was a great friend I had and I'm sorry he had to leave us so early. When I was shooting my movie in Hong Kong, when he was not doing anything at dinner time in the evening he always waited for me to go to a Korean restaurant. He liked the Korean beef, we really enjoyed it.

I was there for three months shooting the movie. I didn't stay in his house because they (movie company) put him in a hotel in Hong Kong, Kowloon Hayat hotel. I never claimed I taught him how to kick, but in Hong Kong when I first arrived to shoot my movie I went to a custom-made shoe store, and when I gave my name for the receipt the sales assistant said, "You're Jhoon Rhee, Bruce Lee's teacher?" I said, "Who told you that?" And he said Bruce Lee was demonstrating kicking techniques on the television and the presenter asked him how he learned to kick like that, because Kung Fu exponents don't kick like that. He told the whole Hong Kong audience that Master Jhoon Rhee, father of Tae Kwon Do in the United States, taught him how to kick like that. That's how I found out he told people that I taught him to kick like that.

Q: Many of those who were close to Bruce confirm he had a great sense of humor. Did you ever detect this quality in him?
Jhoon Rhee: He had a lot of jokes, whenever he gathered with people he would try to make them laugh. So did Muhammad Ali. One time on a television show, he had to pick a small dime from the forehead of the presenter and push it hard. When he took it out the man thought the dime was still there because he pressed it so hard. If you hit the back of your head the dime would fall off, the presenter kept hitting (the back of his own head), the audience kept laughing. He was a very comic person and always liked to joke.

Q: Can you tell me about the photo shoot you did with Bruce on the beach in California?
Jhoon Rhee: That was in Los Angeles on the seaside when we went to catch carbrini. He also brought a photographer with him to take pictures.

Q: What would you say is your most significant memory of Bruce?
Jhoon Rhee: The most vivid memory is when he came to Washington in 1967. He was the special guest at my tournament. I think it was May 7th. We had 8,000 audience members, and in 1967 audiences of 8,000 at a martial arts tournament was never heard of. It was held at the Washington Armory, which holds about 20,000 people. This was the biggest memory of me and Bruce. He did the one-inch punch, two-finger push ups, one thumb and index finger push ups, and one-hand push ups using only two fingers.

Q: Bruce's method of combat related to street fighting and he emphasized this to his students. Did he rather have negative attitude towards competitions?
Jhoon Rhee: He told me he was a natural fighter, when he was in Hong

Kong he was a street fighter. He went to a Boxing tournament when he was attending school and knocked his opponent out with a few weeks of training in Boxing. He was a natural fighter.

Q: Had Bruce lived, which direction do you feel he would have taken his martial arts?
Jhoon Rhee: I don't really know for sure but I don't think he would have expanded his schools around the world, he didn't believe in that. He believed in his technique as being very secretive, and I learned a great deal from him in punching and he learned how to kick. We exchanged ideas - we were teachers of each other and students of each other.

Q: Did you witness his power in kicking the shield?
Jhoon Rhee: Oh, yes. Nobody could take his kick on the kicking shield. He had a 300-pound heavy bag so the student didn't fall down. So when he kicked the bag my back would be touching the bag, so the 300-pound heavy bag would stop my body.

Q: Do you feel Bruce Lee will be remembered for a long time just as someone like James Dean?
Jhoon Rhee: I think   James Dean's name lasted for many years but I think Bruce Lee's name outlasted James Dean's, because   Bruce Lee pictures are everywhere even after 35 years after his death. I don't know how long it's going to last but it's still a very hot name in the martial arts magazines. Charisma is one of the things he had, martial arts became very explosive all over the world. In the Western world there were no martial arts that much, only a little bit of Judo. James Dean was a good actor in the movies but Bruce Lee was not only a good actor but martial artist, he had the advantage in making his name much more popular worldwide. At James Dean's time, East and West were not that close, they were not exchanging much. Now the world's become one global society. Today, everything is like one nation. I really think that soon the cultural thing will be diminished and we'll be living under one God, because mankind must live together.

Q: Do you feel Bruce Lee bridged the gap between East and West?
Jhoon Rhee: I think he did more than anybody bridging the gap between East and the West. I really think that 21st century will make it much closer and there will be no East or West but one happy global society. He never believed in having a chain of schools, whereas I believed in Jhoon Rhee Studios around the world. He was very secretive about keeping his technique and I think Dan Inosanto, who was one of his good students and a friend of mine, is spreading Jeet Kune Do around the world now.

Q: He set the standard for action movie stars, and now we have Jackie Chan, Steven Seagal and all these other action stars. Do you think Bruce was the instigator who set a benchmark for everyone to follow?
Jhoon Rhee: Yes. In the Soviet Union, Muhammad Ali's Boxing wasn't shown because the authorities closed all the American movies, it was prohibited in the country. When the Soviet Union became free, Bruce Lee movies went in and so Bruce Lee became very popular. I would say all over the world two of the well-known faces are Muhammad Ali and Bruce Lee.

Q: Did you ever get to meet any of his celebrity students?
Jhoon Rhee: Yes, his two good students were Steve McQueen and James Coburn. He also taught Stirling Silliphant and Joe Hyams. I met Steve McQueen and James Coburn. Stirling Silliphant visited me in Washington DC at one time when he was on business in Washington because Bruce told him to.

JOE LEWIS

Joe Lewis was one of the few world Karate champions from the Los Angeles area with whom Bruce Lee worked out privately. Lewis met Lee at a national Karate tournament in 1967 in Washington DC. It wasn't until 1968 when both men started to train together - mostly Lewis visiting Lee's house every Wednesday for the better part of a year. It's no secret that Lewis, over the years, has earned quite a controversial reputation. He has been voted the 'Greatest Karate Fighter of All Time' and continues to teach seminars.

Q: Can you please culminate on your background on when and how you got started in the martial arts?
Joe Lewis: Oh, man, I can't remember that far back, I got hit too many times (Laughs). I went out with too many ugly girls, so I try to forget the past. Let me think...I was States champion in 1966, that was the first event I went out to and I cleaned out the house. I only had one point scored on me all day long. I won the Grand Championship first-grade black belt sparring and also first-grade black belt kata. As a matter of fact, I've never been beaten in kata. People say I'm not a traditionalist. I don't know what the word 'traditionalist' means but I think most martial artists use that word traditionalist as a weapon, some excuse for not being a good fighter or not sparring. They say, "Well, you know, that's not traditional martial arts." But that's what traditional martial arts came from, they came from fighting. So if you're not a fighter, in my opinion you're not a traditionalist. Ha! How about that? Anyway, I won the Amateur World Championship in 1966 and I was already a national and a world champion when I met Bruce Lee. I met him in 1967 at a national Karate event in Washington DC, when I went back to defend my title. And later that year we started training together. Up till the point when I met Bruce Lee, I had wanted to be a professional Wrestler since I was a kid.

I was lifting weights for five-and-a-half years, all through my teenage years. I started lifting when I was 14 years old and I got to be pretty big. I was 225 pounds and at that point I went to Okinawa to learn Karate, because that was the only place you could go in mid- or the early 60s. I started taking some Judo lessons and Karate lessons but I didn't like it. I felt martial artists were way out of shape - they were fat, they were skinny, they were weak and they didn't look like athletes. I came from the weightlifting world, and the weightlifting world people look like athletes. They're strong, healthy, muscular. That's the look and persona I wanted to be associated with. One day I met a guy named John Korab and he inspired me because he was kind of muscular, he didn't drink, he didn't cuss and he trained really hard every day for four or five hours a day. At that time he could beat any martial artist in the world. And I felt this was somebody I wanted to be like. So I went to Okinawa and started training at the school he was training at.

At that time they told me I had to quit weightlifting, so that's when I quit weightlifting, I just did straight Karate till I came back from Vietnam. I was taking Judo and Karate lessons. The thing about training in Okinawa in the early 60s is you have to realize in Okinawa all black belts are black belts in at least two different martial arts styles. They teach Judo in the school system there, so everybody is a black belt in Judo or Jiu Jitsu and also Karate. What they call mixed martial arts these days - I don't know where that term came from, I think it's a nonsense term anyway - everybody was doing mixed martial arts in Okinawa, weapons and everything. But when I came back to the United States, it's just a whole different attitude. Everybody was very secular, they would just do straight Karate, Tae Kwon Do or Judo and they didn't mix the arts. I didn't like that. I remember when I put up a school in 1967 and I sold it to Chuck Norris in 1968. I didn't like running the school. In my very first test, which was for the purple belt, you had to learn choke holds, you had to do throws, both standing and from the ground, and you had to break boards. So my first purple belt test was like most people's black belt.

But that was my background before I met Bruce Lee. The first time I met him I was at the magazine called Black Belt, and he saw me inside and he came running outside and tried to talk me into taking lessons from him. To me, I did not like Kung Fu guys. I did not like Kung Fu because most of the Kung Fu guys were really skinny guys who always talked about fighting but they never sparred. They would never come to an event and compete, they never did full contact and they never worked with targets. I didn't like that world. When he was talking to me I kind of put up a mental block because I thought he was just another Kung Fu guy running his mouth. I was very arrogant at the time and I only associated with top fighters, and if you didn't fight and you weren't top and you weren't in really good shape - I mean, good shape where you spar non-stop like 30 minutes without stopping - to me you were a flake, you were a phoney because you didn't really push yourself as hard as you should have. That was my attitude in the old days. Of course, I've changed over the years, but that's the way they trained me in the US marines and in Okinawa: never talk in class, never ask questions, never miss a workout, always be an hour early before a workout, always stay an hour after a workout. And you sparred every single day, and you never quit when you spar and you never counted points - you strictly worked on defense. That was the way I was when I met Bruce Lee.

Q: Did you actually train with the legendary Sugar Ray Robinson in Boxing?

Joe Lewis: I trained Boxing at a gym. There were some guys who owned a car dealership who were kind of in the Mafia, and they were taking care of Sugar Ray Robinson, because he lived in a cheap apartment and he was having a hard time making a living. He couldn't fight anymore. He fought 26 years as a professional, that's a damn long time. And I was down there and he gave me my first Boxing lesson, he was my first Boxing coach, in 1967. How many people can say that they worked with Sugar Ray Robinson and Bruce Lee? How many people on this planet can say that?

I guarantee you that I'm the only person on the planet who can say that, just like Archie Moore is the only one in the world who fought Muhammad Ali and Rocky Marciano. If you go all the way back, in Greece, years before Christ was born, those guys were wearing gloves in the Pankration (Ancient Greek fight sport). Boxing has been around and is the oldest sport, records go back 3,700 years. What other styles of fighting except Wrestling go back that far? And I'll say this: if you can't box, you can't fight. With the mixed martial arts today, you have the cut kicks to the leg and head, the kneebars, chokes, ankle locks, triangle chokes on the ground or the punches to the head. What are the most knock outs caused by? Punches to the head! So what does that say? Use the strategic tools primarily to the head, which are currently the best weapons today.

Q: Can you tell us about your training with Bruce Lee at his house? Am I right in saying you guys would train for six to eight hours sometimes?

Joe Lewis: Nah, that's stuff people misprint. There's a guy named John Little, he wrote a bunch of stuff in books about me which is not true. He also wrote stuff about Bruce Lee that's not true. He claims to be the world's foremost authority on Bruce Lee which I find strange because I need to make this clear: he never met Bruce Lee, he never saw Bruce Lee spar, he never saw Bruce Lee train, he never saw Bruce Lee do a demonstration, he never met me, he never saw me fight. No one on this planet ever saw me and Bruce Lee workout together, not even his wife, that's a fact! I hope that point I've mentioned clears up all the nonsense. John Little's books are full of nonsense, full of what I would call 'intentional deceitful comments', you got me?

I would set up a private lesson with Bruce every Wednesday at one o'clock and I would go over there, it was supposed to be a one-hour class. Sometimes we would be there till seven, eight o'clock at night watching fight films from his library, and he would ask his wife to prepare us food many times. So it wasn't a six-hour class, we kind of liked each other. He liked to work with me and I was beating everybody. As a matter of fact, in 1968, when we were really working together extensively, I won 11 consecutive Grand Championships without a loss. That's still a record today. Most of the champions win one tournament, they lose the next two, they win one they lose three, they win one and they lose four. I won 11 in a row. So, I liked Bruce Lee's stuff because not so much because he's teaching me great techniques but because he was extremely inspirational, he could inspire people. And if you're with an instructor who doesn't inspire you, you're not going to be motivated to train hard, and if you don't train hard you're not going to have everything you've got into your trigger squeeze when you're fighting.

Most people when they throw punches and kicks, when they're fighting, they're thinking how their style looks, they're too much into the artistic nonsense of the mechanics of the motions; they don't move with substance. Bruce Lee would teach me to put the energy - the maximum amount of energy - into what I was doing. He used to call it 'relaxed explosiveness', so you move with intent, you move with conviction, you put your heart and everything into it. Today, in most of the Karate schools it's too commercialized, they're just teaching people bunch of movements. They're not teaching the most important things in martial arts today which is 'how to think' and number two 'how to move with conviction' and how to put energy and passion into your executions. So when a fighter steps into the ring, the two most important things - and this is a self-pitch - in Joe Lewis' Black Belt Manual, two of the most important things - and these are the two things Bruce and I worked on all the time - are 'approach' and 'attitude'. Don't ask me what those two mean because you're not going to buy my manual.

But anyway, most black belts haven't got a clue what attitude or approach is, yet they say they're good black belts and fighters. For example, they say they're teaching kids how to develop confidence. I say to them, "You're a black belt so here is a paper. I looked at your ad in a newspaper, I looked at your ad in Yellow Pages and you say you teach self-confidence to kids. How do you teach something when you don't know what it is?" He says, "What do you mean?" I say, "Here is a paper, write down what's the definition, what's the difference between confidence and the efficacy of your execution and self-confidence?" The guy says, "There's no difference." He says, "Well, can you do it?" Of course I can do it! Confidence is your ability to demonstrate your skills with profound efficacy and with absolute certainty, while being able to maintain not only a realness but eagerness to remain engaged in the face of any adversity and overwhelming odds. You should memorize those definitions. Self-esteem comes before self-confidence. Ask instructors what comes first, self-confidence or self-esteem?Bruce Lee and I would talk about this kind of stuff.

If you say Bruce wasn't a good teacher, I ask why? They say because he wasn't a fighter. Well, Angelo Dundee was one of the greatest Boxing coaches in the world, he had 16 world champions including Sugar Ray Leonard and Muhammad Ali. Angelo Dundee never fought, but he's still one of the greatest coaches on the planet. See what I mean? You don't have to be a fighter to be a good coach. Bruce Lee wasn't a fighter. People say, "Oh, yes, he was, he was a fighter," but we're not talking about street fighters. Street fighters have records down at the police departments. A (real) fighter has a record, he has wins, loses, knockouts and draws. If you don't have a record you are not a fighter, that's it - it's a simple definition.

Q: So you could actually detect Bruce Lee putting emotional content into what he was doing when you were training with him?
Joe Lewis: There's not much to fighting. You could teach a gorilla how to fight. You've got some punches, some kicks, some different stances and blocks, etc. But what most martial artists don't work on is movement. Look up the word 'movement' in the dictionary, it means rhythm. Rhythm with your head, rhythm with your body and footwork. Most great fighters don't do that, they still do that old classical 'standstill' nonsense. Now, you've got to appreciate where that stuff came from. Years ago, the Samurai warriors wore armor, and they had to sit up on a horse or stand upright when they fought with a sword. When you fought with a sword everything was one motion, one movement. A stab or slash, that was it. The Samurai warrior would kill you with one movement, that's where the one point concept in tournament fighting came from. We were copying the same attitude from the Samurai warriors where you had one movement. And when they used to use the sword or the weapon, they had to stand upright because of the armor, that's why most of the Karate styles today still do that nonsense where they stand stiff as a board. It's total nonsense. When you remove the armor, you've got to remove that static position, you've got to get more rhythm into the body. So they're not teaching the rhythm in the martial arts today.

That's the kind of stuff Bruce Lee opened my eyes up to. He said, "Joe, you don't have to be stiff, you can move. Watch Muhammad Ali when he moves, watch Sugar Ray Robinson when he moves, watch one of the greatest knockdown artists of all time and one of the greatest Boxers of all time, Willie Pep, move." He was like a snake, you couldn't catch him. And that's the stuff missing in the martial arts today, and that's one of the things Bruce Lee opened up to me. He was able to conceptualize, he could take abstract phenomenon from that abstract level of consciousness and put it into conceptual terms and break it down.

For example, when you say 'bridging the gap', how do you bridge the gap between you and your opponent? In Okinawa they didn't have names for things like this. If they say 'clear', clear means to disengage. Once you go in and fire, you want to turn your opponent or pull out or disengage. As you disengage you want to make sure you have a clearing technique. In Boxing they teach you the jab, you want to hit him and bump him and you want to displace his defense as you're stepping up so that you don't get caught on the way in. That was what I liked when I worked with Bruce Lee; he had words to describe everything. Even today the vocabulary, I'd say 99.9 percent of all black belts use, is very weak and it's outdated.

Let's take an example. If a fighter makes an attack and he gets hit going in or he misses, those are the two of the worst things in fighting. When I attack I don't want to miss and I don't want to get hit. What's one of the nine steps that you go stick a student through to ensure that's not going to happen again? Have you tested your material to know how to teach that, so next time your student's not going to get hit again, or he's not going to miss? So you see how he's positioned. Maybe it could be the attitude - he's not focused properly, maybe he's thinking about getting hit in the process of hitting, maybe his range is off, maybe he can't squeeze the trigger, you got me? So there's a whole lot of technique other than just throwing kicks and punches. And that's the perfect example of just what I was explaining to you.

There's two attitudes of martial arts. One I would call 'obedient'. There's too many emphasizing the obedience which comes from that totalitarian ideology out of Asia. Such as: I'm older than you, so you listen to me. I'm higher ranking than you, so you listen to me. There's one thing you want to follow in martial arts: someone who has courage, someone who has a sense of bravery. Just because you're older than me or a higher rank than me that doesn't mean I'm going to obey you. Because when I'm out there fighting in the ring and in a realistic situation, if I always learned to have my mind to look at you for advice, look at you for help, look at you for support, you're not going to support me at that moment. But you've brainwashed me into always listening to you, having you hold my hand all the way through class, not getting my butt beat. Or if I'm in the middle of the ring and you're in my corner worried, I'm going to go back and say, "Hey, this guy's kicking my butt. You're the one that got me into the sport, you're the cause of me getting my butt beat because you said I was ready when I'm not."

So what people have to do, instead of 'obey, obey, obey', is to know the instructors must learn how to teach the student to think. When you learn you trust the efficacy of your epistemology. Epistemology is the way we acquire knowledge. Psycho-epistemology is the psychological way the mind knows about acquiring knowledge. Psycho-epistemology is not used in today's martial arts, it's not taught. We teach people to obey but we don't teach them to think. That is the major problem in our martial arts today and that's why we have problems, because we're not teaching people self-discipline. When you have that hyper-ideology, you've got stronger people competing, you have people develop a real self-confidence, confidence which tells them to trust in their own mental process. The same method could be transformed into the other concepts outside of the martial arts arena.

So teach people to be self-responsible and not just obedient. Somebody says, "Are you a person who thinks, or a person who obeys all the time?" I say, "I am not the one who obeys." People who obey, they obey all the time. Sometimes they might think (for themselves). Me, I always think, maybe once in a while I'll obey, but that's not very often (Laughs). You bring anybody in the martial arts face to face with me I'll debate them verbally and I'll step up in the ring and prove what I'm saying. I did my work! Most teachers do not do their homework. We go back to the two words, do you really know what the word self-esteem means? There's six different steps that build self-esteem and without self-esteem you cannot have self-confidence. Self-esteem is the concept which gives rise to the phenomenon which is called 'self-confidence'. How dare you say you're a black belt instructor and you think you know how to teach someone self-confidence when you don't know what the word really means?

Q: Joe, can you shed some light on Bruce Lee's philosophy. Am I right in saying you actually studied Krishnamurti philosophy before you even met Bruce Lee?
Joe Lewis: Yeah, he used a number of different philosopher's quotes, as you can see in the Tao of Jeet Kun Do. He did not write that book. What (the publishers) did was, after he died, they went to his office and gathered a bunch of his documents and they put that book together from those documents. Bruce Lee was very structured and organized and if you look at that book, it is a scraped-up unorganized mess; there's no beginning, there's no end, there's no means to an end. What I learnt

about aspects of Krishnamurti's philosophy is what Bruce Lee used, which pertains to combat.

In martial arts there's a thing called 'attitude' and there's six different aspects of attitude. One is called 'being able to focus' - focusing is one part of what we call 'consciousness'. Within the concept of consciousness we have a phenomenon called 'attention'. When you're fighting, what most people do when they become afraid is they lower the degree of consciousness, they become less aware. People who are self-confident in mid-long range are able to raise their level of consciousness, this phenomenon is what we call 'attention'. There's five different aspects of attention, one is called 'focusing'. I'm not going to get into this stuff - if you want you can buy my Black Belt Manual or go on my website and I can help you out a little bit more - but these are the things which aren't taught in martial arts today, which is a shame. Focusing - I like Krishnamurti's ideology on this - is when you are looking at a target (such as your opponent) what you must be able to do is see your opponent, observe your opponent, but do not identify and do not describe what you are observing. Krishnamurti said, "The thing is never the same as its identity." In other words, the opponent is never the same as its identity. When you look at the opponent, you don't say 'identity' or you're not focused properly, because all concepts and all thoughts are past tense just as all emotions are past tense.

So, when you're functioning on that conceptual moment of consciousness instead of the fluid level of consciousness your timing is always going to be off. When you're going to see something your timing is always going to be off, you're going to be in a responsive reaction when you're going to see something because you're going to react to it. Your timing is off, you're too late. You must be in that reflex mode, the instance you see something, your actions are simultaneously participating in that observation. If you take time to identify or describe of what you're observing, it turns your timing off. That was classically explained by Krishnamurti. You must have that method of focusing down; look at your opponent and not see your opponent but simply observe without description, simply observe without identifying.

So, for example, the gap between me and my opponent. When you see a gap between you and your opponent you think about closing the gap. You're moving in with a concept called 'distance'. Where you can bridge the gap for covering that distance, that will take time. You must first have space. Your next concept is distance. Once you create distance, now you create time. There should be no time between the trigger when you hit your opponent, so you must remove the distance. To remove the distance you must remove what we call the 'space'. So when you throw a kick or a punch you do not see any space between your fist or foot and the target.

That's a reflex of focusing, something Krishnamurti talks about and something Bruce Lee was good at describing very well. But you won't find that in any of Bruce Lee's papers, 90 percent of what Bruce worked on was in Bruce Lee's mind - he never wrote it down anywhere. I worked with him and I got the stuff that he was thinking five years before he wrote it, just like the fight scenes you see in the movie Enter the Dragon. He wrote those fight scenes in detail, five years before he shot them.

I don't want to go into anymore examples but that's a perfect example. Do instructors know how to teach students how to focus? Say that you have that kind of psychology in your attitude, and you have the absence of space when you're throwing a punch or kick, how do you do that? They're always talking about covering the distance and bridging the gap. When you're talking about bridging the gap and covering the distance with punching and kicking, you've already missed the boat! The first thing you must work on is your attitude, ask yourself : how do I remove space so that there's no distance? If I remove the space and eliminate distance, now there's no such thing as time, therefore when I squeeze the trigger and when I land the punch it eliminates any wasted time. There's no such thing as past, present and future, everything 'is'. Bruce used to call it the 'thusness' and the 'thusness of execution'. Think about what that means. I think the only two people he said it to was me and Danny Inosanto, because I talked to Danny about it and he understands what I'm saying.

Q: Joe, you had a weightlifting background prior to training with Bruce. Can you shed some light on your conversations with Bruce which touched upon this subject?
Joe Lewis: He was lifting before I worked with him, I just basically inspired him to get a little bigger. He had small bone structure which made his muscles, especially his back, look wide for his size. When I met him, he was 138 pounds, 5ft 7 and when he died he was 126 pounds. That's what his death certificate said. To me, he was really skinny, but he was really strong. I remember one time he took a 75-pound barbell (standing position) and he held it on his chest and stood completely stationary, then he extended the barbell all the way straight in front of him and locked it for a few seconds. I tried but it's hard. I've got all kinds of tricks people can't do. As a matter of fact, this weekend I was going to set up a world gripping record. You take these grippers - it's the 'Captain Crush', the one all the world's greatest grippers use - and it has a number three and four level.

There's only five men in the world who have ever done it (number four level). I've got one of my black belts who can almost do it. For level three the oldest person to close the gripper - which is 280 pounds - was 55 years old. I was going to close number three on my 65th birthday, so I can't quite do it, but if I do it anytime next year I'll set a world record. I'd like to set a record in my original passion, which was the fitness industry.

Q: Which bodybuilders did you admire of your era of the 60s? Dave Draper, Bill Pearl?
Joe Lewis: I knew all those guys. I met Dave Draper when he was building furniture for Joe Weider. Reg Park, who came out of South Africa, I knew his son who was taking martial arts lessons. Reg Park and Bill Pearl were my idols - as a matter of fact they were Arnold Schwarzenegger's idols. In the 50s, if they weren't your idols you were living in another land. Because they were two of the best in the world. Others such as Mr. Universe Steve Reeves who won Mr. Universe in 1950, Mr. America in 1948 and 1949, John Grimek was Mr. America way back in the early 40s. But the big guys, the guys who had a lot of muscularity as well as the symmetry and the definitions, were the Bill Pearls and Reg Parks. Reg Park had an incredible back.

I've always liked the guys with back and calf development, these were the two favorite muscle groups. Of all the bodybuilders, I got on with Franco Columbu the best, he's a little crazy like I am. I talked to the Arnold people because I'm going to the Arnold Classic this weekend, supposedly Arnold will give me a Lifetime Achievement Award of some kind. The person who is handling the trophies told me that I'm the recipient of it. I met Arnold exactly 40 years ago, in 1969, when he and Franco Columbu were roommates down in Santa Monica. They were training at the World Gym back then. Arnold and I had the same hairdresser and we went to the same acting class at one time.

Q: What does Arnold think of Bruce Lee?
Joe Lewis: I don't think he cares. Some of the bodybuilders are into the martial arts. Mike Tyson was a phenomenal Bruce Lee fanatic. I had a buddy who used to sell DVDs and martial arts stuff, and he said Mike Tyson would order $1,800 worth of Kung Fu tapes at any one time. He loved to watch Kung fu movies over and over again. He had real good legs before he went to prison, but when he came out of the prison he fought McNeeley and he lost his legs, he couldn't explode anymore. He lost the speed and the forward movement of his legs. That's when he started getting beat, because once they figured out his style they could catch him with the straight right hand when he was trying to bridge the gap.

Tyson is short, they say he's 5ft 10 - he's lucky if he's 5ft 1. When a short guy is fighting a tall guy such as Buster Douglas, Lennox Lewis or Evander Holyfield, as soon as he squeezes the trigger to go in, what these tall guys were doing were playing the distance game with him. You know, playing the distance game with a sharpshooter. These tall guys would take the rear foot and do what they call a drop-back or step-back. They'd take a half-step back when Tyson started to bridge the gap, that would throw his distance, timing and his balance off, and they'd nail him with a counter right hand. Then, of course, when he started getting hit he lost his focus and started becoming stationary, not moving his head or hands. Then they would step inside and beat him with their one-two combinations, the jab-straight right hand, or the jab-right uppercut. He only had one style of fighting: exploding and coming forward. If you backed him up or countered him or worked angles on him - pivot in, pivot out, that makes you change the angle - you could beat him. Evander Holyfield is the one who really exposed him.

When I worked with Bruce Lee I realized how important that was. Before I met Bruce Lee, I was physically so strong, so fast, so powerful and I moved with tremendous conviction. If you stood in front of me I'd kill you, you just can't fight me that way. The only way you could beat me is try to figure out how you can make me beat myself. That's how they beat Tyson. Tyson didn't get beat, he self-destructed, make sense? Here's something you'll see in my manual: most fighters train and want to win the next fight, that's how they're focused. Great fighters train for a career. That's the difference between those who become great and those who become mere champions, short-time champions. Do not train for any one fight. You always train for a career.

Q: Did Bruce Lee use any specific principles or methods pertaining to weight training?

Joe Lewis: There's different ways you can train for strength, size or try to reshape your body. Basically, your genes will dictate what your body looks like, like all the great bodybuilders it's 97 percent genes and genetics and three percent of who works the hardest. Bruce Lee had skinny legs, he would always have skinny legs. His ribcage was very flat, he never had a big ribcage and his neck was long which would make me suspicious whether he would have had a good fight career or not. For me, he was skinny. He would admire my body, but I wasn't in his presence to talk about bodybuilding.

I'd given up bodybuilding and as a matter of fact I lost 30 pounds when I was in Okinawa. I went from 223 pounds and two years later when I came back I was about 193 pounds. But I still was real big like a weightlifter, even today my arms look big. When I was with Bruce he had some barbell set in his garage where we would do a lot of training if we didn't go outside or his back porch. I wasn't there to teach him to weight lift, his body was way behind mine and I wasn't there to say, "Hey, you ought to build your bicep." He would show me something, and I would say, "That's really neat."

He had those incredible strong shoulders which a lot of the old class Wing Chun guys had, because they were overworking the shoulder muscles - which they all are going to pay for down the road. It's like Tae Kwon Do guys doing all that stretching on the floor, trying to do the full splits and throwing thousands of kicks in the air and not hitting anything, half of them are going to have hip replacement surgeries before they're 50 years old. It's overworking the hips and overworking the shoulders, which most martial artists do incredibly. Going back to the question, if I was recommending to people what Bruce Lee did, this would be my mandate: you lift weights at least four to six months before you ever, ever start doing any martial arts. And the problem with most martial artists is they don't lift weights, they do these Mickey Mouse jumping jacks and push ups and they call that resistance training.

If you don't do really professional non-consumer resistance, some sort of a high-intensity resistance training, and going in the health club working with real barbells, etc, you're going to sell yourself short when it comes to becoming a great martial artist. Look at the next generation of martial artists today. In my professional opinion most of them can't fight. But the good thing about it is two points: point one is there's real fighting now, not the Mickey Mouse Karate stuff. Number two is a lot of these guys have a pretty much decent body. They look like athletes, they've got a six pack on their stomach, they're more stiff with the shoulders but they live like athletes. So everybody should do some sort of weight training even if it's one time a week, get your butt in the gym and lift weights, you need it! It's the most important thing from the day you were born and to the day you're going to die, not cardio training, not flexibility but resistance training. There's only three things you can do for the body: stretch, cardiovascular and resistance training.

Q: When and how did Bruce Lee ask you to play his adversary in Way of the Dragon?

Joe Lewis: It wasn't one specific conversation, he was constantly talking about how bad all other martial arts looked. For example, say Ed Parker or Jhoon Rhee claim to be masters - can they fight? What kind of fight record do they have? Look at their bodies, what can they really do? He was always making fun of everybody. He would say Mike Stone is one of the greatest fighters of all time, he was the first superstar. I sparred Mike Stone, I sparred Chuck Norris and I know what they can do. Bruce Lee never sparred with any of those suckers. Mike Stone hit real hard and he was extremely fast and he had an incredible intensity. The minute he squeezed the trigger he wasn't thinking about you hitting him, he was going to take you home to your mommy real fast. But Bruce Lee would make fun saying, "Mike is fast but Mike's out of control." Then he would talk about Chuck saying, "Chuck's got real good technique but he's too stiff, he can't move." If you read in the book World's Greatest Fighter Teaches You How to Master Bruce Lee's Fighting Style, I had people say to me, "Why did you do a book about Bruce Lee, why not your own stuff?"

A lot of stuff in that book is my stuff. I wanted to honor Bruce Lee so I gave him credit for a lot of things. People today say Bruce Lee made me the world champion. Hey, sparky, I was the world champion, national champion and kata champion before I ever met Bruce Lee, how come he gets credit for making me a champion? Anyway, I don't care, I've got a lot of glory to last me six different lifetimes, so spread it around. My 'boy' Chuck Norris says he's six-time world champion. I said, "Chuck, hold on a minute, what do you mean six-times world champion? You had one fight, how do you become six-times champion with one fight? You won the World Championship in 1968 and Wallace won it in 74! And Chuck said, "69,70,71,72,73,74 - that's six years. That makes me a six-times world champion." I said to him, "Chuck, it doesn't work that way. Muhammad Ali had 63 professional fights, he's the only three-time heavyweight champion in the world. You're the world champion six times? Muhammad Ali is only three times, he had 62 more fights than you did, explain that to me?" But see, martial artists are so greedy! I'm not saying Chuck's greedy, he's a buddy of mine and he's going to spank my butt.

Don't say something if it's not true! If you say you're a world champion and you're not; you say you beat somebody and you didn't; you start saying you were in a movie and you weren't; you say you've got 800 students and you don't; you start saying you make $100,000 a month and you don't. The green belt in your school is going to leave your school and he's going to pull up all the black belts saying you're a national champion, and now he's going to compete against your school. If he's a better teacher, he's going to kick your butt. So that's why all this garbage starts in the martial arts, no one keeps the record straight, there's no auditing. When someone says something they can base it on hearsay, you don't have to verify anything you say in martial arts and it doesn't have to be supported by verifiable evidence. That's why martial artists that you listened to have lasted for years. Look at the word 'artist' in the dictionary, it says 'one who dwells in deceit'. That's why I don't like the word martial artist. I say I'm a fighter, not an artist...I'm going way off the track I think.

OK, when I worked with Bruce he would make fun of other people but he can't make fun of me, because if you read in my book that I wrote, in the Ted Wong section - I met Ted Wong in Bruce Lee's backyard in 1968, he kind of carries the torch of Bruce Lee now - Ted says Mike Stone was the fastest, Chuck Norris was the technician, but Joe Lewis was the fighter. That's what Bruce Lee said to Ted Wong behind my back, he always considered me as the fighter. I'm the one you don't mess with. You could say I'm dumb - although you can't, I've got a genius-level IQ - or you could say I'm stiff - although when I hit you you're going down. You could say other guys are faster than me - but when they fight me I still kick their butts. But no one could ever say I can't fight, and you don't ever get in the ring with me, and if you're in the ring with me you better make sure you don't ever, ever make me mad. I'll get mad and I'll go through a brick wall. I've never been knocked out or knocked down, not even in the gym when they tried to knock me out when I first started to learn to box.

Bruce Lee wanted that image of me, big, muscular Caucasian, for the movie Way of the Dragon. He would talk all the time about he was mad because the Japanese got all the credit of being the ones to spread the martial arts around the world instead of the Chinese getting the credit. He wanted to show that the Chinese were superior to the Japanese, and definitely superior to the Caucasians. So he wanted to take the one martial arts image, and wanted to put me in because I was bigger than Chuck. I had a lot more muscles than Chuck, so I would look better on the screen where Bruce Lee would kick my butt than have Chuck Norris on the screen and having Bruce Lee kick his butt, you follow me? I just let him know that no way in hell I was going to let some Chinese sucker kick my butt up on the big screen. So I made it clear to him to not bother even asking me.

And in that movie Return of the Dragon (aka Way of the Dragon), where they fought in the Coliseum, Chuck's got a sash in his midsection. If you ask Linda Lee, Bruce's wife, why did Bruce have Chuck wear that damn sash in his midsection, Linda said Chuck had some fat and Bruce wanted him to hide his midsection so he made him wear that sash. Yes, Bob Wall who was in the movie as well, if you ask him, Bob says it's not Chuck's fault. Bruce kept pressuring Chuck to gain more weight, to get bigger. He wanted Chuck to look far bigger than he was, so Chuck ended up getting fat because he kept putting weight on to please Bruce Lee. Since (Bruce) is not here I can't ask Bruce the truth.

Chuck isn't going to say, "I was fat and out of shape when we did the movie," because that's going to embarrass him, so you have to take it for what it is. So it would have been a lot easier just to have someone like me up there on the screen, with Bruce Lee beating the hell out of me. I'm twice the size of Chuck and I've got muscles, not a bunch of hair on my chest. Jim Kelly wanted me to be in a movie where he beats the hell out of me. Over the years I've been asked many times, " Joe, I want you to do a film. You don't mind in the final fight scene the other guy wins?" It happens that for some reason I always said no like I was a dummy. I should have done that movie with Bruce Lee and I could've been a big film star by now.

Q: So you did regret turning the part down?
Joe Lewis: I was stupid, I turned down many parts. Universal Studios at the time was the world's largest studio. In 1970 I had a seven-year contract and I turned it down. A year later they offered me the same seven-year contract again, and I turned it down again. They offered me the contract three different times. My Karate buddies were trying to put me in a movie and I kept turning the seven-year contract with Universal down to do this movie. A big producer wanted me to do a television series, I turned that down because my buddies said don't do it. I was offered a contract by one of the biggest television companies - who do a lot of TV series - and turned that down. I listened to my Karate buddies and my acting coaches said don't do martial arts movies because they're horrible acting, little low-budget crap. They said don't do television because you want to do the big screen; you should be a big star like Montgomery Cliff, James Dean and Marlon Brando, that's where you belong. You've got the rage and the sensitivity and the vulnerability to become the actor, and you've got the looks. Save yourself for the big screen.

So I'd been turning everything down listening to my acting coaches and my Karate buddies, instead of the people who are in the power - the head of the studios in Hollywood - and I blew it. Now I'm too old to go back to redo it. Right now, I've been offered a contract to go to Thailand because all the martial arts film industry moved out of Hong Kong and is now coming out of Bangkok, so they asked me to come over there and start working. I'm going to go over there probably in April. I'm going to do a low-budget film and I'll play a role and choreograph the fight scenes.

If you're familiar with Tony Jaa, a big film star from Thailand, he does the Muay Boran stuff - knee strikes, low cut kicks, the head-butts, the spinning drop elbows and double knee drops - all the stuff Bruce Lee couldn't do and Jackie Chan and Jet Li can't do. The problem with Tony Jaa is he can't speak English, it's hard to do an international movie if you can't speak English. We've got a new kid who is only 21 years old who could do a backflip and land on one foot in perfect balance and throw a kick at the same time. We're trying to make him the next Bruce Lee, me, Jackie Chan and Tony Jaa. I'm going over there to do a film with him. In my life I just wanted to workout and chase women. I didn't care about movies and winning Karate titles, all that stuff was...I just love to train, and nobody loves to train as much as I do. I train 365 days a year, I lift weights and I do martial arts on my birthday, Christmas and Easter. Some people need someone to hold their hands, I didn't need it. I was self-motivated.

Q: When and where did you first see Way of the Dragon?
Joe Lewis: I thought the production values on the movie were kind of bottom of the hill, you know what I mean? But the movie sold on how well

Bruce Lee choreographed the fight scenes, so that was what interested me in the film, the choreography and the fight scenes. The storyline sucked, the production values sucked, I felt the cast sucked but what made it was all Bruce Lee fight scenes. If you go watch and see all Hong Kong movies such as Chinese Connection (aka Fist of Fury) and Big Boss, all those scripts were of films which had already been done in Hong Kong years before. All Bruce Lee did was change the title, rewrote the scrip a little bit and put himself in the lead role. So, when he put himself in the lead role, why did the same movies make millions of dollars and the original ones did not? 'Bruce Lee' is what made the difference.

When you watch Bruce Lee you say, "Whoa, he's good-looking," but other Chinese guys are good-looking. He had the body, well, these other Chinese guys have a body. He's throwing kicks, punches and jumping around, other actors threw punches, kicks and jumped around. But why did his movies make it? Because he had a power called 'presence'. In other words, he looked like he really enjoyed doing what he was doing on film, he looked like a real kid, he was having fun.

You could tell with other actors when they are doing their thing that they're not playing but they're performing to entertain you. When you watch other actors you could tell they're performing with the purpose of attempting to attract your interest and trying to get you interested. When Bruce Lee did that he didn't have to do that, he knew he was interesting, he drew your attention. He was doing it for himself and having fun, that's what separated him from all other people - that's called 'energy'. Very, very few martial artists have that power.

Q: Is it true at one time when Bruce visited your house he wasn't impressed with your heavy bag?
Joe Lewis: Nah, that's a rumor Bob Wall started. Bob Wall made this big, old, fat bag - he says it weighed 300 pounds, I don't know what it weighed because we never put it on the scale - and it was real thick, three-and-a-half feet thick. He gave it to Bruce. Bruce used to have this little canvas bag which weighed about 50 pounds. You can see some old footage that he shot in his backyard when he had a house on Roscomore Drive, up in Bel Air. I think he bought that house in 1969 when he was working with James Coburn. You could see some old footage of him and James Coburn. Coburn sidekicks the bag. It's terrible form on the side kick, he gets way out of range when he releases the trigger. He's lunging in at the bag, you can't do that against a real fighter. You have to get right up, almost just a couple of inches outside of the pockets, so you squeeze the trigger and you've got a chance of hitting him.

Bruce was used to working with little mini-bags, and if you watch him working the bag he's always wearing sneakers. If you want to get tough you have to work barefooted with the bag so you get contraction of the barefoot and not just one kick. You only see him kicking the bag with one kick, the lead leg side kick. When Bruce Lee did a spin hook kick to the head, his knee was always bent, he didn't have that form like you see in Tae Kwon Do or Tang Soo Do stylists when they throw that kick. You've got to remember the Wing Chun style he came from, those are not kicks that have constant rhythm; the Wing Chun does the inside and outside crescent kicks, they do the front hook kick and the little jab round kick. They never do the extended side kick, the spin hook and back kick. Bruce could have worked with somebody to straighten out his kicks - and the knees when he kicked - to get better extension, but he was a little arrogant and thought it was beneath him to go study with somebody. The only martial artist I know that he actually went to take lessons with was Gene LeBell. He asked Gene to show him some grappling.

Q: During the years you knew Bruce what would you say is the most vivid memory on a socializing level?
Joe Lewis: One time he was teaching a kid named Lew Alcindor, who became the great basketball player who changed his name to Kareem Abdul-Jabbar. The three of us went downtown in Chinatown to eat lunch one day. You've got to remember, Lew Alcindor at that time was 7ft tall. So, here I am with a little Chinese guy going to Chinatown where everybody is short, and I've got this giant with me with a big Afro hairstyle; the hair that Kareem had made him five inches taller. We walked in the restaurant and Kareem has to duck down just to get in the damn door. So everybody's looking at us. Bruce was kind of semi-famous at the time, it wasn't like when he was in Hong Kong when he would pull up in a car there would be 50 or 60 people trying to get his autograph. Everyone turned to look, I was embarrassed. I'm with a big black guy and a little short guy, it was a mismatch, it was like the United Nations walking in the door - white guy, the Asian and the black guy! So what does Bruce do? He said, "Joe, let me explain something to you, never trust Chinese cooks." I'll say this also, because I've eaten in Chinese restaurants and they always give you leftovers. I don't care if you're eating in a real hot Chinese restaurant where you're paying $100 for the meal, they're still going to give you leftovers. He makes the waiter set up a table back in the kitchen!

So the three of us go back in the kitchen and we're sitting at a table in the damn kitchen!! He says, "Joe, we sit here in the kitchen because you could keep an eye on the cook, he's not going to give you leftover food." Can you believe that? He made the waiter set up a table right in the middle of the kitchen, that's a true story. Oliver Pang was with us - Black Belt magazine photographer - we went outside and he shot pictures of us. Me and Bruce were dressed in suits. I remember going out in the parking lot,

Bruce Lee is doing his Wing Chun form jumping around in a three-piece suit. He had done a film called Marlowe with James Garner, and they had given him two really nice three-piece suits at the end of the shoot. He had the guys let him keep the suits and he had that suit on the day. He's doing all these jump crescent kicks in the parking lot. Oliver Pang went through at least probably two or three rolls of film that day shooting three of us.

Years later, I called Oliver Pang and said, "Oliver, people always ask me do I have pictures of me and Bruce Lee?" Columbia Pictures have some with me, Bruce Lee and Ed Parker on the movie called The Wrecking Crew, but you have to go to Columbia Pictures to get those. I had Oliver to get me the ones he shot, but he lost his eyesight and was now legally blind and couldn't see. He had taken all those pictures and had a whole bunch of me when I first came back from Vietnam in 1966. He probably took 200 or 300 pictures of me over the years, and dozens of pictures of me and Bruce Lee together. Now I can only find three pictures of me and Bruce Lee, mostly at tournaments. He said, "I've turned all those pictures over to Black Belt magazine." I called Black Belt magazine, and they said, "Joe, we put all that stuff in storage which Oliver Pang gave us. He gave us boxes and boxes of pictures but we have no idea where the stuff is." That's a sad story, because those pictures would be worth a lot of money today.

I know someone who has about 3,000 pictures of Bruce Lee which nobody's ever seen, his name is George Tan. He went over and got all these pictures of Bruce Lee from Raymond Chow. He showed me boxes and boxes of thousands of pictures. I've got to say he must have three or 4,000 pictures no one's ever seen.

Q: What do you remember of your experiences on The Wrecking Crew movie with Bruce?
Joe Lewis: I went in there and I was supposed to do a fight scene. Bruce was the stunt coordinator and Mike Stone was doubling Dean Martin. I was going to be one of the bad guys and Dean Martin was going to confront me. I did a spin hook kick and Dean was going to duck under and foot-sweep me and then nail me when I hit the ground. What was interesting is I was wearing a suit. When I did the spin hook kick, Dean Martin's agent said, "Joe, make sure you don't hit him because he's worth a lot of money." Dean was drinking all day long, and his guy's got a shoulder-strapped portable bar. Between scenes Dean would go drinking the whole time. So he's smashed trying to do a fight scene, so I made sure I did the hook kick real high so I miss his head, and I did it real slow. When we were doing the rehearsals, soon as I did the first kick - the cameras are rolling - my pants split (Laughs). Of course, they got that on film and they didn't have a second pair of pants to replace it. So they go out in the trailer,

take the pants off and stitch the pants up, that was my first fight scene on film.Bruce Lee hired us, he got Mike Stone first.

For that part Mike Stone was making $500 a week to double Dean Martin. I think he worked nine weeks on that shoot. You meet all these actors, Sharon Tate and Nancy Kwan, all those famous people. Dean Martin was real big then, he did two of those Matt Helm films in the late 60s. These films were very popular back then. It was Columbia Pictures who produced them and he was a popular guy. Right up there on top of Hollywood working on the set wasn't small time. Bruce Lee wanted to embrace his friendship with the martial arts world and merge the two together, bring the film industry together with the martial arts industry. So he's one of the first people to do that.

I always say the right timing for Bruce Lee's career was when Richard Nixon, the American president, was the first president to go to China and set up relationship between the United States and China. This opened up the door for the governments, which enabled Bruce to go to China and kick butt and become the first Asian superstar.

Q: Can you explain the intriguing situation when you did a fireman's carry on Muhammad Ali in 1975?
Joe Lewis: I don't remember that too much other than the editor of Karate Illustrated magazine called me up, and he talked to Bob Wall. And Bob Wall called me saying, "Joe, Muhammad Ali is up at the Olympic Auditorium." That's where he first started fighting professionally. Gene LeBell's mother Eileen Eaton owned the Olympic Auditorium. He said, "Let's go down there and see." So we go down there and Muhammad Ali's in the ring, he's wearing that long-sleeved black shirt and black pants, the stuff he always wore, and about, I'd say, 20 photographers standing around the ring taking pictures of him. People were asking him questions and all three networks were there, ABC, CBS and NBC. I'm standing up on the ring apron, and to my left is Bob Wall, and to his left was standing a photographer and the editor of Karate Illustrated magazine.

I turn to Bob Wall and say, "You know what, Ali is talking about how he can beat any martial artist, Boxer or Wrestler." I'm thinking, "You can beat any Wrestler? What the hell are you talking about?" Wrestlers are the best fighters on the planet, because I have a Wrestling background before I was a martial artist. I've always been a Wrestler first and a martial artist second. And I'm thinking, "You can't beat no damn Wrestler. No Boxer can beat a Wrestler." Because I've been in the ring with Boxers, they're like babies if you shoot the legs and take them down. They last maybe 30 seconds. I'm like, "What the hell you're talking about?" Freddie Blassie, the Wrestler, was in the ring with him, so Bob and the editor say to me, "Why don't you ask Ali?" So one of the photographers in the ring came over near the corner, and I turned to him and said, "Ask Ali what would he do if a Wrestler faked a jab to the head and ducks underneath, took the legs and took him down?" He says, "Here, you ask him," and shouts, "Ali! Ali! Come here, come here." I'm thinking, "Oh my God, I don't want to ask him. I'm embarrassed."

So Ali comes over and I'm standing still outside of the ring. Ali is five feet away in the ring, and I ask him the question, "What would you do if a guy fakes a jab to the head and then dives at your legs?" He says, "Come on in here, boy, and show me." So I said, "Nah, I don't want to," but three people shoved me in the ring. At that time I was doing acting and my weight was down to 180 pounds, because I was trying to lose weight because of a film contract, so I wasn't in really great shape. But I was still pretty strong. I could pick up 400 pound deadlift - although I did 550 at one time - so picking somebody up was nothing for me.

So Ali gets in a Boxing stance with his hands up shuffling side to side, doing that movement with his footwork. I could feel the energy of everyone in the room, "Come on, come on. Show us!" So I did a shoulder fake to his head, he put his hands up to catch the jab, and I ducked down and shot for his legs. As soon as I grabbed him I stopped, because I didn't want to take him to the ground. As soon as I stopped, everybody in the arena laughed. There must have been a hundred people there besides the photographers. I knew what he did, he lay on my back as I was underneath holding his legs, and he made that face where he opened his mouth real wide. As soon as he laughed it pissed me off, so I picked him up, spun him upside down and dumped him. I didn't do an armbar or anything on him, I just pinned him. And they grabbed me, Freddie Blassie and two other people grabbed me and took me off him. I stood up and said, "Whoa, whoa. I'm just playing." I thought he figured out I was trying to kill him or something. Which I could have, because what I remember was his body felt like a woman. He was real soft, like jelly, and that shocked me because I'm used to Wrestling and doing weightlifting where the body is hard as a brick. And that just shocked me, he felt really, really weak. No strength.I remember Joe Frazier trying to put 180 pounds over his head, and he was a world Boxing champion, but he couldn't do it, So, Boxers were weak when it came to weightlifting.

Anyway, we stood up and Ali's standing next to me, and they're taking pictures and he puts his arm over my shoulders like we're buddies, and he says, "You were lifting weights when you were younger, weren't you?" I knew what he meant by that question. He could tell that I was a lot stronger than anyone he had been in the ring with before. Then he says, "Come on, do that again." I said, "You're shitting me, what do you mean do it again?" So I faked and dumped him on the ground again, and they took me off him. As I stood up, he was lying on his back where I pinned him and he laughed at me. When they got me off I said to them, "We're just playing," because I did it quite hard and it looked kind of mean. He had his hands on the bottom rope of the ring, and he looked at me and said, "You see that, you would've had to let me up." The point was, when he fought Inoki a couple of weeks later, in Japan, he kept his back against the ropes at all times, so Inoki never took him to the ground. All he did was grab the ropes and Inoki would have had to let him up.

After they finished taking a bunch of pictures of us - that's where you see that picture of him and I where he's got his arm around my shoulders like we're buddies - he sent this white kid who had a suit and tie on over to me outside of the ring. He said, "I represent Muhammad Ali and he would like to invite you to dinner tonight, he would like you to join us." I turned it down. Maybe I shouldn't have done that.

I'm a Vietnam vet and I just never forgave him for not going in the army. I don't care what his religious beliefs were. I have religious beliefs too, but there's a philosophy I live by. It has to do with power, where there's power you have responsibility. America has the power to stop communism, and you hit it right off and not wait till six million people die before you start doing something. You don't wait till ten million people are murdered before you do something, you don't wait till Mao murders 30 million of his own people and you step in to do something. You start early, and I don't believe in silence. I don't care what your religious beliefs are, you don't have to go out in combat and kill people, you could be a cook or do a lot of things. I know the Supreme Court said he could avoid the draft because of his religious beliefs. But in my heart, to me, it's bullshit to this day.

All these other people defend him. I mean, he paid his price when he was out of the ring for three-and-a-half years, he never got his legs back. The last six fights he had, that's when he got the knee damage, and he's got Parkinson's syndrome. My sparring partner Greg Wilkinson was a roommate of Muhammad Ali's personal physician, he was a heart surgeon. Back in 1976, he said, "Joe, Muhammad Ali's doctor told me, and this is confidential, Muhammad Ali's got brain damage. What they're going to do is release it to the media and say he's got Parkinson's syndrome." If you watch his last six fights, when his legs were gone, you see he never had a good defense. His defense was his offense and the rhythm in his footwork. His old style didn't work for him anymore, when his legs went so did his defense. That's where he got the brain damage.

Q: Is it true you thought Bruce Lee was the fastest guy you ever saw?
Joe Lewis: Yes, I thought he was. In terms of the trigger squeeze, initial explosiveness. Not as a fighting technique but as a test of speed. His trigger speed, especially with his hand and footwork, was the fastest.

Q: What about power?

Joe Lewis: A lot of guys are fast, then you've got guys who are quick. Quickness is more important than fastness. Bruce Lee had the quickness. But in the ring could he use that quickness against me or against another fighter, in the line of fire and in combat? No one knows in advance how the nerves of combat are going to affect you. You get people who say they've been doing ten rounds in the gym, and I've been in front of a thousand guys. I ask, "Have you ever been in the real ring or line of fire in combat? Have you ever stood in front of somebody who's trying to knock your head off in the ring to kill you? Could you still make that stuff work?" Then you know whether your stuff works or not. What realistic module did you use to test your ability? If you never used a realistic module and the trigger on other people, then you haven't a clue what you're talking about. Only real fighters know that answer. When it comes to speed in the ring, I have to say Bill Wallace. I've stood in front of Bill Wallace, we were sparring partners for a long time and we came from the exact same school in Okinawa. Bill Wallace, when he squeezed the trigger…other people have his speed, like Bruce Lee has his quickness and explosiveness, but there's something Wallace had. He could do it in the line of actual combat.

When Wallace pulls the trigger he has something extra, he has the confidence that he could fire and hit you, but he'd do it in advance, so you know what's coming. It doesn't matter, he's going to hit you anyway. When he fought he knew he was quick but he also knew he could hit you. Not many people have that incredible accuracy. Speed and quickness does not guarantee accuracy. You have to add the confidence to the speed and quickness, then you have a higher percentage of possibility of being accurate. Accuracy is the 'holy grail' of fighting, not speed or power, not tradition, not muscles, not having a big mouth. Most martial artists have a big mouth, only a small percentage of them can back it up, but the real fighters don't have a big mouth therefore they have nothing to back up. When a guy starts running his mouth, you've got a phoney.

Q: Could you please tell me how you came to write the book How to Master Bruce Lee's Fighting Method?

Joe Lewis: John Graden wanted me to do a book and said, "Let's do one about Bruce Lee's fighting methods." I think he was thinking that commercially it would make a lot of money. The problem I found we ran into is again, if I'm selling the book one-on-one to strangers, they would come over and buy it. Nine out of ten people who bought that book face-to-face said to me, "Joe, I really didn't want a book on Bruce Lee's method, the reason I bought it is because you wrote it. We wanted a book on your system and fighting style." But it was too late, as we had already done the book on Bruce Lee. I wanted to do it as a tribute to Bruce Lee, because he was one of my instructors and I felt like if I could turn around and do something to extend gratitude to my instructors for what they did for me in my lifetime, then that would make me feel better.

I mean, I've got all the trophies and recognition, so I could spread the credit around a little bit. So that's why I did the book. As a matter of fact, every day when I sat down to write chapters I wore a Jeet Kune Do T-shirt for good luck.

HAYWARD NISHIOKA

In the Los Angeles area one of the top grapplers Bruce Lee worked with was the Pan-American Judo champion Hayward Nishioka. Over the years, Professor Nishioka has always been complimentary when it comes to talking about his friend and the extraordinary skills which Lee was able to mesmerize him with. Like most of the great martial arts masters who worked with Lee, Nishioka gleaned as much information from Lee as the Little Dragon did from him. Master Nishioka is a college teacher in Hollywood.

Q: Can you please tell me when and how you met Bruce Lee and what was your impression of him?
Hayward Nishioka: I met Bruce in 1967, because I remember it was right after I had won the Pan-American Judo Championships gold medal at the Pan-American Games. The meeting took place at the Black Belt magazine offices. Mito (owner of Black Belt) said to me, "I want you to meet somebody who is interesting," so I said, "Fine, sure." And then Bruce had come in at that time, that's how we first met.

Q: You often went to visit him at his house, can you talk about the training sessions you both enjoyed?
Hayward Nishioka: I guess I should probably give you some of my impressions of him in the beginning. When we met at Mito Uyhera's place, I was young then and I wasn't thinking too much about what kind of personality a person has, and stuff like that. But now that I reflect back on it, I guess I may have, in the back of my mind thought that he was cocky. I thought, "Wow, he's talking about a lot of things that I also know about," because I had also taken Karate from Mr. Oshima, who was a Shotokan instructor. I didn't even know who Bruce Lee was at the time, because he wasn't all that famous at that time. It wasn't until later when a

lot of his movies came out and he became very famous. So, I thought he was very cocky, but at the same time he was very talented because he would do some of the techniques, talk about techniques, and was a really dedicated martial artist. He was very quick, and I thought, "Wow, this guy's real good." That was my first impression of him.

Q: Over the years you have related a story where he mesmerized you by his one-inch punch, which he demonstrated on you. Can you enlighten me on this subject please?
Hayward Nishioka: That happened! Because he was very talented he invited me to his dojo in Chinatown. I had a hard time finding it because he didn't have a sign up on his place of practice, and actually the windows had been blanked out, you couldn't look in. The area wasn't very big but I could see there were a lot of students, and he was sitting back on a chair. Occasionally he would get up and correct the students. At that time he did the one-inch punch on me. He said, "Let me show you something," because at the time I was questioning some martial arts. Shotokan Karate is different to what he did, which was Jeet Kune Do, and that's his own style. I said, "Well, how effective is the punch?" which was the wrong question to ask him, of course. And he said to me, "OK, just stand here." So I stood there and he put his hand against my chest, and he had his arm fully extended and just punched. I slammed against the back wall and fell down, because I wasn't really ready for that and thought his punch wouldn't be that effective from that close range, having the arm extended out like that.

The strange thing about that punch was it didn't really hurt, or maybe I was used to having taken impact...maybe, I'm not sure. When he hit me I just flew against the wall and fell down. It was so quick and it just lifted me up. At the time I weighed about 150-155 pounds and he weighed probably 135 pounds, and for him to generate that much power, I was just surprised.

Q: You exchanged ideas with him, you being a Judo champion, what did you think of his grappling ability and was he extensively researching this component?
Hayward Nishioka: Well, Bruce Lee was always interested in every kind of martial arts. When I went to his house - I would go there maybe once a month or so - on some occasions when I visited him he would be watching great Boxing matches between champions that existed at the time. He would look at these over and over again, he would point out different things that were going on. He would study the martial arts that way, looking at this and that and then emulating some of the movements. He would say, "A Karate punch kind of sucks, because when you punch the

quickness of the punch goes out, because there's a focus and you stop, whereas in a lot of the Boxing punches there's a follow through which is actually a stronger means of generating force." He would prove this out.

I also did a study on this when I was going to school at the time. I looked up a means by which to look at the forces generated by both punches and it showed that a follow through of the punch would act better. Bruce had a wall full of sports books and he would talk about different types of sports in relationship to his own art. In baseball when you hit the ball there's an interesting thing about it. He said in baseball you don't hit the ball and draw the bat back right away, you follow through. So the follow through is important in punching as well. He said the ball may not be there, also the opponent may not be there, but if you follow through... it's kind of interesting.

As far as grappling is concerned, he did some grappling with an instructor by the name of Chris Kato who was up in the Seattle area, and he also did some grappling with a friend of mine, who since passed away, whose name is Bill Paul who was up in the San Francisco area. He was one of my teammates in the Pan-American Championships. He had worked with both of them for a while considerably up in the Seattle area, he was very conversant and he had the ability to do certain throws. He didn't do too much matwork, he didn't know much on the ground because it does take a considerable amount of time to practice on the ground. In fact, at one point we had a discussion and I said to him, "Isn't that a flaw?" and he said, "It could be." And I said, "What would you do if I just lay down on the ground and you had to fight me?" He turned away and kind of looked at me and the corner of his mouth kind of went down, and he said he'd just walk away. Then he turned around again and pointed a finger at me and said, "But you better not get up."

Q: In your opinion, had Bruce lived would he have evolved and integrated more grappling into his art?
Hayward Nishioka: He did a little bit, not enough. I would imagine given the climate right now and how people are into the martial arts and the Jiu Jitsu scene, probably that would have come about.

Q: Did you start working with him when he was doing Green Hornet?
Hayward Nishioka: The Green Hornet was on TV at the time when these other series were popular like Superman and Captain Marvel from the magazines. In Green Hornet he played the part of a masked person, sort of the modern Tonto and the Lone Ranger thing. I guess that was a spin-off from that. In this case, the modern Tonto was Bruce Lee, who became the star - he was excellent! He could do things that most gymnasts couldn't do. He was able to leap up in the air and kick lamps out, move very quickly

from one place to another, raise his leg up to kick somebody in the teeth, then put his foot down or leave his foot out there. This was the first time ever anybody saw a guy of Asian extraction excel. He was just marvelous!

Q: Bruce Lee was an advocate of relating his art and training to street combat. Why didn't he compete in point-fighting tournaments?
Hayward Nishioka: He said why should he compete? I think in his mind he could. He would practice with people such as Chuck Norris and Joe Lewis who were very quick, very fast and very tough, and also Bob Wall. Actually, he was just too fast for them. He was just so quick, he would go in and out before you could even get started. It is one of the reasons why he is regarded so highly in the martial arts community, even by those who have in the past been not too complimentary. They may feel a little reluctant to say he was really fantastic, but in their hearts I'm sure they know that he was.

Q: Did he ever talk to you about Jeet Kune Do and the importance of fitness? He believed the effective capacity of a martial art lay not primarily on merely technique but attributes of the individual played an integral role.
Hayward Nishioka: Bruce was always running, he was always in good shape. The thing about the martial arts that people forget is it's still a physical activity. If you just feel the touch of technique, where you just practice on technique, then you may not have the successful elements as somebody as Bruce Lee did. But fill the cup of physical fitness, fill the cup of strength, tactics, studying the martial arts like he did, and you fill all those cups up. But you're not going to be able to compete if you're only filling up one cup, which is just technique.

Q: What do you think made Bruce Lee different to all those martial artists of his era, is it because he broke tradition?
Hayward Nishioka: He studied more than anybody else, he practiced more than anybody else and he excelled in his art. He tried to make a technique...how can I put it...he would 'hyper' train in all those areas I mentioned before.

Q: What is your favorite memory of Bruce Lee?
Hayward Nishioka: There are so many, but my favorite was he had all these different kind of tasks he would do, to see how well you can do things. I had been taking Karate with Mr. Oshima and I could move fairly well, and he said, "Watch this, could you do this?" And he held a board in his hand - about one-inch board - then he extended his arm out to the side and he dropped it and he kicked it and broke it. Anybody can break a board

when somebody is holding it, when there's resistance from the back, but hardly anybody can do that by dropping it with nobody holding it and crack it in half. He dropped it and kicked it with a side kick and broke it in half, and then he said, "OK, here. You try it," and he gave it to me. One of my favorite techniques at that time was the side kick. I didn't know whether I could break this board or not but I knew I had to kick it really hard and really fast, so I kicked it and I broke it. That was one of the few times I saw a surprised look on his face (Laughs).

Q: Did you spend sufficient time socializing with him and any interesting stories you can relate to me?
Hayward Nishioka: He invited me to his birthday parties and at his house we did a number of things. I was supposed to be in one of his movies but he didn't live long enough. It was called The Silent Flute, which David Carradine eventually made, but in comparison to what Bruce would have done it was awful. Bruce always surrounded himself with talented people. He had Chuck Norris around him, he had Bob Wall, he had all these guys that were really good and he wanted someone in there with Judo as well. He said, "I'm going to try and put you in the next movie that I have," but he didn't live long enough to do that.

Q: Tell me about your reaction when he hit the box office?
Hayward Nishioka: He was more popular in Asia and then he was imported here (US) and it hit the box office; there were big lines, and I remember that. I had to go to West LA to see it and I thought to myself, "This is really strange, as I'm walking into this theater to see a friend of mine that I know very well." And so I paid my money and went in. I think it was Big Boss, he did very well in it. I'm looking at it and I'm going, "Wow, this is really great!" The action that was in there was really good except for one scene that I started to kind of chuckle to myself. There's one scene where he jumped backwards into a tree (Laughs). I started laughing because I'd never seen him doing anything like that, but it was one of those things where you take a shot and then you run the reel backwards; you reverse it so it looks like he's jumping upwards onto the tree. That was kind of funny.

Q: Did you keep in touch with him when he was enjoying the success with the movies?
Hayward Nishioka: He was still in Hong Kong, he was busy over there so at that point I guess I didn't see him very much.

Q: What would you say to people who say Bruce Lee was just a movie star, not a real martial artist?

Hayward Nishioka: I don't know what to say but it was pretty evident. You just watch him and you know. He just excelled, in life sometimes I think to excel you have to be crazy, and he was in one sense, he was crazy about the martial arts. At that point in your life, usually at a young age when your body could really move, you have to see how well you could move and then work it to the extremes - and he did that. But you have to think about it. If you just do the physical it won't take you far enough, you have to plan out, you have to dream and think of the impossible and try to get there.

Q: Just how much of an influence and profound impact has Bruce Lee had on the world and why is he still so popular?
Hayward Nishioka: I teach a class at Los Angeles City College and every so often one of the students somehow gets hold of some publication and finds my name in it, and I've been mentioned in several of his books as being one of his friends. And they ask me what was Bruce Lee like. To me, for some kid who was born after Bruce Lee had died to ask me these questions is amazing, and his impact has been felt by that. The other things at first which bothered me was when I would be walking up the street and some kid would have a T-shirt with his face on it (Laughs), and I'm going, "Oh my God, this is amazing." So he's had that impact on the world and on society.

I think he stands for excellence, he was really nice to see. And I also told this to Black Belt magazine as well: up till the time of Bruce Lee, Asians were only thought of as a lower marginal scale. No one ever thought of someone being a star of a different race other than whites. Here all of a sudden we have an Asian face on the screen, not someone with a ponytail taking orders from anybody going 'chop, chop', but here was somebody with substance. He led the way socially for many people that are out there today including Jet Li and Jackie Chan. Had it not been for him there would not have been an acceptance of other martial artists. I think he was just great in that respect, and to uplift even for many Asians the idea of, "You know what? We're not going to be a second-grade person in the background, jumping around taking orders from a white man."

Q: Any advice he gave you?
Hayward Nishioka: In some ways it wasn't a student relationship, in some respect it was a collaboration at times, more for him wanting to understand what Judo was like, and for me it was just a fascination at his abilities as a martial artist. He was really fascinating.

DIANA LEE INOSANTO

Diana Lee Inosanto (aka D. Lee Inosanto) is someone most people in the martial arts community will be familiar with as Bruce Lee's goddaughter and the daughter of his top personal student and closest friend Dan Inosanto. A successful Hollywood actress and stuntwoman, Diana made a transition and directed her first movie Sensei which was critically well-received. She cherishes the fond memories of growing up around Uncle Bruce and playing with his son Brandon. Diana is a first-person witness to the Bruce Lee legend.

Q: Diana, what's your relationship with Bruce Lee?
Diana Lee Inosanto: He was an honorary uncle to me and he was my father's closest friend. When I was born, to pay tribute to him, my father decided to name me after him. This is where I get my middle name: Diana Lee Inosanto. My father recently was telling me a story, when I was born I guess Uncle Bruce was so completely into the arts he told him no matter what, the rest of my life I can take lessons with him and he'll be my Sifu - that was really sweet. Uncle Bruce was great, he was very protective, he was really great to all children, it was wonderful. As a child, I used to play with his son Brandon. We both used to have arguments and disputes about playing with toys, it was kind of funny to see Uncle Bruce intervene. He would have to kind of sort things out between Brandon and I.

He was just a wonderful man. I used to see him at our house. He and my father would have great conversations and discussions about philosophy and martial arts and evolution, where Jeet Kune Do was going. I didn't quite always understand but I knew looking back what they were talking about. So I realized it was really a wonderful thing with him. I recently worked on a play called Be Like Water in Los Angeles with a martial arts choreographer. And one of the reasons I was asked to come on board was because this is what I used to do (martial arts). 'Be Like Water' was actually a phrase that Uncle Bruce would use. I think it was rather strange to have to do that. It was about a young girl living in Chicago, she's 14 years old, who's been bullied. She's a Chinese-American. The play itself sends a wonderful message, it really captured the essence of his spirit and his humor and various elements. I remember myself as a little girl in real life growing up around him.

Q: When you were growing up in school how did the other kids treat you when they found out you were close to Bruce Lee?
Diana Lee Inosanto: It was kind of a mixture of both, I actually didn't really want to tell people because I thought they might think I was lying (Laughs), or secondly, if they did find out who I was, I hated it because sometimes I'd get challenged, and sometimes the school bully would want to challenge me and say, "Hey, what can you do?" It's not fun when you have to defend yourself as a kid, but it was kind of a mixture. As I got older it got easier, but it's harder when you are a kid.

Q: When did you start learning the martial arts yourself?
Diana Lee Inosanto: First of all, martial arts have always been around since I've been a baby, there was never getting away from it. It was like having it 24 hours a day, but I started taking it a little bit more serious when I was five years old. I had a couple of kids who tried to bully me around, scratch my face up, hit me, it was horrible. They were much bigger than me and I thought, "Now I understand what my father means by learning to defend yourself." So from that moment on my father took me in his gym in Carson, California, and I started training and from that moment on I took it seriously.

Q: I've seen a birthday card and a picture of you with Uncle Bruce, Linda and your mom, when was this taken?
Diana Lee Inosanto: The picture with my mom, Linda and Uncle Bruce was taken by my dad in our home in Carson, California. The card was given to me when I was born, if you see the Chinese writing on it, what that means is 'America's future Ms. Wing Chun'. Basically, my dad said he was going to name me after him and Uncle Bruce said, "Wow, I'm very honored. She will always have a place learning my art and philosophy."

Q: What do you think Bruce Lee was trying to ultimately achieve, was it more than just learning to fight?
Diana Lee Inosanto: I actually feel he was trying to achieve things on a number of levels. Number one: he was trying to achieve that as an Asian man, he has the right and the ability to be a star on the same level as

Steve McQueen or James Coburn, who were big stars at the time. He was determined to make it. Hollywood wasn't going to open the doors but he was determined to make his own circumstances, he was determined to make his own future, and he did that very well. He was very focused, and so on that level he really changed history, and I think he also had captured the imagination of audiences all around the world and showed that an Asian man can be heroic and can be honorable. He remembered the kind of images of Asian-American performers in Hollywood. They were very few and a lot of the times they weren't really flattering. Uncle Bruce has done amazing for the Asian community worldwide and truly helped and changed the positive image of the Asian-American man. From then on, that's where some of the others like Jet Li and Jackie Chan were thankful to him; he was the pioneer and he was the one who broke down all the barriers.

In the martial arts world, I think it's very clear to me that he was trying to evolve the martial arts. In fact, it was still taboo back then to explore other arts. He really broke those rules and traditions, saying it's one's right to research and allow oneself to explore and become a better martial artist, and really develop the attributes. Today, you can see his influence in mixed martial arts, and see it on film with martial arts being blended.

On a social level, Uncle Bruce made a difference. In 1960s America there was such racism and high levels of prejudice, and this was a man who had a martial arts school which had great diversity. He had whites, Hispanics, Jews, Kareem Abdul-Jabbar who was a Muslim, there were Christians, intellectuals, you had the working class, the middle class and the very wealthy - such a great mixture in his classroom of students. I think it's very important that he understood people coming together no matter what culture they were from. So I'm very grateful for that message, it's had a huge impact on me and on my filmmaking, on my movies and socially.

Q: Any Game of Death stories your father related to you which you would like to share?
Diana Lee Inosanto: When my dad came back from Hong Kong he had a very bad backache. Apparently there was one scene where Uncle Bruce kicks dad and my dad goes flying in the air, he was supposed to land on the mats but hit the floor (Laughs). He kicks in the air and he hits the floor and the mats land on him (Laughs). It was unfortunate, it was just a timing issue. It was funny, but poor dad! He had a backache for a while. My dad was so happy to work with him, and he was one of his best friends. One of the last times he'd seen him was when Uncle Bruce came by the house one time after that, from Hong Kong. It was amazing then and now it's a fond memory.

Q: Did Uncle Bruce have plans on using your dad in other movie projects?
Diana Lee Inosanto: I think yes, actually they were going to work on other projects; it was very good to bring his friends into the business. I think one time he wanted to use Taky Kimura but just never got around to that because Uncle Bruce died. There were other projects definitely down the road.

Q: What do you think he was trying to convey in Game of Death as far as the storyline is concerned?
Diana Lee Inosanto: The problem I have with Game of Death (the finished version after Bruce's death) is what most people see is not really the original vision Uncle Bruce had. I think he was trying to show the evolution of the martial artist who had to adjust to each opponent. My father told me each opponent symbolically represented different stages of his character of evolution, the evolution of Jeet Kune Do and how to absorb quickly and how to adjust with each opponent. That was kind of what he was trying to do in all of his movies, including the Coliseum scene with Chuck Norris in Way of the Dragon.

Q: I remember seeing some uncut scenes of Game of Death, in your house actually, with you and your husband Ron. Can you comment on the epic battle between your dad and Uncle Bruce which involved the nunchaku?
Diana Lee Inosanto: For me, it was exciting to see the footage of my dad and Uncle Bruce. I mean, I understand as a director why it never made it onto the screen for editing purposes and storyline. But for me, from a daughter's perspective, I was absolutely excited to see this footage and it was fun. It was a very euphoric philosophy that was through the fight scene and I was just really proud of my dad and Uncle Bruce, both of them. It was wonderful.

Q: Do you feel Bruce Lee set some kind of a benchmark for fight choreography in action movies?
Diana Lee Inosanto: Yes, I do. I remember a lot of the choreography back then and how he changed it. I think he made it look more organic. Many believed in wires back then, I know it was more flowery in Hong Kong. I guess you can say he really felt strongly that, for him, he wanted to present images a little more combative, more realistic and I think he definitely achieved that quite well. From what I understand from my father, he was very proud of his work and worked very hard. He was the first one to go from striking to Wrestling in Game of Death, from the standing game to the weaponry, then to the Wrestling game with Kareem. So, he changed everything and did it really in a lot of movies.

Q: When Enter the Dragon hit the theaters you were still a little girl. When did you ultimately realize Uncle Bruce was a big star?

Diana Lee Inosanto: I kind of knew from Enter the Dragon. He came by our house and my dad and him were working out in the backyard and a lot of the neighbors were looking over the fence in the backyard. People were like, "Wow, there's Kato from the Green Hornet show." I remember the Green Hornet series, we only had a black and white TV which didn't work well. Everybody found out that Bruce Lee was in the neighborhood, that's kind of when I understood that there was some sort of relevance in accordance to his work. Then eventually my father took me to go to see Return of the Dragon , it's also called Way of the Dragon as well, to see Uncle Bruce on the big screen. I thought to myself he's very important in the Hollywood community. Of course, I was just blown away, it was a good movie and was seen by everybody from Asian-Americans, Caucasians and people from every race. He achieved what he set out to do.

Q: One can speculate what direction Bruce would have taken had he not met his untimely death, but what avenues do you think he would have pursued?

Diana Lee Inosanto: I think he probably would have continued to make movies that were pertinent to propagating his philosophy, such as the original Silent Flute film concept, which eventually was done by David Carradine. I think definitely he'd have picked movies that were philosophically relevant to his message. The Kung Fu series, the original TV show, was his idea and he was going to be contracted, but it was a shame that Hollywood's racism didn't let him do this. I can't think of anything that would have been more devastating than to come up with a project like Kung Fu and have people say, "No, we like the project but we don't like you." How devastating can that be? Yet he had the guts and courage to say, "I'm not going to let this get me down, I'm going to keep moving on." And he made these wonderful movies coming out from Hong Kong.

Q: Can you compare Uncle Bruce to some of the iconic figures that we all admire?

Diana Lee Inosanto: He did a lot for the Asian community in showing that the Asian man can be a star and courageous. What set him apart is you can see him come 'alive' in his philosophy, he was the real deal. A lot of the times these actors were playing parts, but for him, he was the real deal, he really was this top fighter and a very strong man with great vision and conviction. And I think this makes him so special compared to a lot of the other celebrities. He was the real deal.

Q: You were pretty close to Brandon and grew up with him...

Diana Lee Inosanto: I grew up with Brandon, we both were closer in age than Shannon; he was probably one of my best kid friends. I loved being with Brandon because we both came from families that were biracial; we both have an Asian father and a white mother, we both had fathers who were in the martial arts. Brandon was one of these beautiful kids and human beings, he had a great sense of humor just like his father. He was wonderful, playful, very honest about his feelings. He was also very diplomatic and grew up to be an amazing young man. It still is, for me, very sad that he died at the young age of 28.

I know Brandon would have went on to do other great Hollywood movies. I still cry a little bit when it comes to Brandon, maybe because I was a little bit more close to him than my dad was to him. I didn't get to see him very much as we grew older but I could always call him anytime and ask him for advice and get his opinion. I know he had the same kind of struggles - whether he wanted to do martial arts movies or not - because he really wanted to forge his own identity, and people really wanted to see him being him, and not a Bruce Lee's clone, although he was always very proud of his father and his accomplishments.

Q: How did you find out about Uncle Bruce's death?

Diana Lee Inosanto: My mother and I found out before my father. My father was a school teacher in the daytime, so he would teach English, history and physical education. My mother found out on the news but also had a phone call as well. She was the first one to find out in our house that Uncle Bruce died. She made me promise that I wouldn't say anything to my father because she wanted to speak to him first.

When he got home, basically my mother took him to another room, she sat with him and told him what she'd heard, which really upset my father, it was very traumatic for him. It was the first time I ever saw my father cry, and he started calling everyone who knew about the news because at first he didn't want to believe it. It was a very difficult time for my father. They had a very close relationship.

Q: How do you remember Uncle Bruce and the legacy he left behind, which has enriched people's lives all over the world?

Diana Lee Inosanto: I remember him from the eyes of a child, I remember him and his presence. I mean, he'd come into a room and you knew he was in the room, he had quite an aura about him. He was also funny and kind, and he would be playful. I remember punching him in the stomach as a child, his abs felt like stones. He was just wonderful and an affectionate man. He was a philosopher and a strong man, very passionate, very articulate and had hope and could express this. I think he was a human being who set an example to everybody: if we evolve we can do great things. Focus and put our minds to it.

That's a wonderful thing. Most people who lack confidence, I think they can learn something from him. To achieve something in life, and if you focus you can achieve great things, you should never let anything be a hurdle to you because true human beings are capable of great achievements. I think that's the legacy he left.

Also, the social impact he had of just breaking boundaries, the walls of prejudice, the martial arts and Hollywood worlds, which was phenomenal. He's a symbol of great tolerance and diversity, he's special, you honor his image and it's a phenomenal legacy to have. He had courage and taught me I don't have to wait for anybody, I can make the circumstances and go forward. I'm forever grateful for that.

★ ★ ★ CHAPTER THREE ★ ★ ★

CO-STARS AND COLLEAGUES

Bruce Lee's TV career began not long after he moved to Los Angeles. He played Kato, chauffeur to a millionaire newspaper magnate played by Van Williams, in the series Green Hornet. The series ran for 26 half-hour episodes before being given the red light. After a number of years teaching his personal art of Jeet Kune Do to selected Hollywood actors (including James Coburn, Steve McQueen and scriptwriter Stirling Silliphant) and appearing in a number of TV shows, including Green Hornet series and couple of guest appearances in Longstreet and Ironside, Lee made a bold move. He went back to Hong Kong to fully immerse himself in his film career. On the advice of Hollywood actor James Coburn, a close friend and student, Bruce decided his fate lay in Hong Kong. Coburn candidly recalls, " He wanted to be a movie star, he wanted to make more money than Steve McQueen - and did."

Bruce left the United States in 1971 and moved to Kowloon Tong area of Hong Kong, to star in his first major motion picture as the leading man. The Big Boss would turn him into a phenomenon, literally overnight. Bruce was generally dissatisfied by the way films were being made in Hong Kong and single-handedly changed the Chinese film industry. This first film - released in the United States later as Fists of Fury - broke all box office records in Asia and propelled him to superstardom. Lee had taken South East Asia by storm. Suddenly, Lee had set a standard for Kung Fu films which was fresh and unique, with state-of-the-art fight choreography tied into contemporary culture.

By now, part of the Western media had taken note of Lee's success in the Orient, and one man in particular. Pierre Burton, who was a Canadian TV journalist, was the first Western TV journalist to interview Lee in Hong Kong. "He had to change his phone number right away...he was certainly the most intense character I have ever met on television. And I have interviewed at least 2,000 people on television," remembers the late talk show host. The Big Boss was made for a mere $100,000 budget, while his second movie Fist of Fury had a slightly improved budget of $200,000. Eventually Lee's first two films grossed $20 million, which was a lot of money back in the early 1970s.

The Way of the Dragon, Lee's third movie, grossed a staggering $3 million in Hong Kong in its first run alone. Never had there been an actor who caught the public's imagination so fast nor held it more compellingly. By this time Bruce had secured more control over his films and any future projects in the pipeline that he hoped to develop. "Bruce felt it essential that he put his own stamp on his films...the only way he could be assured of protecting his own personal and creative integrity was to write, direct, produce and star - in reality to do the whole thing," Linda Lee states. And this is exactly what Lee did with his third motion picture.

In October 1972, the King of Kung Fu started work on his fourth movie, Game of Death. This masterpiece would have an intriguing plot founded on Lee's philosophy of adaptation in combat. Lee hoped to make Game of Death the cinematic showcase for his personal martial art philosophy. There is no doubt had he completed this film it would have surpassed his previous films in terms of both revolutionary fight scenes and box office receipts. Lee had shot some of the most exciting fight scenes ever filmed on a celluloid camera with his top student Dan Inosanto and the great basketball star Kareem Abdul-Jabbar, who was also one of Lee's celebrity students.

"I hope to make multi-level films," Bruce remarked to a reporter, "the kind of movies that have a deeper meaning beneath the surface of the story." If one penetrates a little deeper, one can see there are key lessons to be learned from all of his films. Lee had majored in philosophy at the University of Washington which lead him to study such notable philosophers and philosophies as Krishnamurti, Alan Watts, Zen and Buddhism. He was able to relate this to his art, which went further and deeper than the kind of action movies that had gone before them.

Hollywood started to take note. Fred Weintraub, who was an executive at Warner Brothers, had been in contact with Bruce two years earlier, before his rise to fame in the Orient. He flew over to Hong Kong to discuss a project specifically developed for Lee entitled Blood and Steel, which later was changed to Enter the Dragon. Weintraub, who produced Enter the Dragon, says, "He had something you can't define - how can you define charisma? He had something on screen were you couldn't keep your eyes off him. His tremendous intensity - something I have rarely seen in films - comes across on the screen."

In August 1973, Enter the Dragon premiered at the world famous Sid Grauman's Chinese Theater (Mann's Chinese Theater) in Hollywood. It broke all box office records in its first week and then proceeded to sweep across the nation in a whirlwind of rave reviews. It even out-grossed Steve McQueen's The Getaway, which was an achievement in itself for Bruce as he finally realized his goal of out-shining his Hollywood friend. Rarely, if ever, has one film with one star loomed like such a colossus over a genre. Made for a mere $850,000, the film was a huge success during its original theatrical release, grossing over $25 million in North America alone and a further $90 million worldwide.

Enter the Dragon not only set a benchmark for action martial arts movies, making it the undisputed classic of the martial arts movie genre, but is one of the most profitable movies in the history of cinema. Bruce Lee acquired almost mythical status. It is unfortunate that Bruce was not able to fully witness the impact of his accomplishment. His ultimate dream of becoming the biggest star in the world was almost in his grasp. Had he lived just a few more months, he would have witnessed it with his own eyes. Nevertheless, Lee had made it. "Bruce was already an icon in a short time…the guy was loved by everybody: cops, bad guys, your sister. He was a phenomenal human being," states former James Bond George Lazenby, who was to co-star in Game of Death.

With only four-and-a-half films completed during his lifetime, Lee elevated the traditional Hong Kong martial arts films to a new level of popularity and acclaim, and sparked the first major surge of interest in martial arts in the West. Who knows what he might have achieved had he lived. After Enter the Dragon, he had the opportunity to channel his abilities into working with some of the top directors and producers. He was offered to do two movies in Hungary for a reported $2 million, which purportedly would have made him the highest paid actor in the world. Carlo Ponti wanted Lee to star with his wife Sophia Loren in a movie. MGM offered him to star with Elvis Presley in a movie, which Lee turned down two weeks before his death. Warner Brothers had at least five scripts for him which Bruce was considering. And no doubt after the sheer success of Enter the Dragon, Warner would have made him an offer that would top any other offers at the time.

Bruce's business partner Raymond Chow had developed a new project, The Shrine of Ultimate Bliss, which was to be Bruce Lee's next film after the duo completed Game of Death. Japanese film star

Sonny Chiba (Kill Bill) and George Lazenby were to co-star with Lee. This was going to be another Golden Harvest/Concord/Warner Brothers collaboration, which was to have a staggering $10 million production budget with a further $10 million worldwide marketing budget. This was astronomical back in the early 1970s. As a comparison, the 1974 Bond movie The Man with the Golden Gun had a $7 million production budget with a $6 million marketing and publicity budget. The producers forecasted a staggering $400 million box office gross worldwide for The Shrine of Ultimate Bliss.

After Lee died, it didn't take long for opportunist producers and actors to jump on the bandwagon for their own motives, which essentially was to cash in on the Bruce Lee tag. Films using Bruce Lee's name and likeness followed in a rapid succession, and films using part of the names of his movies likewise. However, no one has come across to recreating the verisimilitude, dramatic pacing and resurgence of Lee's brilliant fights on screen. Some Western critics may have scoffed at the plots of his Hong Kong produced films. The films may have had some substandard elements to them as far as production values and acting is concerned. But that is made up for by Bruce's on-screen persona and charisma and the magic of martial arts he was able to create, which enthralled the audiences and left them wanting more. Immediately after Bruce Lee's death, as grief and controversy raged across the world, movie theater crowds around the world flocked to see his films in greater numbers than ever before.

In the following segment of this tome, you will discover some of the most insightful interviews ever assembled with Bruce Lee's co-stars and workers. Many co-stars will be instantly familiar to the reader. On the other hand, to your delight you will be treated to some rather rare interviews with some of the co-stars who have hardly publicized their relationship with the legendary movie star.

BILL RYUSAKI

Bill Ryusaki, born in Kamuela on the big island of Hawaii, is a veteran Hollywood stuntman who has worked on and appeared in hundreds of films and TV shows. A master of Kenpo Karate, Bill was regularly used on the Green Hornet series, which gave Bruce Lee his big break into Hollywood. Both men became friends and Bruce would often visit Bill's dojo in Hollywood. Both men would later work on the Dean Martin movie The Wrecking Crew, on which Bruce was hired as the stunt coordinator.

Q: Bill, what's your martial arts background?
Bill Ryusaki: I started at eight years old with my father. I have seven brothers, so we all had to do two arts. Then I never stopped and I kept going. Then when I went to the University of Hawaii, I started Hawaiian Kenpo Karate.

Q: Did you meet Bruce Lee at the Long Beach Internationals in 1964?
Bill Ryusaki: We both were on the exhibition. He was doing an exhibition and I also had my division team doing one for Ed Parker at the Long Beach Internationals. We had a brief meeting, and after that he found out how long I'd been in (the martial arts) so we became friends.

Q: What was your impression of him as a martial artist and his personality?
Bill Ryusaki: He was not doing Green Hornet at that time, he just came from Seattle. So actually he wasn't a high-profile actor yet. When he came down, Ed introduced him to the people who did Green Hornet, and that's how it got all started. Personality wise...I like them (actors), you know. I'm a people person anyway, so I like everybody.

Q: How did you get the opportunity to do stunts on the Green Hornet series?
Bill Ryusaki: I've been a stuntman all my life. I started when I was in high school in Hawaii. And when Green Hornet came on they wanted an Oriental. So I came in and did the fight scenes as a normal stunt job.

Q: Am I right in saying Bruce was quiet and reserved at that point in his life?
Bill Ryusaki: He was quiet and reserved, but then as he became quite a star he became more outgoing; it was the Chinese community that really made him and I think little people identified themselves with Bruce. So he became a superstar. I liked him but a lot of people didn't like him because he held back a lot of things and he would side with people. He didn't want to be disturbed when he was having dinner, stuff like that, but that's typical of stars anyway.

Q: Did Bruce get more fan mail than Van Williams, who was the lead in Green Hornet?
Bill Ryusaki: He had a mask on in Green Hornet, playing Kato. I think what really made him a superstar was when he went back to Hong Kong. When he was in California he was just like a normal Oriental star. Then when he went back to Hong Kong and did all the movies, that's when he became a superstar. In California if you're Oriental you're OK, but you don't stand out like Brad Pitt or the others. What happened was at that point (LA Period) he was a star, but not a major star.

Q: Can you tell me any interesting stories or incidents that occurred on the set?
Bill Ryusaki: Green Hornet was just a working experience. They did a lot of stunts, and they said they had to slow down the camera and stuff like that. To me, it was just like a normal person because I've been in the martial arts and whenever they put you on video or camera, you're faster than you are normally. But to me, he was so dedicated in the arts, because we were at the time in the (martial arts) business but weren't really known. So, then you have a Hollywood star who becomes pretty well known, and the martial arts start spreading around. Ed Parker is my mentor, and I thank him, who spread a lot of the stuff around, and when he brought Bruce in I kind of compounded. Then what happened is our martial arts business became big at the time when he did Green Hornet. Everybody started to know about Karate and they wanted to join. He came down to me twice a week; he came to my school and Ed Parker's twice a week. He was great to watch.

Q: Green Hornet lasted one series. Did Bruce scout for more work in Hollywood after the series ended?

Bill Ryusaki: The Green Hornet lasted one season and he did such a great job that people wanted to find out how come it didn't go on. And then what he did was another movie where he became the stunt coordinator on called The Wrecking Crew. Chuck Norris, myself and some other martial artists worked on it and he was the fight coordinator. When we were working we didn't make so much conversation. He came in and basically said how the fight's got to be and then we did it. We did a lot but I can't really recall it because it's been so long. I know he did a good job and they really liked him for what he did. That's when he and Danny Inosanto became close. Danny Inosanto became his right-hand man so to speak. From there they decided to create The Way of the Intercepting Fist, which is Bruce Lee's theory on the martial arts.

Q: Was Bruce responsible for introducing Kung Fu on the screen to the American mainstream public when he was doing Green Hornet? Before this the movies leaned towards the Western-style of fighting.

Bill Ryusaki: Before that in the movies there was a lot of the old Western-style of fighting, and simply they did it for a reason - because it's better on camera. In Karate the motions are very short, and in the body the selling point of a strike was there. They call it a 'John Wayne punch', which would come all the way round. In a real fight you don't actually do that. So when he did Green Hornet and The Wrecking Crew we used a lot of Karate moves, but again we had to slow it down so they can actually see the motion. After that a lot of people wanted to see the trapping and the close-inside fist punches and stuff like that. What he did was he opened up the motion picture industry to different martial arts moves.

Q: Bruce used to visit your dojo in North Hollywood, could you expand on this please?

Bill Ryusaki: When I first met him he didn't know what I did, but knew I had a mixed division team which was doing real good. What happened was when I came from Hawaii I had to make a name for myself, so we traveled all over doing exhibitions. I guess at the exhibition he liked the idea and the stuff, at that time he was going to start his Jeet Kune Do. I was involved in martial arts for a long time, so people used to come over and ask me different questions as far as the business, how it's going, what people like, stuff like that. And I was into kids. I had a lot of kids at that time. He used to come in and wanted to find out how I worked with children and how I got students. Then he also wanted to expand on what he had. That's when they started the Jeet Kune Do, and so he suggested to me to come on board if I wanted to join them. I said, "I've been in martial arts all my life, what can you teach me?" But we were friends, he came over a lot of times to loosen up, would take his shirt off and condition himself. Also, it was a social thing, we went to Chinatown a lot. We used to go to restaurants in Chinatown because he loved Chinatown. We used to go there late at night, that's when I really got a piece of what stardom is.

One night we were sitting and having dinner and an older Chinese couple came by who were having dinner also, and Bruce said excuse me to us and he went over to talk to them. And when I watched him I could see they were very nervous. Then I said to Bruce, "These are your people. I mean, these are the ones that make you a star," and stuff like that. I just wanted to know what he told them. He told them, "We're here for dinner so don't stare at us." A simple thing, but they got really nervous. That's when I kind of started saying to myself, "I wouldn't let it get to your head." And Bruce and I...he wasn't a star to me, he was just another guy, so I would tell him things because we were friends.

Then I kind of didn't want to go to dinners after that. You know, when you like somebody and then you find out different things about them, it was similar to that. You're human but normal, but you can't do that when you're in the public eye and you're a superstar. It's like anybody now, when somebody comes along and asks them for an autograph you can't say, "I don't have the time," because they are the ones that made you! So that was one of the incidents that kind of turned me off. But that's difficult, I mean, when you become pretty well known people start to bother you and you kind of shy away.

Q: Did Bruce invite you to Hong Kong to take part in any of his movies at the height of his fame?
Bill Ryusaki: When he was in the US after the Green Hornet series and the Kung Fu incident, he just wanted to go home back to Hong Kong. So what he said was, not only to me but a lot of guys, "Why don't you come to Hong Kong, we'll do movies together?" Because that's the Oriental market. But I got injured really bad and had a screw put in my shoulder because of a major accident. I was moving a refrigerator freezer which weighed 800 pounds from my truck. It was going to fall on my head so I turned. I couldn't do anything for six months.

Q: Do you feel he was going to use a lot of the guys he knew in Los Angeles in his Hong Kong movies?
Bill Ryusaki: He was a man of his word, if he said one thing he'd do it. I remember when we were doing The Wrecking Crew with Dean Martin, that's when he said, "Hey, let's go to Hong Kong and we'll do movies."

He said that kind of jokingly, but he's a man of his word - if he said he'll take you, he'd take you. That's what I liked about him, whenever he said something he'd do it. And then another thing is, because he was little or had a short complex, whenever he did anything he had to do it really good. As far as his working out, they did a life story on him which showed his working out and how he used to do this, and I believe that because if he wanted something he'd do it and he'd work hard for it. That's what I really respected him for.

PETER MARK RICHMAN

Peter Mark Richman has starred in many films and TV shows in a remarkable career which started way back in the late 1940s. He played the character of Duke Paige in the Longstreet TV series. Longstreet allowed Bruce Lee to express his personal martial arts philosophy on mainstream TV in the United States. One of the most versatile actors in Hollywood, he has appeared in well over 500 TV shows and movies. He is also an accomplished artist and author, and lives in California.

Q: When did you first meet Bruce Lee and what was your impression of him?
Peter Mark Richman: Bruce Lee was a very nice young man, very shy, very tense and very reserved. I always felt he was like a tough steel wire. If you bend a wire it has a sound to it, but he was always at the apex of this tension. We had a couple of wonderful scenes together in Longstreet, this was back in 1971, where he shows me his Kung Fu and I'm doing the Boxing thing. He was a very inexperienced actor when he came on Longstreet. He improved daily in his work, and then certainly when he went to Hong Kong he got better and better.

Q: You once mentioned that there was always a heavy bag on the set of the show, did you ever witness him working out on the set?
Peter Mark Richman: Yes, he was always doing his Kung Fu, he was not just a guy who hung around doing nothing but was always working out. He was always thinking about moves and exercising and doing stuff.

Q: What do you think Bruce was trying to put across on the Longstreet show?
Peter Mark Richman: It was kind of horseshit philosophy. The producers,

and writer Stirling Silliphant, had the idea that he would be someone who was knowledgeable in Eastern philosophy and gave advice, etc. We had a particular scene which has been sort of made famous in three or four documentaries. When we did our stuff together, there was a wonderful camaraderie and playfulness. The Boxing that I did with him, which was rather extensive, not all of it made it into the film, only the necessities are in there for the cutting of the film. But we did much more, we choreographed a lot of things where he would do something to me and I'd swing back and he would do something else, hitting my arm down and pushing me back. It was much more extensive than shown in the film.

Q: When the camera was rolling how did Bruce choreograph the fights and action?
Peter Mark Richman: He was always the coordinator and did the stuff whatever had to be done. Bruce was always an advisor and would suggest whatever had to be done. It was all choreographed. Because nothing just happens standing still, otherwise it's terribly dangerous. So all the shots were prearranged where he would do this and I would think this way, etc. He was always practicing, he never stopped.

Q: Do you have any on-set stories you would like to share with me, and what kind of a person was he to work with?
Peter Mark Richman: I thought he was...I really liked him very much. He had a terrific thing about him. We would have coffee and tea sitting around on the set. I never expected him to be such a huge martial arts star. He was one of the first people who established the martial arts at a higher plane recognized by millions of people. I don't think there's anyone before him who has done this kind of stuff on an international scale. I don't think even he could have envisioned what happened when he went to Hong Kong. I don't believe he realized how big this was going to become. I think he was open to all ventures.

Q: When Bruce became a household name, after becoming a big global star, did you ever see or speak to him?
Peter Mark Richman: I never saw Bruce again after Longstreet. I was very happy for him and I think it was fantastic. He was a performer and a martial arts expert. I appreciated his efforts to pull it off. I think his demise was related to his extreme tension. The pressure of what he was going through...he was always ready to do martial arts, it seems to me his relaxation was lacking. He would have been even huge had he lived.

MARLYN MASON

Marlyn Mason was born in San Fernando, California, and made her first TV appearance on a 1955 Matinee Theater installment. She appeared in TV shows and several films, which included a leading role in The Trouble with Girls alongside the King of Rock and Roll, Elvis Presley. She played Nikki Bell in the Longstreet series which starred James Franciscus. Marlyn, who now lives in Oregon, admits the short time she worked with Bruce Lee had an indelible impact on her.

Q: How and when did you first meet Bruce Lee and what was your impression of him?
Marlyn Mason: Well, he was fantastic! He was just the dearest man...he changed my life in three words. I don't know what we were talking about but it must've been philosophical. I had no idea but this is the only conversation I remember when he said to me, "Don't say a word, just listen and think about it." And I listened, and he said, "What is, 'is'." I thought, "That's pretty simple," but I didn't say anything. I began to think about it, and I don't think there's a day that passes that I don't think about him because it literally changed my life.

Q: So in Longstreet he would impart his philosophy on and off-set?
Marlyn Mason: I don't remember any of the script or the stories but I imagine it was pretty much along those lines. I'm not a religious person but I think his whole basis was what he taught me: what is, 'is'. Then I guess you can go on and discuss that in more depth, but in reality he kept it more basic than that. I've not read any of the things he wrote, but I think there is a book or two out. There's one book out which he wrote but I've not read it. I just sort of live my life (Laughs).

A young Bruce Lee in Hong Kong demonstrating his versatility

Using the specialized grip exercise machine

KEEP OFF

SIGUNG BRUCE LEE'S WING CHUN DUMMY 1968

SIGUNG BRUCE LEE'S WING CHUN DUMMY

1968

DO NOT TOUCH!

Bruce Lee's original wooden dummy

Bruce using an isometric training device

Bruce was an avid weight trainer always looking to cultivate a strong body

Bruce Lee's original heavy bag

Practicing power kicks on the heavy bag

Practicing kicking on the air shield with *Way of the Dragon* co-star Ing-Sik Whang

A young Bruce Lee seen here with Yip Man, Lee's only instructor

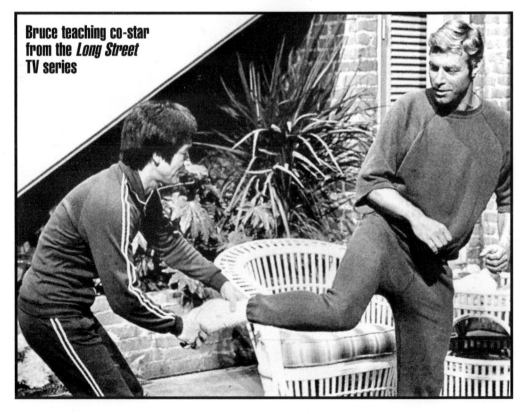

Bruce teaching co-star from the *Long Street* TV series

The final fight in *Way of the Dragon* is widely acknowledged as one of the best fight scenes ever put on camera

Bruce stretching out at the Golden Harvest film studio

Bruce sparring with student in the backyard

A group shot with Bruce on the set of his first movie *Big Boss*, 1971

Bruce Lee's LA Chinatown school, 1969

Bruce in the park for a photo shoot

Bruce spreads his lats. An unbelievable physique which influenced pro and amateur bodybuilders alike

Sharon Tate and Bruce on the set of *The Wrecking Crew*

Bruce with co-star Chuck Norris

At a Karate tournament with Joe Lewis, 1968

Bruce at the airport

Bruce shows who's boss in this promotional shot from *Fist of Fury*

On the set - Bruce directs *Game of Death* co-star and personal student Dan Inosanto

Playful sparring with son Brandon

Enter the Dragon producer Paul Heller and Bruce on the set of the epic blockbuster

Journalist Ted Thomas interviewing Bruce for radio, 1971

Bruce working out with close student Dan Lee at the LA Chinatown gym

Bruce choreographing a fight scene with Bolo whilst John Saxon looks on

Bruce and John Saxon in conversation

Close friend and celebrity student James Coburn joins Bruce at the airport

Being a voracious reader, Bruce amassed over 2,500 books in his personal library

The Little Dragon stretching on the set of *Enter the Dragon*

Jhoon Rhee invited Bruce as a special guest to several of his tournaments

One of many photos shot in the fields for *Game of Death*, the film which would have been Bruce Lee's crowning achievement

With *Green Hornet* co-star Van Williams

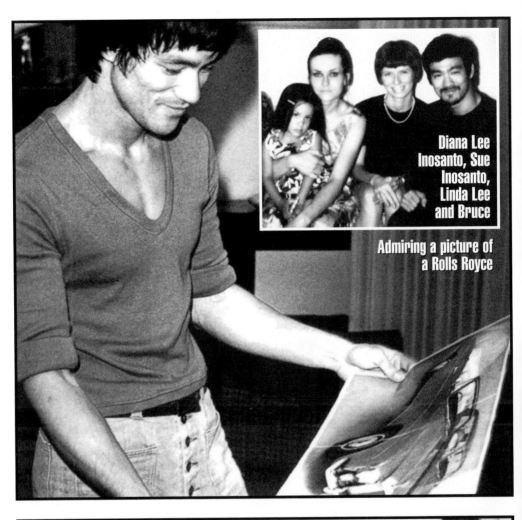

Diana Lee Inosanto, Sue Inosanto, Linda Lee and Bruce

Admiring a picture of a Rolls Royce

Bruce poses with a group of martial artists

Bruce and Kareem Abdul-Jabbar filming *Game of Death*

Sparring celebrity student, friend and NBA star Kareem Abdul-Jabbar

Bruce poses in
front of his
Mercedes Benz

The captivating
opening fight
scene from
*Enter the
Dragon*
depicted what
we now call
MMA

Q: How did Bruce get on with the cast and the crew?
Marlyn Mason: He was like Elvis. I mean, he was wonderful. I mean, I had no idea he was this huge international star and he was trying to become a big star in the United States. I think he was probably one of the first to get the martial arts thing going. I know if I say his name today everybody knows who he is, just like Elvis.

Q: Did you ever see him training on the set showcasing his dynamic skills when the camera wasn't rolling?
Marlyn Mason: They would have to rehearse the scenes, and I do remember one time the cameraman had to ask him to slow down because when he was kicking he was kicking so fast that the camera couldn't see it. The cameraman had to say, "I know we're not supposed to see it but the audience have to see it." So he had to slow down just a little bit, how he did that I don't know. Another funny thing he used to do is he would take all the air out of his body and then he would begin to inflate himself, he would begin to take in air, he would kind of balloon up. And we had such fun watching him (Laughs). We would say, "Blow yourself up, blow yourself up" (Laughs). He was amazing in what he could do, he would let all the air out of his body then he would sort of make a whooshing sound, and you would see his body begin to inflate.

Q: I remember Barbara Anderson - who was a co-star in Ironside - saying once that Bruce was kind of shy at the time. How would you sum up his personality?
Marlyn Mason: Well, I wouldn't call him shy. We did four Longstreet shows together, I just found him to be very sweet and he was quite 'not American' in that sense, he was extremely polite. I just found him to be very, very sweet.

Q: Do you feel he was trying to achieve the American dream of becoming a success there and being recognized globally?
Marlyn Mason: I don't recall ever having any discussions or hearing him discuss it, because when we did the show he mainly worked with Jimmy (James Franciscus). He might be on the set but I didn't work that much with Bruce. I might have been in the scene where we actually acted together. But I just assumed because he was so huge in China and he was becoming this big international star that he and his agents were trying to gain that name in the United States, I think. I'm wondering if he gained more of it after he died.

Q: A lot of people say Bruce was developing himself as an actor, because first and foremost he was a martial artist. Would you say his

acting ability would have accelerated over time?

Marlyn Mason: I don't know, I guess if he wanted to gain fame in this country he had to have learned to act and get better and better. But I think at the time when he was here, in the United States, it was mainly his martial arts in films which were probably the thing which was pushing him along at the time, but I would imagine he would. I think most people who are in the business want to be better so they work towards that, but I can't really tell you the truth as far as he goes.

Q: How was Longstreet received by the viewers and did he receive fan mail when he did the four episodes?

Marlyn Mason: Well, you know the ratings and numbers and all that, they might have been a big thing but it was something that concerned the production office. I don't remember anybody coming on the set saying our numbers were this or our numbers were that. I never really paid any attention to that. I mean, going to work for me was like going to a playground, so I never got involved in any of that business side of it at all. I'm not surprised the ratings would be higher when Bruce was on. Longstreet was an OK show but it got a little silly, sometimes having Jimmy Franciscus do things which probably were a little unbelievable for a blind person. I mean, it's amazing what blind people can do but he was doing some comic book things. But it was a good show of actors and like you say, Bruce probably elevated the show when he was on.

Q: Can you describe the storyline? Bruce plays an antique dealer...

Marlyn Mason: Gosh, you probably know more about it than I do (Laughs). When the show was canceled that was it. I can look at shows now and I can remember the costumes I had on and remember working with certain actors, but there are very few stories I can remember. I think the main thing for him was to teach the Longstreet character how to overcome his blindness, to have a philosophy of life and enable him to do things and be able to live in the world.

Q: How did Stirling Silliphant fit into the picture and was he responsible for getting Bruce in the show?

Marlyn Mason: I would imagine so, it was his show. I understand they were friends and Stirling was studying martial arts with him. I was in the show because of Stirling, and I'm still in touch with the associate producer Joel Rogosin. Not frequently, his wife and I email each other once in a while because he doesn't like the computer (Laughs).

Q: When Bruce exploded onto the international scene after the release of Enter the Dragon, did you feel a great deal of relief knowing that

someone you worked with finally realized his ultimate goal?
Marlyn Mason: I never saw the movie but I'm always very happy for anybody I know who could make it in this business. It's very difficult, because he had a personal impact on my own life. I mean, any kind of success he had I was overjoyed. I always wanted to meet his son to tell him how his father changed my life and how wonderful I thought he was, even though I knew him for a short while. Then, of course, his son had his untimely death, so I never got to do that.

Q: Any final comments on Bruce Lee?
Marlyn Mason: I could only say good things about him, he was very professional. I never got to know him away from the show because I rarely socialized with anybody I worked with. Acting for me was just a job. I would go to work, meet the people, have a good time as I could and try to do the job as good as I could then I would go home. So beyond being on the set, I didn't work with Bruce that much. Face to face we didn't have much conversations. Had he lived he would have probably continued with the martial arts, whether he would have stayed in films or not there's no way of knowing. But I think his philosophy was so deep he would have continued to be the person he was and to live his life.

LOU GOSSETT JR.

Lou Gossett Jr. was the first African-American male to win an Oscar for Best Supporting Actor. His role as Gunnery sergeant Emil Foley in the 1982 film An Officer and a Gentleman showcased the remarkable talent which won him the Academy Award. In a career spanning more than five decades, he has appeared in countless films and TV shows including the earlier episodes of Longstreet. In this rare exclusive interview, he talks about his friendship with Bruce Lee and working on the Longstreet series.

Q: How did you get involved with the Longstreet TV show?
Lou Gossett Jr.: I did a couple of episodes and Bruce Lee was next door teaching Karate (martial arts) during the Longstreet episodes. We were in the same studio. He had a Karate class so all the actors went to study with him.

Q: What was your first impression of him?
Lou Gossett Jr.: He was overwhelmingly wonderful and larger than life. He was great, a magnetic man and in incredible shape! He was a very nice man and I liked him a lot.

Q: Being an avid martial arts exponent, Bruce would often train on the set. Did you witness him perform any incredible feats?
Lou Gossett Jr.: There was a gym at the studio, he was there all the time and he ran the gym. He was in incredible shape and very popular. He would do splits above the ground by putting his legs on one desk and another with nothing underneath, all kinds of incredible things. I studied martial arts as a young man, I wasn't in the army but worked with them. I found Bruce Lee very fascinating. Then I started studying again in

preparation for the movie Diggs Town then, of course, for An Officer and a Gentleman.

Q: His ultimate goal was to break into Hollywood but he had hurdles to overcome because of his race. Were you able to relate to this yourself in some way or another?
Lou Gossett Jr.: He was a magnetic man and very, very focused, and he didn't think that he'd ever fail. There's always been a racial hurdle for me. I broke a lot of doors down. I was the first African-American man to win an Oscar. I broke down the doors even before I did acting. I was just set up that way I guess. I have a Foundation now called Erasecism which makes sure the next generation doesn't practice racism at all. I'm doing this in my latter years to try to help young people grow into a better world, so they don't practice (racism) and get along better. The world needs to study that in the next generation so that we won't have the conflicts. He overcame them and made his martial arts very popular.

Q: Did you know Stirling Silliphant and what was his relationship like with Bruce Lee?
Lou Gossett Jr.: Yes, very much so. He started in theater. He was a wonderful man, Stirling Silliphant. All those writers that came out of theater were wonderful.

Q: What was the most intriguing physical attribute which Bruce possessed?
Lou Gossett Jr.: The physical was (he had) no body fat. He was extremely defined and finely tuned.

Q: What did you make of his philosophical thoughts?
Lou Gossett Jr.: His philosophical thoughts were very healthy, very disciplined and very magnetic, an example of his philosophy.

Q: What was the theme of the show and Bruce's character?
Lou Gossett Jr.: The theme of the show in Longstreet was getting the bad guys. Bruce was the aid, the second, and did most of the physical stuff. Longstreet was blind.

Q: In your opinion, what drove Bruce to succeed? He made a huge impact on the world within a span of two years!
Lou Gossett Jr.: He was a dynamo, very busy and very ambitious. He worked very hard, he worked as hard as Jackie Chan worked to make himself, there was discipline on both of their parts. My hat goes off to both of those men. I call it tunnel vision and great discipline. He never

thought there was anything impossible for him, he was great! Both of them are great.

Q: What did you think of the final result achieved from Bruce's hard work?
Lou Gossett Jr.: It was overdue. He revolutionized movies and he got everybody to copy him, which means he broke a mold, and everybody wanted to try to copy that. They had American Karate people, they had Japanese Karate people, Latin Karate people. Everybody's trying to match Bruce Lee's ability. If it wasn't for Bruce Lee, there would be no Jackie Chan. His charisma was wonderful.

Q: Bruce Lee died as a young man who was on the verge of superstardom. Would he have improved in acting in the pure sense of the word?
Lou Gossett Jr.: Yes. I still have question marks (around his death), but I don't know enough about it. It was a mysterious thing. Of course, he would have improved and he was improving with each movie. I miss him, I miss Bruce Lee. He probably would have got nominated (for an Oscar) by now. He would have his academy and schools all over the place. He's had an enormous impact, even in his death.

Q: Were there plans on continuing the series for much longer than it lasted?
Lou Gossett Jr.: The show would have lasted longer, but James Franciscus passed away when he was very young. He died a young man, he was a very good actor.

Q: Did you know or work with anyone else who knew Bruce Lee?
Lou Gossett Jr.: Kareem Abdul-Jabbar, he was serious (about martial arts) but I was just doing it to stay fit, because of that kind of workout, I was a natural athlete anyway. I moved on and it helped me in my acting. I studied with Benny 'The Jet' Urquidez, he was the referee in Diggs Town, and Jason Randal who trained the LAPD in Officer and a Gentleman. So they kept me fit by working out in martial arts. Of course, I also did a film with Chuck Norris called Walker. Me and Kareem come from New York, and we have basketball in common. He became a professional and I became an actor. We became quite close and I like that man a lot, he's one of the brilliant men in the world. He keeps the discipline of stretching, he made a science out of it, that's why he had such a successful career. He was able to stretch and he never got sprained muscles because of his stretching. He was a very large man but very agile and at over 7ft 3, it was impossible to block

his shots. He was an incredible athlete. I knew Kareem back then and I know him very well now.

Q: Did Kareem share any stories with you about Bruce which fascinated you?
Lou Gossett Jr.: There's a funny picture with Kareem doing a roundhouse over Bruce Lee's head, Bruce Lee's laughing at him (Laughs).They had a pretty good friendship. Muhammad Ali was a larger than life character who, along with these gentlemen, had such discipline and devotion that they had to make it. I idolize all those men who have succeeded with the tunnel vision to make it, and those wonderful men are rare. And they should be saluted, all of them, from Chuck Norris, Bruce Lee, Muhammad Ali and Kareem Abdul-Jabbar to Bill Russell.

ROBERT CHUA

Robert Chua's 45 years television experience spans from Australia, Singapore and Hong Kong to China. He started his TV career in Australia at the age of 17 before making Hong Kong his home. In the mid-60s he helped launch TVB in Hong Kong and created the most successful and longest running live variety show Enjoy Yourself Tonight. Bruce Lee appeared on the show countless times at the height of his stardom. Enjoy Yourself Tonight was the equivalent to Johnny Carson in the United States but with its own theme, which centered around live entertainment.

Q: How and when did you get involved in TVB in Hong Kong?
Robert Chua: OK, I started in Singapore in TV then I started working on TVB in 1967 in Hong Kong.

Q: When did you first come into contact with Bruce Lee? Was this before Big Boss was released?
Robert Chua: When he came to Hong Kong in the early 70s, he appeared on my show several times. This was before his movies came out. He was popular because people knew him from Green Hornet, then he went on TV then later he went to Golden Harvest and produced the movies.

Q: Tell me more about your show. How many times did he appear on it?
Robert Chua: Many time. Many, many times! He was a good friend. On one occasion in one of the shows - I think the 2000th show - we had a celebration, we had a big birthday cake coming out. Usually a beautiful girl comes out of the cake but instead he comes out. In one of the shows he demonstrated things. Another show which I did was the Marathon Charity Show, because there was a disaster and typhoon so we raised funds. He brought his son along to the show who demonstrated with him.

In Hong Kong, at that time there weren't many people who were too intellectual (for us) to do just a chat or talk show, where you're sitting down with the guest and chatting. That represented about 20 percent of the show, the rest was singing, dancing and comedy. It was like a variety show, some singing, dancing and sketches, similar to Saturday Night Live but more wider entertainment.

Q: What was your impression of him from the conversations you had on the show pertaining to his career, martial arts and life in general?
Robert Chua: He was down-to-earth, very friendly, a very nice person. No ego in the head or arrogance, nothing like that. He was a very nice and friendly person. He talked about the martial arts and his experiences in the United States and, of course, his movies. He showed me his speed by kicking at my face, just missing me by an inch. Brandon was on the show and he broke boards. Some idiot erased every damn thing of the footage from the TVB archives; he didn't recognize the value of the footage, in the early days all footage was erased. I think Bruce came on the show about a dozen times, we loved to see him, but unfortunately the footage has been erased.

Q: Were you ever surprised when he broke box office records with his first movie?
Robert Chua: Not surprised at all, we knew he was very good. When we were sitting down, occasionally he would come out with a flying kick to my face. He was so good and hyper. Everybody knew he was a real talent, he was really the best Kung Fu guy who started all this, and in Big Boss he demonstrated the real Kung Fu instead of just acting Kung Fu.

Q: Any behind the scenes stories before or after the show?
Robert Chua: One time he asked me to shoot a movie with him, he asked me as a friend. I told him frankly that I'm a television producer and I cannot be good in a movie, I'm not someone in the movie industry. I've not done movies or films, but he did offer me a part, which was very flattering and nice.

Q: Being involved in the media, did you attend any of the press conferences?
Robert Chua: Only a few, as I was too busy. I did shows five nights a week, three or four nights myself. We would grab a cup of coffee in the canteen and chat.

Q: What's the most intriguing thing he spoke to you about?
Robert Chua: I remember him talking about his passion in what he was

doing, and I remember him as a very hyper person. He loved doing movies. Sometimes when he went to the airport I did attend a couple of press conferences. I was really busy doing my show. Raymond Chow had left the Shaw Brothers so he set up a small company, and at the time Shaw Brothers did not take Bruce so Raymond Chow took him, and then he became a superstar. Shaw Brothers didn't recognize him and this was their loss. Golden Harvest was built on Bruce Lee.

Q: How did the media treat Bruce Lee in Hong Kong? Is it true there would occasionally be stories circulated about him being challenged or dead?
Robert Chua: Very good, very positive. In the early days there wasn't too much of negative press, now it would be terrible. At the time the general media loved him, the whole thing was everybody was really proud of him. I'm a Singaporean Chinese, I lived in Hong Kong and worked on TVB for a long time, so all Chinese - whether you're a Chinese from China; Hong Kong Chinese; Malaysian Chinese or Singaporean Chinese - were all very proud of Bruce Lee.

Q: Bruce Lee movies were breaking box office records all over Asia, not just Hong Kong, starting a new wave of interest in Kung Fu flicks...
Robert Chua: He broke records everywhere and people started following in his footsteps. And when he died they mourned for him and there were such a lot of people at the funeral parlor to give the final farewell. He was such a big superstar. When he died, I think someone told me when I was at the studio. At the funeral parlor I was one of the people covering the event, seeing what we can do to cover the whole event for the public. It was a very sad time which shocked people.

Q: What was the atmosphere like at the funeral in Hong Kong?
Robert Chua: That was one of the biggest funerals for a very long time, that was the kind of funeral no other important person in Hong Kong ever got, he was a real superstar. No leader of a country gets that kind of treatment.

Q: Any final comments?
Robert Chua: Certainly he was one of the big stars, it's a shame we lost him. He was the first international Chinese star. He told me he wanted to be the world's best Kung Fu person, so when he did the films he actually was also perfecting his skills at the same time, he had a unique method of doing it. He had a scream which we know, Bruce Lee's scream. I'm doing a health and lifestyle show now on TV, Bruce would have liked it. He was

a strong and healthy man, it would have been wonderful to have had him on the show, to talk to people and tell them how to be healthy and strong. What I would wish if he was alive - he would be 68 years old now, he would still be very strong - now that I've got a health and lifestyle channel, he would come on my channel and talk to people on how healthy and strong he is. I'm sure he would go on the show and show how he looks and how healthy he is. I don't think anyone can replace him, his personality or his skill. One thing people like is to match him with someone like Muhammad Ali or someone really famous, and ask who would win. I'd always put my money on Bruce to win, he was powerful, strong and too fast for them.

TED THOMAS

British broadcaster Ted Thomas arrived in Hong Kong in 1954. He worked for the Hong Kong Standard as a journalist and later was employed by RTHK. Later, he became involved with public relations and founded his own PR and publishing company. Born in Cheshire, England, Thomas was the first Western journalist to interview Bruce Lee in Hong Kong. Thomas was one of the few Western journalists to interview Lee at the height of his fame. He has a unique insight and perspective into the martial arts movie star's most compelling story.

Q: Ted, please tell me how you first came into contact with Bruce Lee?
Ted Thomas: I was in Hong Kong working for a dubbing company. We did all the Shaw Brothers movies and then the Golden Harvest movies. Bruce, as you know, was working with Raymond Chow. He'd been acting in Green Hornet in Hollywood as a Chinese chauffeur, and Raymond Chow had signed him up as the new star of Golden Harvest.

Raymond Chow had worked before for Run Run Shaw on the Shaw Brothers movies. Then he was being groomed as the Run Run Shaw's next successor. However, some difference of opinion took place and then I suppose he changed his mind. Raymond decided to start up his own company Golden Harvest. Up until that time, Shaw Brothers had been the premier and the only really existing maker of quality movies in Hong Kong in the Mandarin language, because all the previous were in Cantonese. Now suddenly Run Run Shaw had a competitor, Raymond, and although Raymond was well behind, being the new boy on the block, he brought Bruce Lee. Bruce Lee caught on so well with a young American guy called Andre Morgan, who is a big producer now in Hollywood, they groomed him to become an instant star. This pulled a lot of business away from Shaw Brothers and towards Golden Harvest. That was in the early 70s.

Q: Let's talk about the success of his first two films, you were the first Western journalist to interview Bruce. What was the reaction in Hong Kong?

Ted Thomas: I think the first thing was the script idea. The movie showed China, after many hundreds of years of being subdued by Western countries such as Great Britain, Germany, France, America, etc, is no longer the sick man of Asia. This awakened the national pride in Chinese, along the lines of: yes, we are a big country and successful, why should we be regarded as a country every Western country comes and exploits? And that awakened a lot of Chinese not just in Hong Kong but all around Asia, like Singapore and places like the Philippines where there are a lot of Chinese people and, of course, Malaysia and Indonesia. He awoke a national pride among the Chinese, that they were indeed a nation who could stand up to anyone else, and because of his superb Kung Fu and action skills he was able to represent the Chinese as a recognizable nation.

Q: Can you describe your first meeting when you first interviewed him for radio?

Ted Thomas: We met well before I interviewed him, of course. We had a big argument. I was a very enthusiastic Boxer in my youth, and I was a bit skeptical about the martial arts the Chinese did. I always thought a basic move of martial arts is a kick to the head, which at the time, would leave a fighter off-balance. The Kung Fu man would only have to be caught by someone with a quick reflex, capture the leg and get him on his back and it'll be the end of him. Bruce and I played around in the dubbing studios a few times. I said to Bruce that I felt - and this had been tried several times against Japanese, especially Jiu Jitsu and Judo practitioners and Karate - that an Eastern-style of Kung Fu or martial arts expert would not beat a Western-style Boxer; if the Boxer had no rules and didn't have to wear gloves. We often tried hitting each other and I caught him off-guard at one time in the studio. The day I interviewed him, I cut his lip with the edge of my hand and if you look at the interview picture, he's covering his lip.

Q: How would you describe his personality and what made him different to all the other celebrities you have interviewed?

Ted Thomas: He was very cocky, which is very unusual of a Chinese guy. The national characteristic is to be very shy and reserved. Bruce had been to Hollywood and had a lot of success with Green Hornet and, of course, in Hong Kong he was an instant star. He was getting a lot of attention from Chinese movie stars. He was getting a lot of attention. Bruce was

Raymond Chow's piggy bank, his bank account. He was the major star in Asia and he was owned by Raymond Chow, so Raymond wasn't going to allow anybody to get in the way of that. He watched Bruce Lee carefully. He was alleged to have been with Bruce the day he died, walking up and down the garden of a house when we first got the report. In fact, that turned out to be entirely untrue. He was a cocky young actor, as you might expect at that age when suddenly surrounded by glamour and a success which probably was unparallel for an Asian actor at that time.

Q: When Bruce was enjoying tremendous success from his movies, how did the press treat him in Hong Kong?
Ted Thomas: They were very cautious because the first movies here, up till Bruce came along, were Cantonese movies and they were very, very bad. For example, in one of the scenes on the balcony there's someone in the back, you could see a piece of string he's holding in the background, it was things like that (Laughs). What Raymond Chow achieved was he recognized there was a wider audience for Chinese movies, and he chose the Cantonese language, which is the local dialect for Hong Kong. The films could be exported to places such as Singapore, Malaysia and Indonesia and places where there's a substantial Chinese population. And that included the UK where, of course, there's London, Manchester, I think Yorkshire and Liverpool as well, with a substantial Chinese population.

Q: How did Bruce acclimatize to the fame?
Ted Thomas: It went to his head to be honest, not surprisingly because it was all so much more than he expected. He expected to come to Hong Kong and get better parts. Becoming a star virtually overnight would be a shock to anyone. Expecting some better parts and develop your art, your craft or whatever you want to call it, and instead of that suddenly becoming not just a famous Asian movie star but international movie star. That, of course, is a tremendous strain on yourself. And you think you're someone rather special, instead of just a good personality which translates exceptionally well to movies. Very good actors do nothing in movies at all. Look at Richard Burton, he never made a really great movie. He made one good one I think, when you consider that with Lawrence Olivier. I suppose Albert Finney was an exception, another Manchester boy. He was a good stage actor. Ultimately, after many failures I have to say he transcended into becoming a great movie actor as well.

Q: Am I right in saying when Bruce became famous he started keeping people at a distance, because he found it very hard to trust anybody?
Ted Thomas: I believe threats were being made to him by the Triads who

had enormous influence on the movie industry in Hong Kong. They said he better align himself with them, and they would dictate what sort of films he made and how they were made. The movie industry in Hong Kong was not run by guys who made movies - Run Run Shaw and Raymond Chow - but the Triads, a bit like the Mafia. They had a lot more of an influence and were prepared to emphasize to people what sort of movies were to be made.

Q: What is one of the most interesting conversations you ever had with Bruce?
Ted Thomas: He said, "There are people in this industry who think they own me - and they don't. I'm my own man." Which is the character he portrays in Big Boss too. He was not somebody else, he was going to be a man who was going to be his own person. And in this he managed to convey that a Chinese could do this and not only the Americans, the Brits and the Germans are going to be the movie stars. There was going to be a Chinese movie industry with Chinese characters and Chinese stories, and it would be great movies.

Q: How often did you see Bruce? Would you just call him up when you wanted to conduct an interview with him?
Ted Thomas: I had complete access to him and, of course, a lot of our dubbing was done at Golden Harvest. In those days it would take five or six days to dub a movie, and if he wasn't specifically filming he would wonder into the studios. He was very much a Westernized Chinese, he liked chatting. He had a middle type of an accent which was American and British, and Bruce really thought he could dub his own voice, but he couldn't. He wasn't a terribly good actor but he was a very good Kung Fu fighter. When it came to his voice, he had a rather flat, emotionless voice which wasn't very good for the type of characters he portrayed. So what we had to do was to persuade him that this wasn't his 'bag'. One day he came in when we were dubbing in the dubbing studio at Golden Harvest up on the hill, and he wanted to do a voice. So we gave him the voice of one of the extras, some black guy who was a Kung Fu fighter, that's in the original dubbing. Of course, the films have been dubbed many times after that.

Q: Bruce was not the type to be self-satisfied or complacent when it came to moving up the ladder of success. Can you recall any conversations where he spoke about pursuing his dream by capturing the worldwide audience?
Ted Thomas: This was his obsession and he was good at it, of course. One was the martial arts, he was annoyed that the world seemed to think the

greatest martial artists were Japanese with Jiu Jitsu and Judo and the Koreans with their Karate. He wanted the Chinese system or style of martial arts to be recognized, which was originated from the Shaolin. He wanted to show that the Chinese were good at this, and they weren't people who were gardeners, barbers or houseboys. Of course, what was happening on the mainland at the time, the mainland itself was beginning to assert itself. Bruce wanted to show that the Chinese were a great nation. And, of course, claim paper, writing and gunpowder, all these things that made civilization advance thousands of years ago. So he had a bigger mission than just being a good movie star and attractive to ladies, that sort of thing. He wanted to show the Chinese are well-rounded people who could also be aggressive and tough and self-assertive.

Q: Did he have certain hurdles when making his first movie Big Boss? As we understand he had a problem with the director Lo Wei?
Ted Thomas: Lo Wei was regarded to be connected to some organization, and that would have been a problem. Later, he had influence which was far wider than his position in the movie industry. The other thing was I think Bruce, by the time he made his second and third film, thought he knew better than the directors how to do it, so he wasn't a good actor to direct. I'd seen him on the set a few times and there would be gossip around the studio that Bruce had an idea of a specific shot, and he would want to play it that way but the director, of course, had a different idea all together.

Q: Bruce set up his own company Concord Productions after the success of his first two movies. Where did Raymond Chow fit into the picture?
Ted Thomas: Bruce wasn't stupid. He knew what sort of money these movies were making and realized that a very large percentage of Raymond's money was from (his) two movies, and the others were sort of minor. I would imagine Raymond would not be agreeable to giving him shares from Golden Harvest, which by now was a well-established facility of movie making. To him Bruce was a good actor. So I think what happened was the idea of having his own company, Concord Productions, and everything Bruce did would be through this company, if not equally then a substantial share of it.

Q: Bruce was losing weight near to the end. Do you feel he burned himself out with the demands of filming and the stress that came with all the complications?
Ted Thomas: He was. I was discussing this with another martial arts guy. But certainly he was losing weight but wasn't losing muscle mass because

he was still exercising very regularly. But when he died, a lot of so-called 'wise guys' said it was all the drugs he was taking. I've no way of knowing whether that's true or not because it's hearsay. But I think, in effect, a guy in superb physical condition should not have to go to bed halfway through a dinner party and end up dead.

Q: Do you remember where you were the day Bruce passed away?
Ted Thomas: I was having dinner, at that time I was with the director of public relations for the Royal Hong Kong Police Force. I think the previous day someone committed suicide. It wasn't my main job, I wasn't a public relations man at all back then, I was a broadcaster, a sports broadcaster mainly. But I was put in this position until they found a suitable man for this job. At that time the police were being accused of - quite rightly in fact - corruption. In fact, in the homicide squad the Senior Superintendent was arrested for corruption and sent to jail short after.

I was having dinner with the Commissioner of police, who was a rather tough, very straight Yorkshire man. He hadn't done his early policing in Hong Kong, so he wasn't exposed to corruption like most local expatriate inspectors were. Johnny Sutcliffe had done his early policing in Africa. He had two of the most important cases, including the homicide I mentioned. I had a phone call from one of my Inspectors or Superintendent friends, because I had told them if any news story broke that was likely to end up on television or in newspapers I was to be told about it at once. All enquiries would then be passed on to me, then we would decide what was said about it. So I got a call at Johnny Sutcliffe's house - I can't remember the time now, it was nine or ten at night - and I had to go down to headquarters and start preparing some material. Luckily I did because Bruce Lee had not been reported as walking up and down the garden with Raymond Chow.

Q: Do you feel Bruce Lee in the end achieved the ultimate goal which he had set out to?
Ted Thomas: He was a national hero, not just an actor. I've met a lot of movie stars and I've worked on a lot of movies myself, and they're actors basically, you don't see them as the epitome of a hero of their country. Bruce had achieved a position where he was more than just an actor. He represented hope and improved conditions and reputation for Chinese all over the world. Chinese all over the world were working in substandard positions as house maids, laundry men…all meager jobs were done by Chinese, that was perfectly normal. Bruce's view was: no, we're not going to be like this, we're going to be this, we're going to be people like British, American, German or French or Italians. So he wasn't just a Kung Fu fighter, he was a national hero in many ways. Forty years later he's still a

name, and as I said in a story in the paper yesterday, his former house which had been used as a brothel has been bought by the government and it's going to be a Bruce Lee museum.

Q: After Bruce died, do you feel the media has done its bit to keep his legacy alive?
Ted Thomas: I think they're very decent about it, they didn't do what the tabloid media in England would have done, which is to delve into a few little bits he had on the side. They did subscribe to the legend of Bruce Lee and they built him up in that way. In that respect the media, especially the English media and to lesser extent the more responsible Chinese-language media, were prepared to make him their Lord Nelson or Lord Wellington of China, not just Hong Kong. Of course, Hong Kong wasn't part of China at that time.

Q: Had Bruce lived, what path do you think his career would have taken?
Ted Thomas: People often make the mistake of mixing up the person and the character who comes across on the screen, who's not necessarily a great actor but becomes a great movie star. Very few of the great movie stars were great actors by the way, they were themselves. For example, John Wayne and Clark Gable, you could never see John Wayne of being a pedophile or drug addict, he was always a big husky hero, a man's man, a two-fisted, hard-hitting American guy in same way Clark Gable was. Then you get a really good actor, I suppose someone like Robert DeNiro, he could do any part. He could do a priest in one movie and the next part he could be a savage killer. I think in this respect, Bruce did not have the range of acting skills to be able to do that sort of thing. He was just 'Bruce Lee the hero' and I think it could have taken him a long time, if he could possibly achieve it, to develop into a great movie actor, he was never that.

Q: Do you feel he would have got involved in more American productions after Enter the Dragon?
Ted Thomas: Absolutely. Once he had achieved international fame he was looking over his shoulder at going back and establishing movies with Chinese storylines and Chinese settings. But, of course, Hollywood was and still is the center of all movie making, that's where 90 percent of the world's movies that have international distribution come out of.

Q: Anything significant you would like to share after Bruce died?
Ted Thomas: Well, I suppose it has to be the way his son was killed, and that was an accident on the set. And anybody who knows anything about firearms knows that a blank cartridge of any revolver or rifle is not really

a blank. If you hold it within two inches of your face and pull the trigger, a sharp blast comes from the cartridge and is carried to your face at about a thousand miles per hour, and that's how he was killed. They said they substituted a real bullet without a cartridge, but that wasn't true at all. I know a bit about firearms, and all that hassle about (a real bullet) was American tabloids suggesting it was done by the Triads and people who wanted to destroy the Bruce Lee legend. Then there's been occasional attempts to create another Bruce Lee, someone looking like Bruce. There's a lot of lookalikes by the way, movie extras in Hong Kong with the hairstyle and the attributes in martial arts. To this day, he's a very admired person and a role model. I think to be fair to the media here, they've more or less kept out of the bad media and headed towards positive side of his life.

Q: Did you ever visit him at his house and socialize with him?
Ted Thomas: If he had a charity event or something, where you needed some movie star to turn up because you were collecting money for a home for blind babies or disadvantaged children, he would give his time to that very generously. A lot of movie stars nowadays, I won't mention any names, want to attend but they'd be looking at $100,000 for a ten-minute appearance.

Q: When was the last time you spoke to or saw Bruce, was it at the time he was getting ready to promote Enter the Dragon?
Ted Thomas: I suppose about a month or two before he died. I had the feeling it was a movie he wasn't happy with, there was a rumor he was having director problems. I don't know but it's hearsay. I was never on the set watching him having problems. But he had reached a stage like a lot of actors, he realized people are paying to see a movie and they're paying to see Bruce Lee. I might go see Robert De Niro or someone like that of caliber, people have heroes even if some of them are the worst actors in the world, but you go and see them. He had his following, which was not necessarily focused on his ability as an actor.

Q: In your opinion, do you think Bruce Lee had to go to America to achieve the success he ultimately did on a global basis?
Ted Thomas: I don't think he had to but then I think he got a bit of fanfare. Obviously, there's so many actors in Hong Kong, but he was one Chinese, if you like, in a massive industry where 99.9 percent were Caucasians. So he was something different there (US), and as something different, if you were a Chinese watching an American movie with a Chinese in it you'd be attracted to the idea. Again, he would need to stand out from every other expatriate, Caucasian or European, so he was very different in America.

That's how he was noticed. Again, he was never a great actor by any stretch of the imagination. But he knew if he went back once he was established, and everybody agrees with this, he was the most famous Chinese person in the world, including Mao Tsung and all the great politicians. Bruce Lee was the 'name' on everybody's lips. If you want to talk Chinese success, he could've gone back to Hollywood with really talented producers and directors, surrounding supporting actors and scriptwriters who could have made much more impression.

Q: Being a regular at Golden Harvest did you meet Chuck Norris when he was filming Way of the Dragon?
Ted Thomas: I met Chuck Norris several times, yes. I mean, most of the times I saw Bruce sitting watching movies and whenever he came into the dubbing studio it was because he wanted someone to chat to.

Q: Can you talk about the time you interviewed him for the radio after his first movie Big Boss smashed the box office records?
Ted Thomas: Without being bitchy about it, Bruce had developed into an arrogant person. As they say: fame takes to different people in different ways. He had only made three or four movies and really began to think he was God's gift to acting in the movie business. He justified feeling that because he certainly had become the most famous Chinese in the world, and he was a bankable star. If you had him play the lead you were going to sell a lot of tickets, more than if you would use someone else who was around at the time, I don't know, Jackie Chan or somebody like that. There were successful Chinese before but there weren't any that helped Westernize. He appealed to both audiences, the Western and the Asian audiences.

Q: There seem to have been rumors circulating in Hong Kong when he was alive about challenges to fight. Were these made up?
Ted Thomas: No, I think all Kung Fu actors get that. I think Jackie Chan gets it still. The point is anybody who doesn't know about the movie industry thinks that a Kung Fu fighter who's an actor is going to be the best hand-to-hand combat fighter in the world. As you know, tough guy movie stars have always been challenged in bars in Los Angeles and New York. They get all this, "You're such a tough guy?" and, of course they're not, just because they can portray the hard man. I'll give you an example in the UK, you've got a guy like Vinnie Jones, he's a hard guy anyway, but some actors who act murderers or tough guys are just good actors. But it brings the worst out in people. They want to challenge him when the girlfriend is out (with them). "Who's that guy at the bar? It's Bruce Lee! I'm going to go up there and challenge him." The last thing you want if you're working

in acting is to be in this kind of a situation, because some prat comes over pissed (drunk) and challenging you to a fist fight (Laughs). He did get rather impatient with people like that, yeah.

Q: Final comments on your relationship with Bruce Lee?

Ted Thomas: I knew him well, we greeted each other if we met in bars and restaurants. And he'd come to the dubbing studios just to talk because he wanted contact with people, which he wasn't getting with the Chinese actors, a lot were terribly envious of him. So he would mix with the dubbing crew quite freely. Although people said on the set he was sometimes show-offish, I honestly thing Bruce was more at home with Westernized people because of his Hollywood experience.

There are a lot of phonies around the world today who profess to be his best friend, who probably appeared as an extra in one of his movies (Laughs), as close as that. And that's not just the Caucasians but Chinese as well. It's quite often the case if someone's doing well, it's like, "I'm your friend." I publish books and the amount of people I get coming to me and say they've worked with such a such star and had a relationship with a star. One actor's mistress came to me and she couldn't produce one single photo of the 30 years she claimed they had been together. She's obviously lying and exaggerating.

Bruce brought a revolution, there's no doubt about it. The world started recognizing Chinese movies. Run Run Shaw started filming in Mandarin, Raymond Chow, who originally was working with the Voice of America as a clerk more or less, joined Run. And I think if their relationship got better and they stuck together it would have been better for everyone concerned, but it didn't. I think even at that time Run was 70-something, nobody could envision him living till a hundred. In any case, Raymond would have never been his number two because at the time he was involved with his lady, who later became his wife and who was running the studio practically. He was a significant figure, in fact the primary figure in Chinese movies recognized overseas by Chinese actors and directors, etc. Now Hong Kong is part of China and is capable of making really high-grade movies itself, but before Bruce Lee there was nothing of that quality.

JON T. BENN

He is best known for as the menacing Mafia boss in Bruce Lee's cult classic movie Way of the Dragon. Benn's cocktail party conversation with Golden Harvest producer Raymond Chow led to the role and a friendship with the Little Dragon which would go beyond the confines of the studios. Benn has spent most of his life living in South East Asia, and has appeared in well over 50 movies and TV series. Today, he makes his home in the city of Shanghai where it's not unusual for people to come over to him and ask, "Were you in a movie with Bruce Lee?"

Q: Can you please recall when you got the part in Bruce Lee's Way of the Dragon?
Jon T. Benn: I met Raymond Chow, who was the producer of Way of the Dragon. I met him at a cocktail party in 1971 in Hong Kong. He asked me if I would like to be in a movie with Bruce Lee. I didn't know who Bruce Lee was at the time, but I'd never done a Chinese movie so I said, "Sure, why not?" I lived in Hong Kong for 30 years so I would occasionally see him (Raymond Chow). If we happened to be in the same function we would greet each other.

Q: Was this your first ever experience in the film industry?
Jon T. Benn: Well, I had a small part in Magnificent Seven. I was studying in Mexico at the time. I was riding with two friends, the three of us were horseback riding and we were on the set of Magnificent Seven. Elli Wallach was horse riding and he was passing us, and we got the job.

Q: Can you recall the first day of shooting on Way of the Dragon, did you film in Italy or at Golden Harvest?

Jon T. Benn: All of my days were in Golden Harvest at various lots. I did not go to Rome. Raymond Chow and I came from a meal and he (Bruce) called up saying he had already hired a Big Boss. This was when I was sitting in Raymond's office. Raymond called up Bruce and said we don't need that guy because I've found another one. And they picked me up the next morning at eight o' clock to take me to the studio; that's when I met Bruce and we shook hands. He told me what to say and in 15 minutes we finished the first scene.

Q: Was he a vibrant person?
Jon T. Benn: He was a very fun guy, always laughing and having a good time, and he liked to show off on the set. There were some pretty girls on the set and he liked to flirt, and when we were ready to shoot he was a perfectionist! He made sure that everybody knew what they were doing and we rehearsed a lot, which included the fight scenes. His English was better than his Chinese. He spent so many years in the United States, most of the extras spoke English. His Cantonese wasn't that good, but he was conversing in both languages. Bruce would sing his favorite song and Neilson Larson would play the guitar. We would be having a good time on the set as the lights were being changed, etc. Neilson Larson gave me that guitar.

Q: When the cameras weren't rolling how did he spend the time at break times?
Jon T. Benn: He would show us some kicks. He would kick 500 times on one leg, then he would stand on the other leg and kick 500 times. He could drop down and do 100 push ups on two fingers. He did a lot of hand tricks, he could make coins disappear. He was always very active, non-stop. He loved to show his physique. He was an amazing guy. One of the reasons he passed away was he was non-stop, he would workout on the set on a eight-hour shooting and then he would go home and workout eight hours in his gym which was in the basement of his home. He was active 16 hours a day. And that's what killed him, he was right on the edge all the time.

Q: Any funny incidents on the set which you would like to share with me?
Jon T. Benn: One time when I was in my office, I was standing up and he hits me with his shoulder. He hit me so hard that I fell back and the chair fell back. I did a backward somersault. He said, "Oh, my gosh, I'm sorry," and pulled me up. He didn't know just how strong he was. So for the next take they put a big guy behind the chair just to hold it in case he hit me too hard again.

Q: Were you on the set when they filmed the nunchaku fight scene in the backyard?
Jon T. Benn: Yes, I was standing behind the camera. That scene was cut (originally) in the UK for a long time. I was invited to a Bruce Lee fan club where they, for the first time, showed Way of the Dragon in full uncut version. There were hundreds of people there, there was a line of 200 people waiting in line for my autograph.

Q: How did Bruce Lee choreograph the fight scenes and instruct his co-workers in regards to this?
Jon T. Benn: In the office scenes there were a lot of guys fighting, he put everybody in places and they knew what they were doing. Everybody rehearsed so they don't get hurt because there was a lot of swinging and kicking going on. One Chinese guy who was supposed to get married that afternoon got hit, a friend of mine who was an extra swung at him and the Chinese guy didn't turn his head fast enough so he hit him in the eye. He had the biggest black eye I ever saw. We were all invited to go to the wedding right after filming. He had a big black eye and a swollen lip at the wedding.

Q: How many takes would Bruce Lee do for a typical fight scene?
Jon T. Benn: He called me 'One-Take-Benn' because I was going to do all my takes in one. And as far as the fights go, he choreographed them so well he didn't have to do it many times. Everybody knew what they were doing. He could usually do it in one or two takes. We shot in 16mm with no sound.

Q: Did you see him sitting down jotting down ideas on paper and did he get involved with all aspects of the filming process?
Jon T. Benn: The script was written as we went along, there was no formal script. If he had an idea he wrote it down, and told me and other people what to say. So it was very informal. This was his 'baby', this was his number one and favorite movie, no doubt about it. And he was proud of it. This was his favorite.

Q: Some say you see the real Bruce Lee in the movie. Linda Lee has gone on record to say this too. Did his real personality shine through in this movie?
Jon T. Benn: Yeah, actually Linda said the same thing to me one time. This was his first opportunity to show what he could really do.

Q: Did you witness Chuck Norris and Bruce Lee film the fight scene on the set?

Jon T. Benn: Bruce asked Chuck in Los Angeles. Chuck was one of his students, even though he had retired competing - he was a six-time world Karate champion and had never been defeated - he still learned a lot from Bruce. They were very good friends and very close. I was not on the set, that was all done on the set in Hong Kong and not in the Coliseum in Rome. In the outdoor lot when they were fighting, a lot of the fights with the Korean guy and Bob (Wall) and all the Chinese, he said what we were going to do here and then jump to the next scene. He choreographed everything. I drive down in a red Mercedes which was Bruce's car which he bought the day before. He told me to be very careful as it was his new car, so I was very careful as I drove down the hill.

Q: How did Bruce spend time during break times?
Jon T. Benn: He would just be eating noodles (Laughs). Everybody had pot noodles at breaks and he would talk to everybody, always laughing and telling jokes. He was having fun.

Q: Did you see him working out on the set and displaying his extraordinary skills?
Jon T. Benn: On the set he was non-stop working out. He would punch 500 times, always moving, never stopping. He'd do push ups, stretching, every now and again he had these migraine headaches and he would just collapse on the floor. He'd say, "Oh my God. I've got a headache." Ten minutes later he'd say, "Sorry about that," and he'd be rolling again. That happened several times. That's why he went to Los Angeles, to get experts to check it over but they couldn't find anything wrong with him.

Q: Did Bruce demonstrate his power on the set using a kick shield with Bob Wall or Chuck Norris?
Jon T. Benn: He put a shield on me one time to give me a one-inch punch just to show the people on the set how effective it was. I flew back about five feet. Bob and Chuck knew what they were doing, they knew how to turn and move, etc.

Q: How often did Linda come on the set?
Jon T. Benn: She would bring the kids Shannon and Brandon, not every day but every few days they'd come to watch.

Q: Am I right in saying Bruce said to you he was going to make you famous but not necessarily rich?
Jon T. Benn: Yes, he said that, and it was true! Nearly 35 years later

I'm still recognized in the city of Shanghai, probably every other day somebody walks up to me and says, "Were you in a movie with Bruce Lee?" Because I haven't changed that much, even after 35 years I still look more or less the same. Now I look white, before I was gray (Laughs). One thing I asked him one day, "Hey, Bruce, will I get credit for this movie?" and he said, "Yes, everybody's going to get credit in my movie." When I went to the premiere I saw I didn't have credit, that was not very nice, he did not keep his promise. I went to the premiere with my girlfriend, the theater was packed and it was a red carpet deal with thousands of people outside watching people coming in. I was kind of embarrassed seeing myself on the big screen, but it was something to watch. And afterwards everybody went to a big party - I don't remember where. It was fun, it was like a Hollywood premiere, afterwards the audience stood up and applauded.

Q: Did Bruce have any plans to use you in any future movies?
Jon T. Benn: No, they never talked about it and I never really thought much about it. The last time when I saw Bruce was in the coffee shop in the Hyatt Hotel, I think a day or two before he died. He was with Fred Weintraub. He called me over and introduced me to Fred, and I remember at the time Bruce looked really thin, he did not look healthy at all. I was surprised. He just called me over to introduce me, and I hadn't seen Bruce for a while. They were obviously talking about Enter the Dragon.

Q: What is the most interesting conversation you had with him?
Jon T. Benn: He was a philosopher, he was always writing in his diary. He was one of the smartest guys I ever met, he could talk philosophy, he could talk about goals in life. He was a fantastic guy and the most interesting person I ever met.

Q: He digested knowledge from books which included filmmaking books and was always learning...
Jon T. Benn: I've been to his house where he had a library with thousands of books, if you pull out a book out of the shelf you'd notice everyone of them was underlined, words written in the margins. He read every book and he studied every book, he digested every book. He had thousands of books, I couldn't believe it. He was just an amazing guy, non-stop learning. He had a big gym in the basement with devices that he had made. One had four holes in it, one was big enough for the fist, four fingers, two fingers and one finger. They were very, very sharp metal and he would stick his fist in there, and there would be a shock because it was electrified. So he would punch in there a 100 times just to perfect his aim, if he aimed

wrong he'd cut his arm, finger or hand, so he would pull it out fast. That's how he got so fast.

Q: Did he talk to you about what he was ultimately trying to achieve within the scope of the film industry?
Jon T. Benn: We would talk about various things, he was very upset, of course, about not getting the David Carradine part for the Kung Fu series in America. He was supposed to have that part but at that time, in the 70s, Hollywood would not take to Oriental actors so they put David Carradine and put a little makeup on his eyes, and Bruce was very upset about that. His whole vision was to show the world the Chinese should be proud of themselves. I think he was really the one who made Chinese proud of themselves, before they were working in laundries. He was the little Chinese guy who takes on the gwailos - the white guys - and beats them, and every Chinese guy in the world at that moment became proud of himself. It was very significant.

Q: How did you find out about his death?
Jon T. Benn: I happen to be walking down the street in Kowloon and I just saw the newspaper with big headlines 'BRUCE LEE DIES'. I was totally shocked like everybody and couldn't believe it. I was in Hong Kong at the time. He was certainly very famous there, he could not walk down the street without having hundreds of people around him asking for autographs. I had a beach house on the island, he used come over just to get away from the crowds, he couldn't walk down the street. I traveled a lot all over the world, out of curiosity I've asked women and old ladies if they've heard of Bruce Lee, everybody I've talked to has heard of Bruce Lee. He's famous all around the world!

Q: Tell me about the Bruce Lee Cafe in Hong Kong which you opened.
Jon T. Benn: I had a number of his items and I worked with Media Asia, who had rights to all his films except Enter the Dragon. We had a lot of the original posters and photographs. I put them all together and made a museum, I had a three-story building with a very large bar downstairs and a restaurant upstairs and a swimming pool on the top. We made it into a museum and had the menus like in Fist of Fury. We made it a fun thing and it was very colorful with all the posters and nunchaku and different things in plastic cases. It was a combination of cafe and museum.

We had over 20,000 people come from all over the world. We had 200 items, six scrapbooks full of articles, over 200 publications from all over the world doing stories about the museum. 28 TV crews came from different countries to film there including the BBC and channels from Japan. I'm doing interviews all the time and, of course, the Japanese were the biggest ones, big crews of bus loads of Japanese tourists would come over. All the young girls loved it. I'm having my picture taken with them and it was great and a lot of fun (Laughs).

Q: Did Bruce give you any items?
Jon T. Benn: He gave me a set of his nunchaku.

Q: Finally, anything you would like to add?
Jon T. Benn: For me, it was an honor to know him and be able to be in the movie with him. Because as we were making the movie I realized just how great a guy he was, it was a real pleasure to do that. I didn't make much money out of it but it certainly made me famous around the world. I mean, here I am doing interviews 35 years later.

ING-SIK WHANG

I ng-Sik Whang is one of the foremost Korean Hapkido masters in the world. Contracted to Golden Harvest studios in the early 70s to train actors, in 1972 Whang was invited to appear in Lee's third movie Way of the Dragon. He moved to Canada, where he is currently based, in 1976. In this very rare interview, the Korean master recalls his experiences working on the classic movie and his friendship with the greatest action movie star of all time.

Q: Master Whang, could you please highlight your martial arts background prior to meeting and working with Bruce Lee?
Ing-Sik Whang: I started martial arts when I was 14 years old, so it's been over 50 years. Whether it's Korean, Japanese or Chinese martial arts, the root of your martial arts is very important. Martial artists were stubborn and very concentrated in one-dimensional thought, they do not move around. Those martial artists are proud of the martial art they're involved in and they never mix two different martial arts together. One martial art is not inferior to the other, for cultural reasons I stuck to only one martial art. These martial artists learn from one grandmaster or teacher and see him as a father. Just as sons cannot replace their fathers, martial artists do not replace their teacher or master. That's why I learned Hapkido and stuck with Hapkido, and I still study Hapkido.

Q: When and where did your first meeting take place with Bruce Lee?
Ing-Sik Whang: Bruce Lee came from the United States and became very successful with Golden Harvest production company. The company invited me to become an instructor for martial artists. I was not invited as an actor, but as a martial arts instructor and action director. I was introduced to Bruce Lee with the same company I was affiliated with. I cannot remember exactly when I first met him in

Hong Kong, but I believe I met him right after the first Bruce Lee movie (Big Boss) was made.

Q: How did you get involved in Way of the Dragon and was it Bruce Lee's suggestion to use you?

Ing-Sik Whang: I was affiliated with the same company. I really didn't want to star in movies. However, Golden Harvest wanted me to star in the movie as a special guest. They added me into the script as the movie was filming, as a special guest. I was published in a lot of newspapers in Hong Kong as a martial artist and I had a big-name value as a martial artist. I think Bruce Lee asked for me to be part of the movie for the name value, because in movies you want somebody who's famous. At that time in Hong Kong martial arts movies were becoming big and they wanted big names such as Chuck Norris and Kareem Abdul-Jabbar - the NBA player - because they would be good actors and good for the movie business. Those people who star in the movies become superstars. Those people like Chuck Norris and Kareem Abdul-Jabbar, and those starring in the movies, they end up ruining their career. The reason I accepted the role was because it was a Golden Harvest company project to whom I was affiliated with.

Q: Can we talk about the fight choreography between you and Bruce Lee?

Ing-Sik Whang: Bruce Lee was a passionate and famous movie star. In the movies the value of his martial art comes from the Chinese Kung Fu. Prior to Bruce Lee no one had ever kicked like Bruce Lee. Imagine where he learned how to kick like that, because there was no such martial art in Hong Kong. If you research all the movies prior to Bruce Lee's movies, and see how they kick, you'll realize the difference. Kung Fu is usually used, and some swords. But Bruce Lee incorporated the kicks in his movies. Prior to him there was no such (style of) kicking in Hong Kong movies. Kicking came from the Korean martial art and he changed the Chinese Kung Fu. It was not Korean martial art before that, it depends on how one can evaluate Bruce Lee's martial art or other martial arts. I'm happy that Bruce Lee's impact was felt the way martial arts became famous. I honor Bruce Lee because he made martial arts famous around the world.

Q: On the film set did you make time to workout using kicking shields, etc?

Ing-Sik Whang: Prior to filming we used a lot of kicking shields to practice and we practiced with targets. Because he was not just a movie star but he was a martial artist, and we used real martial arts and not just choreography. I brought joint locks, kicking and punching into the Jackie Chan movie which I did later. Truthfully, what he wanted to do was martial arts on a practical level. When you saw Chinese movies you saw actors and actresses flying around with swords, he wanted to bring real martial arts into movies. It's not just one person attacking and beating someone up, but rather how do you defend when the other person is attacking you or counter-attacking you? He really tried hard to incorporate that in his movies. And in his movies, rather than making a movie beautiful in terms of articulating or stretching the reality, he wanted to bring the reality into the movies - real martial arts.

Q: How much of concentrated effort did Bruce put in this movie, which he was directing, producing and acting in? Would you say he was a perfectionist?
Ing-Sik Whang: Before Bruce Lee, there was no person who was as passionate about movies. He wanted to bring out his personal best. He did a lot of weight training, working on his speed and agility, messing and joking around. Because he was quite short, sometimes he wore high heels to cover his height. I believe stars such as Jackie Chan, Steven Seagal, Sylvester Stallone, Dean Martin and Steve McQueen, once they become famous in the media they become like a balloon in the air, you never know when it's going to come down. They have this anxiety. I'm not one of them. I believe when they become too stressed or scared...Bruce often would call me in the middle of the night for a drink.

These stars cannot show that side of them to other people, because they are heroes of Hong Kong, China and Asia. In reality the Asian star is very small in terms of body size. Sometimes those stars are weaker than normal people, more lonely, especially Bruce Lee. His friends in the past used to call him 'Big Boss' and he started to lose friends as well. He called them friends but in reality he believed that they weren't truly his friends, because he was a foreigner as well. So when he started to get lonely he used to give me a call.

Q: Did Bruce Lee ask you to be in Game of Death, the movie which was going to propagate the major defining aspect of his martial arts philosophy?
Ing-Sik Whang: Yes, Bruce Lee asked me to star in this movie. I don't remember clearly, but in the movie there were different stages as Bruce Lee increased the level of difficulty of his enemies, they got progressively harder and harder. And I was in one stage where I would be fighting Bruce Lee, but I don't recall because it's been a very long time, but it was in one of the latter tougher stages. Before I was able to star in the movie, Bruce Lee passed away.

Q: Bruce Lee was going to use many other gifted martial artists and actors in this movie. Did he dispense any information to you in regards to who else he was going to utilize?

Ing-Sik Whang: I don't remember clearly but I know he was using NBA star Kareem Abdul-Jabbar. As for other martial artists, I don't remember clearly. Whilst I was asked to be in the movie, I was filming another movie. I was part of the casting but I never stepped my foot in the production process. I did visit the set once or twice and exercised and fooled around with Bruce Lee, but was never there when they were shooting.

Q: What was Bruce like as a person?

Ing-Sik Whang: Bruce Lee really loved Korean barbeque. He used to always bring orange juice in a cooler, and drove a Mercedes Benz sports car. Because Hong Kong was so hot back in those days, he used to drink orange juice. Hong Kong was Bruce Lee's hometown and he was very successful there. However, despite his fame, money and honor he didn't have too many people around him to share this. He was lonely so he always talked to me.

Q: Did you ever visit him at home?

Ing-Sik Whang: Bruce Lee always called me and we would go outside, but I never visited his house. When I was in Hong Kong shooting movies I always stayed in hotels.

Q: How would you describe his personality?

Ing-Sik Whang: He was a very sharp person. As one can see from his action in the movies, he was good at incorporating a lot of other martial arts into his own. Bruce Lee either studied psychology or philosophy, he was a major in one of these. He wasn't a calm person, he was a quick person, he was a wise person.

Q: Were you on the set when they were filming the double nunchaku scene in Way of the Dragon?

Ing-Sik Whang: The nunchaku Bruce Lee used comes from Philippines, and he articulated it in a way where he made it his own. People who use sticks in their martial arts are brilliant, he used it in a way where he made it his own and he adapted things and tried to incorporate everything in his Kung Fu. People who studied one style of martial arts, these masters devote themselves to one art, in a way they had a strange feeling about Bruce Lee. However, on the other hand they were glad Bruce Lee allowed martial arts to become famous around the globe. I don't remember being on the set when that scene was done.

Q: What is the most interesting conversation you ever had with Bruce Lee?

Ing-Sik Whang: We had common conversations. Bruce Lee always talked to me about the other martial arts such as Tae Kwon Do, Karate and Hapkido. He said there were too much exaggerated movements which weren't realistic. So he said, "Why not practice hard?" And that way I made an agreement and all the time we would go practice on the targets.

Q: Was Bruce an inventive person when it came to fight choreography?

Ing-Sik Whang: He was inventive because he incorporated a lot of different martial arts and made it his own.

Q: After appearing in the Bruce Lee movie and having known him for a number of years, how much of an impact did he have on you?

Ing-Sik Whang: Of course, a lot of impact on me! There were a lot of rumors, one such rumor was that somebody beat him to death. Since we worked with the same company, I was very uncomfortable about these. He was a successful actor and a very successful martial artist.

CHAPLIN CHANG

Chaplin Chang was hired by Golden Harvest to go to Italy with the cast and crew of Bruce Lee's directorial debut Way of the Dragon. His next project with Lee would be as assistant director on the global blockbuster Enter the Dragon, which propelled Bruce Lee to superstardom soon after his untimely death. Mr. Chang was an integral part of the crew and played major roles as a crew member on the Bruce Lee films he was involved in. His recollections and insights are refreshing and intriguing.

Q: The first movie you worked on with Bruce Lee was Way of the Dragon on which you were the production manager, is this correct?
Chaplin Chang: I wasn't working with Raymond Chow at the time but with another film company called King Hu Production. This was one of the big Chinese film companies. Hu directed some big movies. I was the manager of that company. Raymond Chow asked me to help him and go to Italy for Way of the Dragon. At the time when he asked me, I did not even know Bruce Lee. Raymond Chow introduced me, and that was only a brief meeting. Then after we reached Rome, we started our conversations. Before we went to Rome I didn't have any real conversation with Bruce Lee. Actually, because I was so busy I didn't go to the movies or pay attention to the movie world. So when Raymond Chow introduced me to Bruce Lee, I didn't even know who he was (Laughs).

Q: Was it difficult shooting at the Rome airport? Is it true you had to shoot between 45 to 60 different setups?
Chaplin Chang: It wasn't hard, we had a lot of shots but it wasn't that difficult.

Q: After you finished the first day of shooting, did you typically go to dinner and wind down with the cast and crew?

Chaplin Chang: Normally we did have dinners after work, but for that particular day I can't remember. I think that particular day there was something different because Chuck Norris was arriving that day. We had to shoot at the airport as he enters, at the same time. We waited for Chuck Norris to come out of the plane in the airport hall, he was to come out much later than other passengers. So he came out by himself. That was prearranged. Of course, he had Robert (Bob) Wall with him.

Q: So Chuck Norris arrived in Rome when the crew was already there filming?
Chaplin Chang: I remember when Robert came with Chuck Norris. Bruce wasn't expecting him to come, and Bruce didn't ask him to come. It seems that Bruce did talk to me about this. When he arrived in the evening, Bruce talked to me about how he wasn't happy about Robert Wall. At the time I didn't know who Chuck Norris and Robert Wall were. Bruce did talk to me about how he wasn't happy about Robert Wall coming. Later on, it was said that Robert Wall paid his own airfare to come.

Q: Tell me about scouting locations in Rome and the places you visited.
Chaplin Chang: We went to the Leaning Tower of Pisa - this was before the shooting - and we went up the tower. During the filming we didn't really go to places other than the ones where we were shooting. When we went to the Pisa Tower, Nora (Miao) wasn't there, it was Bruce Lee, Raymond, myself and the cameraman (Tadashi) Nishomoto. He (Nishomoto) was the one who was responsible for Hong Kong film industry starting with color films, he was good.

Q: Were you on location for three weeks or was it much longer than that?
Chaplin Chang: Yes, I was there for three weeks. The shooting was for two weeks but I stayed there for one extra week for my own personal time. The things that I remember the most is the Vatican, and I watched a film which was shot by a lady film director. I don't remember her name but she was an Italian film director. That film was very impressive to me because I didn't know the Italian language but I could laugh with all the other audience all along, it was very impressive.

Q: Did any actual filming take place at the Roman Coliseum?
Chaplin Chang: We shot there, we went there very early before the tourists came in. We started the shooting, and at the same time we shot a lot of still photographs which would help us to make the studio back in Hong Kong.

Q: Were there any hurdles in getting permission to shoot at the Coliseum?

Chaplin Chang: We didn't get the permission, we went in there like tourists. Before that we went to a water fountain and shot there. We pretended to be tourists; we had the camera, lighting equipment and everything and packed it in bags. Each one of us, including Bruce, came there with bags and we just paid the entrance fee to go in there. We talked to the guards inside and they said, "OK, but don't bring the camera out until you're ready to shoot." So we rehearsed and when we were ready we got the camera out, then told them we were ready to shoot and then we would disappear.

Q: Did you shoot any actual fight scenes in Rome or were they all done back at the Golden Harvest studios in Hong Kong?

Chaplin Chang: They did have a couple of fights, a few shots but most of them were shot in the studio. So we did film a few shots in the Coliseum but most were done at the Golden Harvest studio.

Q: Was Betty Ting Pei on location? There are some photographs of her on the set of Way of the Dragon.

Chaplin Chang: Betty Ting Pei was not involved in that film, she wasn't involved with any of Bruce Lee's films, although Bruce was prepared to have her in one of his future films, but he passed away.

Q: What was Nora Miao like?

Chaplin Chang: Well, they were very close and very friendly.

Q: In Rome were there any Caucasians involved in the movie?

Chaplin Chang: Yes, we had one location manager who was very tall and a big guy, who was working as a location manger. He also played the bank manager in the film.

Q: What was Bruce Lee's relationship like with Raymond Chow at the time?

Chaplin Chang: Well, it was kind of an 'on and off' thing. If things didn't go Bruce Lee's way they would be shouting, cursing, swearing. Raymond had a way of angering him. When Bruce calmed down, Raymond would then start to reason with him. But in a way Bruce did depend on Raymond and Raymond depended on Bruce. They equally needed each other. Had Bruce not appeared at Golden Harvest they would have been bankrupt. Bruce didn't know much about the film business and industry in Hong Kong, so he needed Raymond. One day he wanted to become a producer himself but he still needed to learn.

Q: What major role did you play as a crew member on Bruce Lee's masterpiece Enter the Dragon?
Chaplin Chang: On Enter the Dragon I was the assistant director. Actually, I started reading the script and breaking it down, making the budget and then working as assistant director.

Q: Who did you work closely with?
Chaplin Chang: I worked with Robert Clouse and Charles Lowe (cameraman), who at the time was introduced to me by Roy Chiao. Roy Chiao was a very good friend of mine and in the film he played the master monk to Bruce Lee. Roy Chiao told me Charles Lowe had just come to Hong Kong and needed a job. At that time he told me that Charles Lowe was working as a cameraman. In the beginning there was no need for a second camera, so I took him in and asked him to go into the camera department and get involved with the people, so there's no problem to work as a second cameraman. Later on he was given the job as second cameraman.

Q: When Bruce was rehearsing and shooting in the dungeon how did Bruce keep pumped up and in shape?
Chaplin Chang: He didn't really do anything, he was always active. There were people who wanted to do particular physical things before the fights, he didn't do that.

Q: Any behind the scenes stories when the cameras were not rolling?
Chaplin Chang: He would be joking around. Most of the time when we were shooting one of the big fights, at one of the places, the time that we had to spare was lunchtime. I went with Robert Clouse and the rest of the American crew to the Bay Hotel for lunch, but Bruce insisted on staying on location eating out of a lunch box together with the other fighters and crew.

Q: What was Jim Kelly like to work with?
Chaplin Chang: Jim Kelly was brought in by Robert Clouse. When he went on the set, somehow something had happened, at one time he was sick or something. So he stopped filming for more than a week. At the time when it happened, we didn't know what had happened.

Q: Did you ever visit Bruce at his house?
Chaplin Chang: Yes. Personally, I wasn't into fighting or anything like that (Laughs). Usually when the work is finished I go home. I don't get involved with people getting together having a drink. I went to his house, in the sitting room. Bruce was always active, he threw a punch so fast and his fist stopped about half an inch from my nose - very good control!

Q: How often did Raymond Chow visit the set?

Chaplin Chang: He would come sometimes and watch and he'd be talking to Bruce, which I didn't get involved in. I don't know what they talked about, but there was once when something wasn't going Bruce's way and he exploded, shouted and so forth, and asked me to get Raymond Chow. So I went down to the office, there was some distance from the location to the office. I said to Raymond that Bruce Lee wanted to see him and that he was shouting and so forth. Raymond didn't go right away, he waited till Bruce would be calm and cooled down, then he would talk to him. The way it appeared to me, at that time, when Bruce Lee saw Raymond it was like a little boy sees his mother, that's the feeling I got. When Raymond had come down Bruce was already calm. It appeared to me, but I don't know how other people may have looked at it, it was like a little boy who had done something and he wanted his mother and the mother came.

Q: Was it difficult shooting the scenes on the boats?

Chaplin Chang: Because the space was so small the scene was difficult to setup, and the ship was swaying.

Q: It's been common knowledge that Bruce didn't get on with the screenwriter Michael Allin. Did Bruce have problems with the scriptwriter?

Chaplin Chang: I was involved with Enter the Dragon from the very beginning, which included reading the script. What I mean by this is, when Raymond got the script from Fred Weintraub he didn't read it, but asked me to read it. So I read it and I told him that this couldn't be shot in Hong Kong - the original script wasn't quite fit for Hong Kong. In the beginning it was called Blood and Steel, and by the end they'd changed the storyline all along. Bob Clouse, and I think with Raymond as well as with Bruce Lee, talked about the changes. I think Bruce Lee did give a lot of suggestions to Robert Clouse.

Q: What was Bruce Lee's working relationship like with the director Robert Clouse?

Chaplin Chang: Quite good, quite good. Bruce Lee wasn't that easy to handle, but I think Robert Clouse worked quite well with him. At one point, there was a fight scene between Bruce and Robert Wall. Robert Wall was using two broken bottles which Bruce Lee was supposed to kick out of his hands, but Bruce got injured. I was there and watched it. So right away I took Bruce Lee, with Wu Ngan - who is now in England - to hospital. But afterwards Bruce was very angry with Robert Wall! And he said, "I want to kill him." Whether he said it and meant it or not, I don't know. Robert Clouse said he wanted to do something to calm things down.

He said, "We still have shots left and we need Robert Wall in the story, so we cannot kill him" (Laughs).

Q: Did Bruce get involved in other aspects of the movie besides the action?
Chaplin Chang: For this film he wasn't the director, although he was very close with Robert Clouse on the fight scenes. He would try to do his best but he didn't really see the camera, the men behind the cameras were Robert Clouse and Gil Hubbs, the cameraman.

Q: How fast was Bruce Lee and did you really had to speed the camera up to capture the dynamics of his actions?
Chaplin Chang: Yes, in some cases we needed to speed it up.

Q: How would you describe Bruce Lee's working relationship with the stunt guys?
Chaplin Chang: One special group was working very close with him, someone named Ching-Ying Lam, who is a famous stuntman, was working closely with Bruce Lee. When Bruce Lee fights in the first scene, he was more or less choreographing with him, at home and on the set.

Q: Do you remember Jackie Chan, who was one of the stuntmen on the set?
Chaplin Chang: He was nobody, nobody knew him. I'll tell you a story. As I mentioned earlier, I was the manger of King Hu Film Productions, and at the time we were shooting two films side by side and we used a lot of stunts. And Jackie Chan - at that time he wasn't called Jackie Chan - came to King Hu and said he needed money, so can we give him more jobs? So Hu told him, "If you want a job as a stuntman, and in the scenes if you show your face and you die, you cannot work anymore in the film. If you want to work I'll give you more work but we cannot show your face." And he agreed. On the film, The Valiant Ones, he was working for nearly 30 days, which is very rare for a stuntman.

Q: I have come across something which said Bruce Lee filmed more footage in the mirror room. Is this true?
Chaplin Chang: In the beginning of the film the scene with Sammo Hung, that was the part which was shot when the American crew was gone. It's possible he shot more in the mirror room because the mirror room was still there and there were shots of him...it's possible. Charles Lowe told me that when Bruce was shooting the extra scene, every day he would drink a lot of Vitasoy, which is a juice made from soya beans. Charles Lowe was the cameraman when the America crew went back. Each day Bruce would

order several cases, each case had 12 bottles. Bruce said it was very nutritious. When they were shooting and they cut, he would drink this, and all the time he was drinking it. I believe you may have noticed in the scene where he's fighting Sammo Hung, he was very skinny, he's sort of not himself. At the time I think he himself must have built his physique from getting low in weight. I was shocked watching the beginning part of the film, he was not the Bruce Lee I saw.

Q: Did the majority of the filming of Enter the Dragon take place on the tennis courts and the studio?
Chaplin Chang: All the fight scenes where people are doing the martial arts so forth were on the tennis courts.

Q: When Bruce Lee had his dialogue scenes what was your impression of him as an actor, and did he have to do many takes?
Chaplin Chang: The film was shot in English and he was well-versed in English. Although some people said he had a Chinese accent. But to us it's all English.

Q: What is the most interesting conversation you had with Bruce during your working relationship?
Chaplin Chang: The most interesting one was when we were in Rome. Raymond had left for Hong Kong, and I think about two days after Raymond had left Bruce asked me to call Raymond. So I called him. I let him talk and walked to the side, and they were talking and later on in the conversation it became louder and louder, swearing in English and Cantonese, it was shocking. And when the phone hung up he talked to me and cursed Raymond. He said Raymond promised to send him San Chin, who was an actor who was in his two previous films.

Bruce wrote the script in Way of the Dragon with San Chin in mind. He put his name in the script because he wanted him to be in the picture. When Raymond went back to Hong Kong he said he'll send San Chin to Rome, but when Bruce was talking to him over the phone Raymond told him something along the lines of San Chin was busy or something. To Bruce, Raymond was playing certain games with him, politics or whatever. He sent San Chin to Lo Wei because Lo Wei was going to shoot a film in Japan, and at that time Lo Wei and Bruce Lee weren't on good terms. So Bruce Lee was very, very angry about that. He told me, "Chaplin, Raymond didn't give me what I deserve, so that's why I wanted to organize and set up a company, Concord (Productions), myself."

MALISA LONGO

When Bruce Lee was in Rome scouting locations and shooting for his directorial debut Way of the Dragon, he happened to see a photo of a young model named Malisa Longo in a magazine. He contacted her agent and offered a role in the film. Although the part was a minor one, Malisa is still known worldwide as the 'Italian beauty' in one of Bruce Lee's greatest films. Malisa, who still lives in Italy, talks about working with the iconic action film star.

Q: How did you get the part in Way of the Dragon with Bruce Lee?
Malisa Longo: My agent introduced me to him via some pictures. But he already had seen me in a picture in a magazine, I don't remember which one.

Q: How would you describe Bruce Lee's personality?
Malisa Longo: I didn't know who he was before I met him, so I didn't know what his real personality was like. But from my knowledge, he had two personalities: one on the set, one after shooting, at relaxing time. When I met him in Italy, I didn't realize who he was. In Italy he was nobody and totally unknown (apart from people who loved martial arts). Honestly, I had doubts about working in that film, because the role which was offered to me was too small. At that time I had already participated in many films, mostly in leading roles. Bruce Lee was very involved on Way of the Dragon because other than the acting, he was also the producer. So on the set he was very touchy and strict, not only with actors but with himself too. The film was shot in nearly two weeks on location, and every scene was shot running from one location to another location, so we didn't have too much time.

He didn't want to spend too much money outside of the budget, so he wanted to save every single penny. Nevertheless, he desired the best and more expensive locations. At the end he had everything he wanted. Really, he made miracles. For example, Bruce Lee got to shoot on location at the Roman Coliseum, where it is impossible to shoot, both back then and still to this day.

Q: Is it true the scene you filmed in the hotel room was cut in the final film?
Malisa Longo: The scene we filmed in the hotel room was quite long. They cut it out in the editing to protect Bruce Lee's image. At that time but I think still now, Asian and American market films were very pure. I think Bruce Lee made the choice. In my opinion, he cut the scenes because the film was intended for family viewing. The nude hotel room love scene could damage the positive image of Bruce Lee, since his career had started. His image leaned towards a good, pure man who defends the weak people but is always ready to combat the bad men, in the name of justice, with the only weapon he had: perfect knowledge of martial arts. He wanted to create his own style. Don't forget that he was very ambitious.

Q: How was Nora Miao to work with?
Malisa Longo: I never really had much to do with her. She was very reserved. After she finished work on the set she always disappeared. I didn't know if it was from shyness or for the difficulty of communication between each other. My English was very bad and I was shy too.

Q: How was Bruce Lee to work with on the set?
Malisa Longo: He was very professional. I didn't have to read the script because the only script he had was in the Chinese language. And sometimes he changed dialogue. He had all the complete script in his own mind. During the shooting he explained my part to me, so when I shot the Piazza Navona scene I was ready. Because the production team didn't have permission to shoot there, we rehearsed and filmed the scene only one time, without any problem or the need to shoot a second take. It was not the same for the scene in the hotel room. Bruce was very nervous and electric, as you can see in every frame of the scene. Anyway, with me Bruce was very gentle and sweet, even if he was shy because of my bursting out appeal. That's the way I am, this voluptuous 'Italian beauty'! Aren't I?

Q: Did you socialize off-set?
Malisa Longo: Yes. Many times in the evenings when we finished shooting we went to dinner together in a Chinese restaurant, along with most of the production team and the other actors.

Q: What conversations did you engage in with Bruce regarding movies and life in general?
Malisa Longo: General conversations. Even when he was with many other people he was always seeking my eyes. I know I liked him very much.

Q: When Bruce Lee died and his films started to play in Italian cinemas, what was the reaction there?
Malisa Longo: When he died the success of martial arts films increased, so Bruce's death made his films a great box office success. So everybody knew him immediately. And he started to become a legend.

Q: Any last words on Bruce Lee?
Malisa Longo: His death is still a mystery. The media have written many things about him. The one which I think is true is that he was killed.

ANDRE MORGAN

Former Golden Harvest executive Andre Morgan was the first Westerner to be involved in the production of Asian martial arts films. He worked closely with Bruce Lee, who at the time was the most popular personality in South East Asia. Morgan was promoted from office boy to producer within three months of arriving in Hong Kong. He would later take his skills to Hollywood, producing the Martial Law TV series and many other movies which appealed to both the Western and the Eastern audiences.

Q: When did you start working at the Golden Harvest film studios in Hong Kong and when did you meet Bruce Lee?
Andre Morgan: I joined Golden Harvest studios in the summer of 1972. Bruce Lee had already made his first two films for Golden Harvest, Big Boss and Fist of Fury. Those were the first two Bruce Lee movies. I met Bruce Lee the week after I joined Golden Harvest, when he returned from location shooting in Rome for the movie that became known as Return of the Dragon. And actually, I went on to work on that movie with Bruce Lee and Chuck Norris for all the filming they did in Hong Kong. In Return of the Dragon, Bruce Lee has the climatic fight with Chuck Norris in the Coliseum in Rome, which we actually rebuilt on the sound stages of Golden Harvest in Hong Kong. That was in the summer of 1972, and we released the movie at Christmas time of the same year.

And then I went to work with Bruce Lee on preparing for the shooting for Game of Death. After we shot that for a month, a decision was made to put it on hold. We prepared to shoot our co-production Enter the Dragon. I was the line producer on Enter the Dragon for Golden Harvest, which we shot as a co-production with Warner Brothers, starting in January of 1973. We started shooting in March of 1973, then we went back to work on shooting for Game of Death.

Q: Did you have discussions pertaining to the plotline of Game of Death with Bruce?

Andre Morgan: You have to understand his goal and his intentions, all the way along, were to build one success and one strength to the next. If you look at the evolution of Bruce Lee, both as an actor and in the filmic sense, what he was showing about the world of martial arts, he was progressively trying to expand both directions at the same time. First, the introduction to the world with Big Boss, which is a fairly straightforward and simple story in which he co-stars, to Fist of Fury which was written and designed as a vehicle for Bruce specifically as a star, and it showcased his martial arts skills. He also changed the way Hong Kong cinema was portraying martial arts on the screen. And with the success of Fist of Fury, obviously he tested his wings as a director and a martial arts choreographer in doing Return of the Dragon. He also started to call on his friends who were also exceptional martial artists.

Ultimately, the goal was to make bigger and more complex and more intense films. Enter the Dragon was the beginning of his transition into Hollywood, but by no means was it going to be the end of Hollywood for him. And Game of Death was to be an exploration of the strength and weaknesses of various schools of martial arts. Also to show what a young student of martial arts would learn in that progressive journey to what we called, in those days, 'The Tower of Death' culminating in a fight that now everybody knows and has seen between Bruce and Kareem Abdul-Jabbar. Unfortunately, beyond shooting some of these fighting scenes, we didn't have the opportunity to go back and shoot rest of the story which would have played out what the journey was and the progression to getting to 'The Tower of Death'.

Q: There is some footage of Dan Inosanto fighting outside of the pagoda - among other outtakes - can you shed some light on this intriguing footage that never originally made it to the film, which was eventually completed some years after Bruce's death?

Andre Morgan: Yeah, I knew very much about this because I ultimately ended up producing the final version of what became Game of Death. The problem was very simple: we didn't have enough footage with Bruce Lee in it that would allow us to tie those scenes together. And after talking to the distributors and exhibitors around the world, we gave those distributors the option of releasing the footage in the form of a documentary or releasing it in the form of a reworked story using the footage that existed. The collective wisdom back then, 30 years ago, was that the audience of the world would prefer to see the footage that existed in the context of a story and not see it as documentary footage.

Now, in fairness to the distributors and exhibitors of the 1970s, I don't

237

think anybody at that point in time realized what a cult figure Bruce Lee was destined to become. These were the early days immediately after his death, and before he managed to become part of the youth culture around the world. It was over a period of 20 years since his death in 1973, that all the myths and stories that grew up about him that allowed people to look back and wonder whether we made the decision at the time. I can assure you, as one of the people involved in the decision-making process, that the consensus from the theatrical distributors at the time was: please try and complete this as a full-length feature film and not as part of a documentary footage. So, when you try to construct a story and you don't have the leading man available to tie the story together, you have to make some choices on which footage you can use and which you can't use.

Q: Can you tell me about Bruce's business relationship with Raymond Chow and which direction they were planning to go to further elevate Bruce's appeal beyond the confines of the Orient?
Andre Morgan: Of course, you can read all the notes that get written but at the end of the day, in truth, it was Raymond Chow and Golden Harvest who gave Bruce Lee the platform to become the star that he ultimately became, by giving him the opportunity to star first in Big Boss and then in Fist of Fury. And out of that box office success came the joint venture with Concord Pictures that was used as a vehicle for Bruce Lee to develop his directing and acting skills.

So the plan, at the time of Bruce's death, was that he would hopefully do one English-speaking movie a year with the studios, as a co-production between Hong Kong and the United States, and he would do one Chinese-language picture a year in order to build up the Hong Kong film industry and remain loyal to his fan base, which became so extensive in Asia. So the long-term plan was to continue to explore opportunities to make films in conjunction with Hollywood, and at the same time to expand his directions and opportunities and making films for the Chinese markets of South East Asia.

Q: Did the success of Game of Death, when it was finally released, surprise you in any way?
Andre Morgan: I wouldn't say that it surprised us. I think for those of us who had been on the journey from the beginning, from 1972, we were pleased with the reception the movie received from the audiences around the world, if not the critics from around the world. Because ultimately, Bruce Lee was a popular star, he was never a film critic's star. Remember, film critics tend to be snobs, and it's only after the fact that they'll look back and recognize those kind of films which gained popular appeal and became part of pop culture. They seldom recognize

those type of movies when they're first released. But the general public's support and the box office success meant the movie was a fitting tribute to Bruce Lee's impact on the world of cinema. And speaking in the context of the late 1970s, the legacy which was born from that brief career, I think it's quite amazing. It certainly puts Bruce Lee in the same league as other young talented actors who died in early stages of their careers. He's right there besides James Dean.

Q: Can you recall Bruce's day to day activities when he used to arrive at the Golden Harvest studios when he wasn't actually filming?
Andre Morgan: Well, the truth was me and Bruce kept offices at the studio, which he used for production meetings or script or planning meetings, etc - projects he was working on. Bruce basically had a very straight regimen where he would wake up every day and he would workout a couple of hours, depending on what he was focusing on in terms of enhancing his physical stamina or improving his speed and agility as a martial artist. Then he would come to the studio at around 11 in the morning to discuss meetings and business at hand. Then he'd usually go to lunch, and depending on what the rest of the day had in store for him, he would adjourn to the studio for the meetings in the afternoon. He might go off for a press conference or he might go off to meetings off the studio lot, or do a photo session or visit foreign press that were wanting interviews with him.

Q: Please tell me about your experiences on working on Enter the Dragon.
Andre Morgan: I talked to Bruce Lee on a daily basis. I think you have to understand the significance of the movie. Enter The Dragon got released four weeks after Bruce Lee died. You have to put it into context that even though Bruce got to see the finished film, he never got to see it play to the audience in America or Hong Kong. So he could only imagine to what extent the movie would be successful. However, the goal and the ambition of making the movie in the first place was to find a vehicle which would allow Bruce Lee to act in an English-language movie, which would be released in America by an American studio and treated in the same respect as any movie produced in Hollywood starring a Caucasian.

As far as Bruce's point of view, there were no Asian stars that had managed to gain international acclaim on a long-term basis. And therefore there were no role models for young Asians growing up to see within the context of Hollywood and the star system which Hollywood represented. So one of his goals was to achieve that kind of status, a role model for young people and an example for other people, inspiring minority actors all over the world that were trying to break into Hollywood. But you have to put this into the context of 1973, long before there was a Jackie Chan or Jet Li or any of the others that have come since in Asia. The truth was in those days the only Asian actors that had any serious following was perhaps opera stage actors, and that was in the context of working around the world with a very limited audience. Bruce's goal, as he told me on several occasions, was to be as a recognizable face as Steve McQueen.

In those days, in the 1970s, Steve McQueen was the most famous actor in the world. He was the definition of 'cool', long before Paul Newman or Clint Eastwood. So Bruce's goal with Enter the Dragon was to find that vehicle that would allow him to be introduced to broad audiences of young people around the world. They can tell you that he succeeded beyond the wildest of his dreams with his first film, even though for him it was just a starting point. The dream was that the next movie would be even bigger, with more fantastic action scenes and more interesting stories. But the journey of a thousand miles must start with a first step, and Enter the Dragon was certainly the first step of that journey.

Q: Do you vividly remember Jackie Chan, who was one of the stunt guys in Enter the Dragon, on the set?

Andre Morgan: I remember the set very well. To be very frank about it, Jackie was one of a 150 action martial artists we had working as extras on the film, there was nothing special about him. If you look at the film, he's only in few scenes in the film. One is the cave set and then in the end battle scene in the terraces. So in all honesty, I can't say Jackie stood out from all the other martial arts extras we had on the film set back in 1973. Obviously, he went on to be successful in his own right because of the enormous talent and skill he has, he managed to very quickly distance himself from all the other extras which were his contemporaries. It didn't take very long for Jackie to join Golden Harvest. I worked with Jackie after he joined Golden Harvest.

Q: Did Bruce talk to you about future projects and who he wanted to work with as far as actors are concerned, and did he mention any particular names?

Andre Morgan: Absolutely! Yes. You have to remember that Bruce Lee came from Hong Kong to Seattle and then to Hollywood at a relatively young age. And before he returned to Hong Kong he had made is acting debut in Hollywood in Longstreet TV series with James Franciscus. The truth was he had a number of friends that were actors of some repute in Hollywood that he had taught as a martial arts instructor. This included Steve McQueen, James Coburn and some others. So it was only natural as his success, his fame and opportunities improved, his mind gravitated to the idea of working with some of these well-established actors in

Hollywood. Obviously, had he lived longer I'm sure he would have achieved that. There were a number of scripts in development at the time Bruce died. Had he lived longer I'm sure they would have found their way into production, and he would have worked with a number of major American action stars of that period. Remember this predates Chuck Norris, Arnold Schwarzenegger and Sylvester Stallone becoming stars by nearly a decade.

Q: When Bruce died and Enter the Dragon hit the theaters and became a big box office success, can you recall the atmosphere and reaction from the public who were all mesmerized by this powerhouse?

Andre Morgan: I was in Hollywood for the opening of Enter the Dragon. I stood outside of the theater on Hollywood Boulevard watching the lion dance team performing around the block. But it was all bitter and sweet because on one hand, as a producer, you're thrilled and the public is receiving your movie well; on the other side you're sad because as a friend, Bruce and the journey that this movie represented and the wonderful work was not there to share it. And the truth is when the movie opened up in America, Bruce's funeral had taken place in Hong Kong which had attracted global news attention. And the funeral in Seattle also had made Bruce's death into something of a cult story and the beginning of the year of the paparazzi.

So there was a certain electricity and anticipation on the opening night at the Mann's Chinese Theater on Hollywood Boulevard. The audiences were lined up along the block waiting to get in. And watching their faces when they came out of the theater, you could see they were obviously very excited and very taken at what they had seen. It was a very gratifying feeling. However, knowing the man you started the journey with was not there to enjoy the benefits of the satisfactions on those smiles on the people's faces made it a sort of a very sad feeling.

Q: From the perspective of someone who knew and worked with Bruce, what was the depth of his character?

Andre Morgan: Like any other gifted and talented person, he had very strong opinions and a very clear vision of who he was and what he expected of others, and very high standards in terms of both demanding perfection of others and demanding perfection of himself. But at the same time, he was a very fair and open person which made it relatively easy to work with him. If you didn't bullshit him he didn't bullshit you.

Q: What sets Bruce Lee apart from other action stars and propels his status to iconic level?

Andre Morgan: He's become an icon, and I think part of him is that he was the first Asian actor to break into the international scene. Secondly, he was an incredibly talented martial artist and he was a reasonable actor who was growing as an actor with each performance. But most importantly, I think it was the tragic early death of somebody who had so much promise that put him up there with those who died young.

Q: Do you feel Bruce was going to lean more towards directing and producing as his career developed, and did he talk to you about this?
Andre Morgan: The truth was Bruce directed only because he was finding it difficult to communicate with Hong Kong directors at that point of time. Because most of them were much older than he was and he had no references from another generation. Bruce Lee was of the Billy Jack generation, so he was part of what we would call the 'new wave' sweeping the world in those days. He came up in the era of Billy Jack and Easy Rider. Now, that generation of filmmakers went on to change the way Hollywood makes films and the way the world defined entertainment. His problem in Hong Kong was the directors that worked with him were much older, just as most of the directors in Hollywood were at the time, so it was difficult for him to express his vision, and realized this vision working through those directors. He directed in order to defend his vision of what he thought entertainment should be.

Q: What direction did your career take after Bruce died?
Andre Morgan: Well, I would say I was very fortunate to be in the right place at the right time. Golden Harvest, in 1973, was certainly an established entity in Hong Kong and was expanding rapidly from production to distribution and foreign sales. I was very fortunate to be part of that very rapid expansion from 1972 to 1984. I was given the opportunity to explore the many different sides to the film business, in terms of making Chinese-language films around the world on location and working with virtually every young talented actor and director who would go on to become that next generation in Hong Kong in the 1980s. And at the same time, to help and build Golden Harvest the franchise it became. It's become the largest film entertainment company in Asia.

I had the opportunity to use Golden Harvest as a platform to enter Hollywood and start what became a trend for a long time, doing co-productions on a global basis, with part of the financing coming from Hollywood and the rest of it coming from international sales from Europe and Asia. So I can say that I was very fortunate to be there at the right time. After Bruce Lee, at Golden Harvest we went on to do Cannon Ball Run movies and the people I worked with and trained went on to do the Ninja

Turtle movies, and to build on the prestige of Golden Harvest's dynamic force in the film business.

Q: Another gentleman you worked with is Sammo Hung who, of course, appeared in Enter the Dragon.
Andre Morgan: Actually, Sammo and I, our journey began before Enter the Dragon. Sammo was working on a movie called Hapkido in Hong Kong in the summer of 1972, with a young actress named Angela Mao, that's when I met Sammo. I cast Sammo in Enter the Dragon. In the beginning of the movie we see a very young Sammo Hung fighting.

He and I became friends and stayed friends throughout the years of Golden Harvest, and his career took off. We worked on many films from the 1970s going to the early 1980s. When Sammo became an established star in his own right and a very talented and gifted director in Hong Kong, our careers drifted apart and I came back to America to set up Ruddy Morgan with my current partner Al Ruddy. Then the Hong Kong film directors and actors picked up momentum in the early 90s, not just Jackie Chan coming to America but also John Woo, Stanley Tong and Michelle Yeoh coming to America.

One day Sammo actually called up out of the blue, he said he was in Los Angeles and that we could get together for a coffee. I sat down with him and his wife and we had coffee at the Beverly Wiltshire, and we were chatting about what sort of career he could have in Hollywood. Unknown to Sammo, at the time I was developing a TV series for CBS because we were also producing a TV series called Walker: Texas Ranger with Chuck Norris in it. And it was a very successful TV series. They put it on Saturday night on CBS, and the president of CBS said he needed a companion piece to go an hour before Walker: Texas Ranger - I was working with Stanley Tong - which ultimately became Martial Law. Over the course of the next few months, while I was developing Martial Law, we came to the conclusion that Sammo was one of the three possible candidates to play the Chinese detective. And ultimately, we took him to CBS and shot the test and Sammo got the job. As we say, the rest is history.

Q: Bruce Lee will be remembered with an esteem equal that given to the any other memorialized legendary figures of the past. Final comments on Bruce Lee?
Andre Morgan: Final comments on Bruce Lee? No, I don't think the final words have been spoken about Bruce Lee, (it will be a) long time before that could be said. The only thing I can say, as someone who knew and worked with Bruce, is I think he would be very proud of the fact that his legacy has transcended 30 years of updating the film industry, and that to this day he still remains inspirational to young Asian filmmakers and

actors. And his impact on how action scenes are designed, choreographed and shot transcends his expectations at the time he was making these films. So to that end, he should be very proud.

And the other side of it, which was very interesting for me, was when Japanese newspapers were doing their end of the millennium selection of the 100 most influential people in the world. It was fascinating to me that two of them came to the conclusion that Bruce Lee was one of the most important people for Asia in the 20th century. He did provide a positive role model for these young generations of Asians who grew up, but who had never had the opportunity to see an Asian actor as a leading man in performance in an international film.

Before Bruce it was Japanese in Japanese-language movies and Chinese in Chinese-language movies. And the first time it was somebody playing on a global stage and receiving recognition. I'm sure in conversations with that generation of actors in Asia he became an inspiration for them - if Bruce Lee could do it, they could do it too.

KAREEM ABDUL-JABBAR

Kareem Abdul-Jabbar, widely considered one of the greatest NBA players of all time, was one of Bruce Lee's celebrity students and friends. Lee's terrific fight sequence with Abdul-Jabbar in Game of Death still remains as one of the most climatic action fight sequences ever filmed. Since retiring as a player in 1989, Kareem has balanced his love of basketball with his love of history, authoring six bestselling history books pertaining to African-American contributions to American culture and history.

Q: Kareem, when did you first meet Bruce Lee?
Kareem Abdul-Jabbar: I first met Bruce Lee when I was attending the University of California in Los Angeles, UCLA. I was studying Aikido but I wanted to continue training in the martial arts during the school years, and someone recommended I go meet Bruce and train with him.

Q: Bruce had a unique and dynamic personality, how would you describe his personality?
Kareem Abdul-Jabbar: Bruce was a very outgoing guy, he really was very curious about all aspects of life, and he liked to engage with people in conversations and find out what people knew. He was very curious and very gregarious. He could engage with anybody in a conversation, he was very good at it, and finding out what they were all about. He was always reading. If someone came down and knew something he didn't, he would talk to them about it.

Q: How would you describe Bruce as a teacher?
Kareem Abdul-Jabbar: Bruce was what I call a very pragmatic teacher.

He taught by example and then he taught by having you do what you were trying to learn, especially about martial arts. It wasn't about theory, it was about: can you do this? If you can't do this then you have to find out how you can substitute something for whatever you're trying to achieve. So he covered this aspect of what he was trying to teach you. He didn't believe that one size fit everybody, every different person had their own solution to the martial arts situation, because we're all different sizes with different skills, etc.

Q: Would you say Bruce was one of the first to combine martial arts with state-of-the-art physical training methods, also integrating philosophy into his martial art?
Kareem Abdul-Jabbar: I think Bruce tried to convey all the different philosophies and find what was legitimate, and he would hold on to that and he would throw out the stuff which was useless. Also, it had to do with physical techniques and useful techniques, he'd find ways to incorporate these into his art because it was something which worked, and it was pragmatic for him. And the other things he'd get rid of because they weren't pragmatic.

Q: Let's talk about the backyard workouts. What elements did you and Bruce work on during these private sessions?
Kareem Abdul-Jabbar: With regard to Bruce's backyard workouts, I mainly worked with Bruce. There were a couple of times when Danny Inosanto and one or two guys from the Kwoon (school) would come out to work at Bruce's house. But I mainly worked with Bruce alone. We just worked on specific things, footwork for example, how to use the dummy or hitting the bag. I remember one time fooling around breaking wood blocks. He would just pick a different aspect on what he wanted to work on and sharpen it and move on to the next thing - it was never any set routine. The routine he had, he would work certain amount of time each day, at least an hour and a half.

Q: Bruce weighed only 135 pounds, how was he able to generate the explosive power and speed?
Kareem Abdul-Jabbar: I think Bruce's size was really something that he maximized by weight training, and he worked on his quickness so that he was all 'business' - there was no excess there. One thing he always would mention to me was: if you think someone is supposed to be a great master and they're big and fat and out of shape, they shouldn't have a lot of credibility. Because whoever that person is, they're not training hard, their mastership is based on different techniques which may or may not be effective in a real fight.

Q: Did your conversations touch on philosophy?
Kareem Abdul-Jabbar: I have my own philosophy and I gave Bruce books to read on Islam, and Bruce knew Chinese Muslims. They have a lot of Wushu techniques that are unique to that, and from the martial arts of Indonesia and Malaysia. He was aware of Islam and it was not beyond something he investigated. He investigated different techniques from the Islamic part of China.

Q: Did he ever talk to you about becoming a movie star?
Kareem Abdul-Jabbar: Bruce never talked to me about becoming a movie star, he talked to me about how I can be the best basketball player. And one of the things he suggested was I do a session of weight training over one summer, which I did and it certainly helped my game. He said being in the best shape you can be will absolutely enhance whatever I was trying to do on the basketball court, and he was absolutely right.

Q: Did you think he would ever become as famous as he did eventually?
Kareem Abdul-Jabbar: I was surprised that Bruce became so famous that it really didn't take much time. He left America and went to Hong Kong and within two years he was an international star. I wasn't surprised with that, he had a good background in acting, his dad was an actor, he had been a childhood actor and the work he did on Green Hornet. So I knew Bruce was well-versed in that and all the pieces just came together when he got to Hong Kong.

Q: How did you get the part in Game of Death?
Kareem Abdul-Jabbar: Bruce had spoken to me while I was training with him here in America, stating that if we ever get the opportunity we would make a movie. So when the opportunity came where he could call the shots, he gave me a call and said, "How would you like to make a movie with me?" That's how all that came about.

Q: What was Bruce's original concept behind this movie and what was he trying to ultimately achieve?
Kareem Abdul-Jabbar: Bruce's original concept in Game of Death had to do with trying to show how one person dealt with different forms, one martial artist going up against people using different fighting styles; he has to overcome in each of them. In order to do that you have to be versatile, you can't take the same approach to dealing with different problems, and that's mainly what that was all about.

Q: What was it like working on the climatic fight scenes with Bruce?
Kareem Abdul-Jabbar: It was a lot of hard work doing the fight scenes because we had to shoot everything from different angles. So we'd do exactly the same thing for this camera and that camera, and then reverse things, so it took a lot of time. And Hong Kong is very warm, so working on the sound stage, it was still warm in September. So it was very hard going.

Q: Can you recall any on and off-set incidents?
Kareem Abdul-Jabbar: I remember one time Bruce almost fell out and I had to catch him, and we had a good laugh about that because he ended up in my arms like a little baby. Another time, one of the actors decided he wanted to challenge Bruce in the middle of a discussion and Bruce had to deal with him and put him on his back pretty quickly. People decided not to try that any more.

Q: Bruce integrated a lot of grappling into this movie, do you feel this was an avenue he would have evolved in?
Kareem Abdul-Jabbar: Bruce did know fundamental Jiu Jitsu and was well-grounded, it was something he knew how to deal with fundamentally. He didn't have an advanced degree in Jiu Jitsu but just basic concepts of it. If you look at the fight scene with me, we box a little bit but he ends up getting the advantage because I can't see, he gets me in a choke hold and that's how that fight ends. Basically, he was foreseeing something which was 30 years to come, with how things have evolved with the concept of mixed martial arts that we aspire to today.

Q: Did you ever talk about future movie roles?
Kareem Abdul-Jabbar: Bruce said he wanted to do a variety of roles and he was looking forward to working with some American screenwriters, who have a different approach to what they do in the Hong Kong movie industry. He felt that the American writers could write interesting stories that the people in Hong Kong wouldn't necessarily think of.

Q: When his movies hit the theaters in the Western world how did the audiences react?
Kareem Abdul-Jabbar: I remember seeing Big Boss and everybody was impressed that people weren't flying and jumping over buildings and stuff like that. It was reality based and not something unbelievable.

Q: When did you hear about his death?
Kareem Abdul-Jabbar: I heard about Bruce's death when I was at the airport in Singapore. I was on my way to see him that day. I was in

Singapore and had spent some time in the Middle East, and before going back home I was going to Hong Kong to visit him. When my plane got to Singapore, it was in all the newspapers that he had died the previous day.

Q: Bruce's superstar status popularized and raised the visibility of the martial arts and the action film genre. Had he lived do you think Bruce would have achieved much more in the martial arts and the film industry?

Kareem Abdul-Jabbar: I'm sure Bruce's movies would have been very successful. He had all the charisma and the physical abilities to be a star that would have lasting power. I'm pretty sure of that. I'm sure he would have been able to promote his concept of mixed martial arts which is now the way everybody sees the martial arts these days. He was way ahead of everybody in that respect.

Q: We've got Arnold Schwarzenegger and Sylvester Stallone, the modern action heroes. Do you think there will ever be another Bruce Lee?

Kareem Abdul-Jabbar: I don't think there will ever be another Bruce Lee in so far as he was the pioneer in the whole concept of mixed martial arts and training eclectically. I think he really distinguished himself. I think Bruce and the senior Mr. Gracie (Helio Gracie) in Brazil were way ahead of everybody in understanding that the martial arts have to be pragmatic and useful, you can't just stick to one style above everything else. I really think those two people were unique and way ahead of their time, by taking those positions and forming their art around that concept.

Bruce was very pragmatic. It's funny that Bruce was more of a Boxer (striker) and Gracie was a grappler, you have to combine those two things to be a successful martial artist today. So I think he has a unique place here. I don't think Arnold Schwarzenegger or Sylvester Stallone really distinguished themselves as athletes, they've distinguished themselves as actors. Arnold was a bodybuilder, he said he did it using steroids and it's a thing which really doesn't get that much respect.

JI HAN JAE

Bruce Lee met Ji Han Jae in 1969 when the Hapkido master was on an official visit to the United States. One of the highest ranking Hapkido masters in the world, he was a personal bodyguard to the Korean President Park Chung Hee. Bruce Lee, impressed with the skills the Korean master possessed, invited him to star in his new film Game of Death which would feature a plethora of talented martial arts masters. It is very rare you will see an interview with Master Jae talking about his relationship with Bruce Lee. This is a very rare interview indeed!

Q: As I understand, you met Bruce Lee in 1969 on your visit to the United States. Could you tell me more please?
Ji Han Jae: The first time I went to the United States was for a government-to-government exchange teaching program. American government personnel would teach the Korean government bodyguard techniques, and I went to America to teach hand-to-hand combat techniques to the bodyguards. In May 1969, Jhoon Rhee had the International Karate Championships and I went there to do a demonstration, and this is where Jhoon Rhee introduced me to Bruce Lee. I showed him some of my techniques and he liked my techniques. Then he invited me to Hong Kong. We were involved in three movies. The first one was Game of Death, the second movie which was produced by the same company was called Hapkido and Bruce Lee was involved in this to a certain extent. When this movie was exported out of the country they changed the title to Lady Kung Fu. Bruce Lee's best friend Unicorn and I made Fist of Unicorn.

Q: On the set of Game of Death who choreographed the fight scene at Golden Harvest?

Ji Han Jae: When I was filming my fight scene with Bruce Lee there were several extra guys there. He was a good movie actor. My level and his level was different, so that's why there was a little bit of a gap. But he was a really nice guy and a good martial artist. Some stuff for the fight scene we worked out together, some were my ideas and some his ideas, then we worked out the fight scene together.

Q: In Game of Death you implemented grappling moves, and so did Bruce, did you talk about or teach him anything specific?
Ji Han Jae: Yes, of course. I showed him techniques. Hong Kong movie stars at that time didn't know Hapkido techniques so I showed Hapkido techniques, and everybody started using Hapkido techniques. Sammo Hung, Angela Mao and several other Hong Kong movie stars came to Korea for three years, in and out, and I taught them Hapkido. Then they made a Hapkido movie. After that the Hong Kong movie stars were using my techniques - joint locks, throwing and kicking and everything. Do you know who made the spinning kick? I made the spinning kick! Right now around the world people are using the spinning kick - it's mine! Nobody could say this technique's theirs, only I can say it's mine. I made a spinning kick, handkerchief and the cane techniques. In the Hapkido movie they used 100 percent my techniques.

Q: In Game of Death Bruce Lee was using many top talented martial artists. Dan Inosanto, Kareem Abdul-Jabbar and Bolo were part of the casting. Did he mention any other names to you?
Ji Han Jae: I don't want to comment on the other people, I can only talk about Hapkido. I don't want to comment on the others. Different martial artists, they have pride. I don't want to talk about other martial artist's pride.

Q: Can you tell me about working with Bruce Lee and what it was like to work with him?
Ji Han Jae: I was in and out of Golden Harvest for three years, from 1972 to 74, and I made three movies.

Q: Which floor did you fight in the pagoda?
Ji Han Jae: I was on the second floor. The next floor was the long, tall guy Kareem Abdul-Jabbar who was on the third floor. Inosanto was on the first floor.

Q: What was your impression of Bruce Lee as a person?
Ji Han Jae: A good and nice person, yeah. Very kind. He was a very hardworking individual.

Q: What language did you speak to communicate with him?
Ji Han Jae: Of course, English, but my English was very bad. I grew up in China and sometimes I stayed in Hong Kong on vacation. I speak the Chinese language, that's why they liked me.

Q: Any off-set stories you would like to share with me?
Ji Han Jae: Most of the days we would go to dinner or whatever. I talked to him about martial arts only.

Q: Did Bruce Lee ever come to Korea and did you see him there too?
Ji Han Jae: No, he didn't come to Korea.

Q: On Fist of Unicorn was Bruce hired as the fight choreographer?
Ji Han Jae: Fist of Unicorn starred Bruce Lee's best friend (Unicorn) who invited Bruce Lee to get involved in the movie, they were very close friends. Bruce Lee was teaching/coordinating fight scenes on this movie. It's been over 35 years now, that's why I have forgotten a lot of the stories.

Q: In some rare footage you can be seen fighting other actors in the pagoda whilst Bruce Lee is watching. Also fighting outside with Korean fighters...
Ji Han Jae: One of my students worked with Bruce Lee on many movies, then after that many people understood my techniques, that's why before the movie shoots they learned techniques which they could integrate into the movie when shooting.

Q: How was the crew to work with?
Ji Han Jae: Golden Harvest had a good Korean language interpreter, mostly my interpreter controlled the other side. I didn't converse with Golden Harvest staff directly.

Q: When you were not shooting scenes did you train or learn techniques from each other?
Ji Han Jae: I didn't train but Bruce Lee introduced me to a Kung Fu master and we went to this dojo where they were doing Choy Lay Fut techniques. I didn't teach, they showed their techniques and I was just watching.

Q: What did Bruce Lee think of your grappling techniques and did he plan on integrating more in future projects?
Ji Han Jae: You must understand in the future the martial arts do not just rely on those kind of techniques. Future martial arts is to do with 'mind

technique'; if you develop the mind power then you control the mind, not just physical techniques.

Q: Why did Bruce Lee wear a yellow cat suit in Game of Death?
Ji Han Jae: I don't know. I don't have an idea, it was probably just for the movie.

Q: How many weeks did you work on Game of Death?
Ji Han Jae: I was shooting on the film for three months. One day when I was in Hong Kong, he came to my hotel room and said to me that me and him should do a fight scene, and the scene will be a one-cut and finish. I said, "One-cut and the camera finish?" I said OK. But I was there for three months. After that he died before the film was finished. Jhoon Rhee is a friend of mine who introduced me to Bruce Lee.

Q: How did you feel about being in a Bruce Lee movie, were you excited?
Ji Han Jae: (Laughs) It was exciting, yes.

Q: Finally, how would you sum up Bruce Lee as a martial artist?
Ji Han Jae: He was a good martial artist and good movie actor.

PAUL HELLER

Paul M. Heller's first film as a producer was David and Lisa, which received two Oscar nominations and innumerable awards. In 1973 he founded Sequoia Pictures, a production company affiliated with Warner Brothers. The company's first production was Enter the Dragon, a film which set off the explosion of interests in the martial arts genre and the film which catapulted Bruce Lee to international superstardom. Paul Heller co-produced the movie, which is one of the most profitable movies ever made.

Q: Paul, can you shed some light on how the concept of producing Enter the Dragon came to light?
Paul Heller: Well, I was an executive at Warner Brothers. Shortly before, my partner Fred Weintraub and several people such as Stirling Silliphant and a few other people brought Bruce Lee to our attention. And we met him and were very impressed with him. Stirling Silliphant had written a part for him called Silent Flute, then we decided to come up with a project for him. I think it was called Way of the Dragon, Sign of the Tiger; but we just couldn't get anyone to base a film on a relatively unknown Chinese star. The story of it was a young Chinese monk comes to the States and ended up the champion of all the Chinese railroad workers, and this then became the television series Kung Fu.

Even in a television series, they wouldn't give it to Bruce, and he was quite discouraged. He went back to Hong Kong and certainly did a couple of films and became an international celebrity. So having known him and met him, you'd be very impressed at how successful he had become. We decided we would do a film with him and came up with the idea of Enter the Dragon, which was initially called Blood and Steel. My partner Fred went over (to Hong Kong) and Bruce and Raymond said, "Yes, let's do it." So we went out there. We started to do it originally on our own. However, we were under arrangement with Warners and they'd have a first look at whatever we did. At that time we had left and set up our own company, and they decided they wanted in. So we went and made it. It all happened really quickly.

Q: Before meeting Bruce and making Enter the Dragon, you were aware of Bruce's success in Hong Kong. What was your impression of his first movie Big Boss, which hadn't been released in the West?
Paul Heller: They weren't released yet but we saw them through Warner Brothers. We arranged to see the films, they were so amazing, his talent was jumping off the screen. There's no question why he was so successful and why he had built up such a reputation.

Q: What was Bruce Lee really like?
Paul Heller: He was all energy and the most energetic person. He had this aura and intensity. I've never met anybody in my life who wanted to become a star more than him. Everything he did was directed towards reaching that goal of being a star. One of the people he admired was Steve McQueen, he wanted to be a bigger star than Steve.

Q: Did your relationship with Bruce filter over on a social level?
Paul Heller: There wasn't much time to do that, but we went to dinner and lunches often. I went to his house once, we were working very long hours. Whenever we would go to a big restaurant, he was as big as the Beatles were here. We would go to a restaurant and there would be a big crowd of tables watching, and the chefs would come out and make special dishes for him. He was a major, major star.

Q: Did Bruce's contribution to the movie go beyond the confines of an actor and fight coordinator? Was Bruce involved in every aspects of the film?
Paul Heller: Bruce was very concerned about the script, although he didn't make any changes on it. We did things and when we saw some of the things he could do we would adapt the script to capitalize on those amazing things. But he was also very involved, he choreographed all of his stunts. In other words, together with the director they would workout any of the fight sequences between them. Bruce would, in essence, choreograph with his team of stunt guys so that they were effective as they were.

Q: With all the problems which are associated with producing a film, what hurdles did you have to overcome in making the greatest martial arts movie ever made?
Paul Heller: The biggest one was the communication we were making

with a crew that spoke very little English. We had translators. Actually, Andre Morgan, who is now a very successful producer himself, was our translator for us. Originally he had worked for Raymond Chow doing subtitles for Chinese films. He was quite helpful. The cameraman developed his own sign language in Chinese with his lighting crew.

Q: What made Bruce's fight choreography so unique and visually stunning?

Paul Heller: The thing that we did was we tried to work towards all of Bruce's strengths. When we would come up with a fight scene, or something of that sort, we would design the set and he went on to the point of changing the set and things of that sort, so it capitalized on what he could do so brilliantly. It would show him off to the best advantage. It was all of us working together.

The mirror room scene came about - as I said, I used to be a designer - when we were having lunch at a hotel, we saw this mirror section with little things which gave a multiple image. So we thought, "Oh my God, it looks so exciting," and we then designed the set for that scene which became the secret mirrored room of Han. That whole sequence came about all of us working together and coming up with ideas on how best Bruce's skills could be put to use; the idea of breaking mirrors to break the reflection so you know which was the real and which wasn't. Then for the final death of Han we worked out with the mirror on the door and the door swinging around. All of that sort of came about through very concentrated effort to get the very best out of each sequence and capitalizing on Bruce's strengths.

Q: Bruce had a brilliant innovative mind, he often used stick matches to choreograph his fights for the movies. Did you see him actually prepare like this?

Paul Heller: I didn't see him doing stick matches but he did make little sketches. I think there is a script that was his. I haven't seen it myself but there is a copy of it. But he did make tiny diagrams of what he wanted the fights to look like, and what he was thinking about in fights.

Q: What schedule did you adhere to daily filming?

Paul Heller: Oh, mostly we would get things done in 12 or 13 hours, some of it was very complicated and took a lot longer to do, other things went quickly. When we filmed in the street there was always a problem because of the crowds. Sometimes we had to do a diversion where we would set up a camera, lights and the whole thing so people knew we were shooting there, but that was fake and we would go somewhere else. We couldn't get the scenes done with all those crowds. Sometimes the crowds stood on the roofs of cars and they crushed the cars.

Q: How would you describe Bruce's working relationship with the cast and the crew?

Paul Heller: It was amazing, he was a very generous actor. His stunt guys would have jumped in boiling oil for him. He was a wonderful person and excellent with the crew. It was always a pleasure to work with him.

Q: It's interesting to note that Jackie Chan was an extra and stuntman on Enter the Dragon, do you remember him?

Paul Heller: I certainly remember him back then, but I don't remember anything specific. He was part of Bruce's stunt team. I've seen him since and he's been very appreciative and grateful for the chance he had working on the film. He is into his own stardom now.

Q: Did Bruce direct the scene which appears in the beginning of the movie (when he's fighting Sammo Hung) himself when you left for Los Angeles?

Paul Heller: That's true. It was hard to get Bruce started on the film, even though we started to shoot, he hadn't shown up on the set. So we went off and shot a lot of stuff, and finally when the day came for him to come on set he was very, very nervous because he knew this was important. But once we got through the first day, we couldn't stop him, he was there early and left late and worked so hard. Even when we were done, Bruce had this idea for the opening fight scene in the temple. It was a lovely thought, it was a wonderful scene to do. He got Sammo to come and do the fight with him, he shot that on his own and brought it to us.

Q: Did you see Bruce working out? As I understand, he often worked out with John Saxon and also used weights to keep his physique in tune, as we can see from the definition he had in Enter the Dragon.

Paul Heller: I was never there when he was working out, but he had a weight training gym at his house, his body was hard like a hardwood. He was in such an amazing shape. He was incredible. One other thing to note is that he worked so hard during the film, when we shot the opening scene at the temple, when you see up closely you can see Bruce had lost I think 10 pounds. He was very, very lean.

Q: Can you recall filming the nunchaku scene in the dungeon?

Paul Heller: That was done by Bruce, we didn't speed anything up. He actually did it at that speed, we were so amazed at his skills. The nunchaku scene is just as you see it and there's nothing done or added to it.

Q: Enter the Dragon premiered in August 1973, can you recall the premiere at Mann's Theater?

Paul Heller: Warners did a wonderful thing, they had a Chinese Dragon race on Hollywood Boulevard - Los Angeles and San Francisco Parade Dragon before the screening. I was so excited that everything was a blur to me. To see that audience at the first play, they were just screaming out and everybody was excited. It was the most exciting event of my life.

Q: Had Bruce lived what avenues would he have taken? Were there any other offers on the table?
Paul Heller: I don't know exactly what he was offered, but I do know that Run Run Shaw was very anxious to do something with him. He would have given Bruce anything he wanted. Bruce and I talked about his career from time to time, and I tried to tell him certain things because he wanted to be a serious actor. He wanted to be more than just an actor, and we talked about it several times (about) modeling his career of that of Clint Eastwood, who started his way into more serious roles. Bruce was very impatient as he wanted to do that quickly. We had talked about it.

Q: Bruce was catapulted to worldwide fame after Enter the Dragon was released. What sets Bruce apart from other action stars?
Paul Heller: He was great! There was no one like him and nobody ever since. His talent, I think everybody in the world recognizes Bruce, he was like James Dean - it's true, he was. I think anybody who has worked in the action genre recognizes the brilliance he brought to it, he was truly, truly brilliant. He was on the scene for a short time and he was gone. The impact that he made goes on because it was so incredible. You have Jackie Chan, a big star, Clark Gable and those big stars, but it was tragic that Bruce had a short career. Not tragic only for him but the world audiences who loved to see him grow and give us so much satisfaction.

Q: Paul, people tend to never get bored watching a Bruce Lee movie over and over again, why is that?
Paul Heller: That's true, it's absolutely true! He had an intensity which the camera caught. Some actors can be brilliant actors but the camera doesn't love them - the camera loved Bruce. In other words, there's something about stardom the camera sees into their souls, something that even probably most people don't know they even had, and the camera embraces that. Bruce's energy, his raw talent and his excitement all came through the cameras and onto the screen. Very few people have that; very few people are totally successful in communicating that.

LALO SCHIFRIN

Lalo Schifrin is a true renaissance man, a musician of exceptional imagination and skill. He has composed music for many hundreds of films and TV shows in Hollywood, and has won four Grammy Awards and received six Oscar nominations. It is safe to say Lalo Schifrin gave Enter the Dragon the final touch, composing the music which left an everlasting impression on all those who witnessed the magic Bruce Lee portrayed in the movie theater. In this rare interview he discusses his connection with Lee and the blockbuster box office smash hit.

Q: How did you get involved in doing the music for Enter the Dragon movie?
Lalo Schifrin: I remember when I met Bruce Lee. The producers Fred Weintraub and Paul Heller called my agent. My agent called me and said that for the first time it's going to be a martial arts movie here in Hollywood. Bruce Lee was making movies in Hong Kong, they were big, but this was first time an American production company started to make a martial arts movie. I think he came to Hollywood and said he wanted to meet me. We had lunch and he said he had a dojo where he practiced with the rhythm of my Mission Impossible music, which he liked.

Q: Tell me more about this meeting and any significant conversations you had.
Lalo Schifrin: Well, he told me that he broke the traditions. Martial arts started in India 5,000 years ago. Indian monks were attacked by the bandits so they developed an empty hand form of self defense. So, from India it went to China, different forms of martial arts were created from Kung Fu to the Korean and Japanese Karate and some other forms. He

said he broke the rules and created his own style. And I said to him, "You know something? I studied 2,000 years of European music which also had traditions, and I broke the rules." So we had that in common.

Q: Can you reflect on his personality?
Lalo Schifrin: It was very sad that he died, he was doing a tour promoting Enter the Dragon. He had something in the brain which killed him. First of all, he was a great, great guy. Secondly, he was starting a career here in Hollywood, in the United States, which could've made him bigger than he was.

Q: Upon its release how was the movie received in the United States?
Lalo Schifrin: It was fantastic, there was a great, great reaction. Later in my career, I did work with Jackie Chan on the Rush Hour movies.

Q: To what extent and lengths did you go to for scoring the music for Enter the Dragon?
Lalo Schifrin: I didn't have too much time after our lunch meeting because I had to come back to my studio to complete work on a movie, doing the score. We used contemporary rhythm of the 70s combined with the music of the Orient, especially music from China, Japan and Korea. I studied music and one of my thesis was musicology, so I knew music from all around the world. I don't want to brag about it but I studied music from all over the world, all tunes, different people, so I'm very familiar with them. It's my job to make it work and feed it into the movie. I create the right music. Basically, I was inspired by the movie and I did something different because it was a different kind of a movie .

Q: How would you define his martial arts abilities?
Lalo Schifrin: Bruce Lee was amazing! He moved like a dancer, it was really amazing. As a form of exercise I was playing tennis at the time. I stopped doing tennis and I started to study martial arts and I became a black belt, because he made an impression on me. I didn't know that he was teaching Hollywood celebrities otherwise I would have taken lessons with him too.

Q: When he died how did you find out and how popular was he in your native Argentina?
Lalo Schifrin: I was very sad, everybody was very sad. I know that the movie was very popular in Argentina, because I do music concerts all over the world and when I do it in Argentina I made a suite of Enter the Dragon, and I play the music and the public like it. He was popular all over the world.

Q: Had Bruce lived which direction do you think he would have gone and what would have been the focal point of his career?
Lalo Schifrin: I cannot answer that. The possibilities were infinite, so it was a sad thing he died because he could have developed an amazing career. He had charisma and personality which was very appealing on the screen.

JOHN SAXON

lthough John Saxon's career spans more than five decades with hundreds of movies and TV shows under his belt, Enter the Dragon is the film which he is known for. Whilst working together on Enter the Dragon, Saxon and Lee became good friends and would often workout at Lee's house during the shooting process. Of all the cast and crew on the film, Saxon was one of the men Lee trusted the most. He is still active as an actor and makes his home in California.

Q: John, could you start off by telling me when and how you formed an interest in the martial arts, and the first day you met Bruce?
John Saxon: In those days you may see martial arts once in a while in a book or something, but eventually we found a dojo which was (teaching) the Japanese style - I forget what it was - it was a governmental situation that sent people to trainers like Nishiyama, who I trained with for three or four years. Anyway, that was all going on and in time I got interested also in the Chinese thing, like Tai Chi and stuff like that. So I'd done a little bit of everything but I never wanted to be a martial arts star. The only time that came up was actually when I was less interested in the martial arts.

The movie came up - Enter the Dragon - and I read the script and I'd heard of Bruce Lee but I'd never met him at that point. I saw what was happening in contrast to what I was telling you in the late 50s, when nobody knew what the hell the martial arts were in America. All of a sudden there was a little dojo on every little corner of Los Angeles, you know. And I realized that the world had come to taking this kind of thing very, very seriously. So I decided to do that film. I hadn't really trained a great deal in the couple of years before that time, but I thought: well, it's a movie and I can do it well enough in a movie. My assumption was right, but not quite right as I expected. I mean, in a sense I felt Enter the Dragon was going to be OK.I had an agent who said to me, "Oh, it's a little crappy thing with a Chinese actor that nobody will ever see it." But it became a huge hit! It was beyond my expectations.

But I never wanted to do another martial art movie. I mean, by the time I did Enter the Dragon I was approaching 38 years old, so it was just a thing I could do at the time. Also it was something I could do to the extent there weren't many actors who could do martial arts. There was a small group, but I had probably been the most prominent of them. I found out many, many years later it had something to do with Bruce Lee seeing me training with the Shotokan group, in the university we did a demonstration. I did a demonstration and broke a board and sparred with some young Japanese kid. So Bruce at that point decided that I should be the other character in the movie with him, the one called 'Roper' which I played.

But I've always been interested in the martial arts, and in the last year or so I've been working on kettlebells. I had one kettlebell way back in the 60s, and as a matter fact the very first day when I was in Hong Kong Bruce Lee asked me to come over to his house, so I went over.   He had a home gym with lots of equipment, some of it which he had built or had built for him, and so on. He also had these American-style kettlebells, same as the ones I had, which were really just the way a dumbbell shaft is, with a handle, not the Russian type with the solid iron.

He had them too, and he used them too. He used them for muscles by swinging and holding a heavyweight up - so you have a moment to do something, like a strike. Afterwards, nearly two years ago I started to read in some magazines about a Russian called Pavel. He was a Russian who'd come to the United States and he'd trained the Armed Forces with kettlebells. I went to a seminar and I watched them and then they asked me to participate. From then on, I've been using them. Primarily I do a little bit of Tai Chi and other Chinese things, and also kettlebells, which has become something very, very prominent now. A few years ago you couldn't find them here in Los Angeles, now every sporting shop has kettlebells.

Q: Am I right in saying before you met Bruce Lee you'd seen him on the TV in an interview on a Boxing match?
John Saxon: That's true. It was called the Olympic Auditorium which was in downtown LA. It was a Boxing venue, actually it was owned and operated by Gene LeBell's mother. I watched Bruce at the Olympic Auditorium, there were some minor Boxers fighting, and in between that he was brought to the commentator with a microphone, and he started talking. And standing on the steps he began doing things like kicks and

stuff like that. He was saying something like he has four weapons and I thought this guy's very sharp. Then I think I saw him only once in a movie called Marlowe where he leapt up and kicked a chandelier. I thought, "Wow, this guy's really fantastic and athletic." Then I heard a lot of people talking about him, then not long after I went to Hong Kong and I met him the first day.

Q: I understand later on you studied other arts...
John Saxon: In between the Karate I was doing, I met Rorion Gracie on a movie set. Then I started working out with him when he was just beginning to get noticed. He had a little garage gym, before they became important and famous. Royce was 18 I think, a small skinny kid, and I worked out with him when Rorion wasn't available. I did that for a while, the Brazilian Jiu Jitsu. You know what, all of this stuff...let me give you an idea.

Bruce Lee initiated such an interest in the martial arts. And one of the things he always prominently mentioned is, "Don't show me your Japanese way of doing something, don't show me your Korean way - show me your way!" What he did was he made an amalgamation of everything, including Western Boxing. He had books in his library on Fencing. I think he had a cousin or a brother who was a Fencer. What I'm getting at is the next step, what has now developed into something as big and important as the UFC. What happened was, I think they all of a sudden realized that striking and punching was not enough, so it became a mixture of all these things. And it reminds me of what Bruce Lee was saying, which was: show me your way. What it amounted to now, with the UFC, was that it was grappling and punching, it's almost outclassed regular Boxing in America.

In the beginning, when the idea of UFC came to light, Rorion called me and he wanted me to come down to his studio, which is a drive away from where I lived. So I said, "What is it about?" And he said, "You must come, you must come." What it was they wanted me to sit on the sideline of the UFC and talk about what I was seeing, and when I saw some of the footage of stuff like that, I said I didn't want any part of it (Laughs). I don't want to stand there and say, "Oh, look at that! Awww !! Oh God, he's got the guy's eye out!!" I had no desire to be part of being a commentator.

Q: You, of course, visited Bruce at home, there are many pictures of you both sitting and talking in his room. What did the conversations lean towards?
John Saxon: Sure, well, two things basically, martial arts and...I said to him that I kind of lost interest in really serious training. But I did get all

excited even before I met him, because I kind of got the feeling from what I'd heard and little bit of what I'd seen him in, a movie or television, that it was something which was kind of relighting my interest. So we talked a lot about the martial arts. I told him I was interested in Tai Chi and he thought that was funny. He said that's a 'head trip', as he called it. But I was still interested in things like Bagua and so on. We talked about the martial arts a lot and we also talked about the movies. In the beginning he was kind of nervous. We had a sense of friendship from the start.

I told him I'd hurt my leg prior to going to Hong Kong, actually after doing a scene in Los Angeles for Enter the Dragon. I tore a muscle in the back of my leg, so I was very nervous. I said, "You know what, I've not worked out a whole lot, and I got hurt." And I said, "Let's try to help each other." He said, "OK, I'm nervous too because I haven't spoken much English in a movie." We became friends and got along very well.

Q: John, you experienced the power of Bruce's side kick when he demonstrated on the kick shield. Could you express to me what it was like being on the other end of Bruce's kick?
John Saxon: Oh, yeah, talking about that many times, which was kind of funny - you already read it somewhere? This was again, the first day I'd met him. He said show me how you do your side kick. Well, I stood up and just bent down and I raised my right leg and pushed it out.

He said, "OK, let me show you how I do mine," and he walked over and he got a shield which was inflated with air. I looked at it and he said don't worry I won't hurt you. He began moving things around and he positioned me. I stood there and checked the shield. I'd never experienced it before, and he came and leapt at me and banged right in the shield which knocked me, I'd say six or eight feet back, and I fell right into a chair and the legs broke. Because I weighed 170 pounds, when I hit the chair one or two legs broke. Bruce came over looking worried. I said to him, "I'm not hurt, I'm not hurt." He said, "Well, you broke my chair." He said, "I've done this a dozen times but nobody broke my chair." This was a gag he used to do, he used to set it up with a chair behind and he'd kick you into the chair. He kicked me so hard that when I hit the chair it broke. He said this was his favorite chair.

Q: Could you please talk to me about your experiences on the set of Enter the Dragon?
John Saxon: Most of the times we were talking about the things I indicated to you. I think he also liked me because I had no desire to upstage him; he was often feeling people were friendly with him and then would talk behind his back, like saying, "Yeah, well, I could beat

him up if necessary," and stuff like that. I had no such desire (Laughs), so we got along very well. He had a little anger here and there with other people in the cast, but I got along with him very well.

Q: Any hurdles or obstacles in shooting the fight scenes?
John Saxon: There was an accident in a fighting scene. I don't think it was done purposely. You know when he fights Bob Wall in that movie, at the end Bob Wall's beaten up so badly that he gets hold of two beer bottles and cracks them together. If that had been in America they'd have been made of sugar, but in Hong Kong at the time they used real beer bottles. He broke one and he held it in his hand, Bruce came in and they just happened to meet and Bruce's wrist got cut. Bruce was angry as hell!

Q: Can we talk about the fight choreography pertaining to your fight with Bolo?
John Saxon: Once when Bolo knocks me down and puts a scissors grip on my neck with his leg, Bruce said, "Bite him! Bite him!" It was acting, it wasn't real but that was a thing which Bruce introduced. Also, he had somebody doing things that I couldn't do, in some cases doing things he couldn't do, like that kick where he jumps over acrobat overhead; he didn't do that, it was done by a Chinese stuntman who was an acrobat. The same guy did the thing when I get back up with a backflip in the fight with Bolo.

Q: How was Bruce handling success at that point of his career?
John Saxon: He started, as I said, rather nervous, even on the first day of work, the scene of the big party with Sumo Wrestlers, he was rather tense. I was making additional dialogue and he was looking at me like: Is he trying to upstage me or something. But he caught on pretty quickly that wasn't my intention in any way. I was there about 12 weeks, but at the time apparently some footage was shown to him by Warner Brothers - they were contacting him I think - and suddenly he was coming on the set feeling all happy. I think they were telling him the stuff looks really good. So he got a sense of happiness.

He would say to me that we were going to go on nighttime television. At that time I was doing some musicals and Summer Stock, and I was vocalized. He said, "You're going to sing a song and I'm going to do this." He's making all these plans first for the promotion of the film. He worked extremely hard! He really started to get worn out I think towards the end of the film. The end of it is this: I had my wife and two-year-old son with me when I was in Hong Kong, and when I finished I went down to the set and said my good-byes to everybody and we were traveling to Japan and Thailand.

I was back home after several weeks and all of sudden I got a call one day. I picked up the phone and I said hello, and it's Bruce. I was so happy to hear from him. I'll tell you, you can be friendly in a movie and it often happens, people go from a movie, to a movie to another movie. Your best friend's somebody who's lasted maybe six weeks and you don't see him for six years. So I was very pleased that he'd called. I asked him what he was doing here, and he said he was going to see a doctor. I asked why, he said he'd been fainting. I said, "What!? Fainting?" That sounded very strange to me. Then he said, "Maybe there won't be a Bruce Lee," that made me rather nervous. We talked a little further and I asked where he was staying, whether he was staying in a hotel, he said he was staying at a friend's house. I said to him, "Why don't you give me the number and I'll give you a ring back later." And he did, he gave me the number.

He was going to take some physical tests because he'd been fainting. So I waited about a week then I called and he answered. I said, "How's everything going?" He said it was great. The doctor said he had a body of an 18-year-old. I said to him if we can get together, and he said he was leaving tomorrow and that he had to do some work on editing and stuff. I never saw him again or spoke to him again. Then maybe a month and half later somebody said Bruce Lee died. I said, "What are you talking about?" I called Warner Brothers and the producer said it was true. That was the last I saw or heard from Bruce Lee. When I was doing the publicity for the film I was sent out by Warner Brothers to go to New York, Philadelphia and other places.

Q: Were you supposed to go on with Bruce on the Johnny Carson Show to promote the movie?
John Saxon: He was talking about that, I said that's a great idea and so on. Had he lived we would have probably done that, because what I'm getting to is in New York I was being taken by a limousine to various radio stations to do interviews and so on. I remember lying back of the limousine, and I looked out on Broadway and I saw lines of people. Then I looked and looked and the line wasn't ending, and at the end of the street the lines of people turn on the street. I said, "What's going on there?" and the driver said, "That's your movie." I realized what a success it was, there must have been hundreds of people lined up to see it. I thought it was a pity, this is exactly what Bruce wanted so much in his life.

You have to understand something, when I first met him he talked about having been not given a chance in Hollywood when he expected to do a TV series called Kung Fu. He told me about that. The funny thing was I had been offered that part. What I'm getting at are two things here. Bruce was bitter because he said the part was built and prepared for him, but the television network thought differently. The look of the matter was: would people want to see a Chinese actor every week? And that's what he was told. They didn't think the American public wanted to see a Chinese actor every week. He was bitter about that. Enter the Dragon would have been for him the breakthrough that would have made all these other people who said nobody wants to see a Chinese actor every week think again.

The great success of Enter the Dragon had an effect on many people. These little kids now, five or six-year-old kids, who are taken by their mothers and fathers to the dojos, sometimes I see them and I say to them, "Why are you doing this? Mommy wants you to do this?" They say, "Because I saw Enter the Dragon on television, that's why." In India, in 1975 I did a film. I watched a bunch of Indians, I think it was in Bangalore or somewhere, there were a bunch of stuntmen and they were doing Karate. So I walked over to them and said, "Where did you guys work this out?" they said, Watching Enter the Dragon 22 times." That's what happened, that's the pity.

Once I said, "Listen, Bruce, could you imagine playing the role of a mild-mannered bank employee?" And he looked at me and said, "Hmmm…" (Laughs). What I was trying to say was: could you do martial arts movies all the time? I think all of them martial arts stars, Jean ClaudeVan Damme, Steven Seagal and Jackie Chan, have carried on doing just martial arts films. What I was saying is: what are you going to do when you're 55 years old? Are you going to be a martial arts hero, jumping the walls and things like that? One day I said to him, "Bruce, what would you do if you were 6ft 4 and a 190 pounds?" He stopped and he seriously thought and said, "If I was 6ft 1 and 190 pounds I'd rule the world." He had great ambition.

I got something from him. I've got it somewhere here in my little office in my house, he wrote all the plans he had. He expected by this and this year: I'm going to do this and that and by the time I'll be worth $10 million. And in fact, one day he asked me if I would come with him, his wife, and my wife and we'd go to the Run Run Shaw's studious. I said OK and that I'd be interested. So Run Run Shaw sent a Rolls Royce and Bruce was telling me, "Run Run Shaw wants me to do a film for him and he's offering me $500,000." I said, "Wow!" He said, "If Marlon Brando can get $2 million, so can I." He was very, very ambitious. Very ambitious.

You know what? One of the things about the Kung Fu series is that I was considered for it when they didn't want Bruce Lee. I was second in line. I couldn't do it because I had a contract with a studio where I was expected to do the television series about doctors, so I had a contract already. And they couldn't get me out of the contract so I couldn't do it. I would have not done it the way they did it, the mysterious, spiritual way David Carradine did it.What I'm getting at is when Bruce spoke about having been placed aside, I can't remember honestly, either whether I was shy on saying, "The producers wanted me after you." I can't remember whether I did say it to him or not, still to this day I can't remember. I remember asking myself if I should say it to him (Laughs), or maybe I'd rather not say it to him.

I would have not done anything like David Carradine did it. The idea was the spiritual stuff was almost beyond reality. I did an episode because I knew the producers and the directors, who asked me to come on as a guest star. What happened was I played a tough Western guy, a bounty hunter who grabs Cane. Then we have a fight. I told the director, "Listen, I'm the rough, tough cowboy type of a guy and I just chained him." I said, "Let's see what he can do to release the hooks." They said, "No, that's crazy, nobody could fight against him." I said, "OK, nobody could fight against him then." In other words he was beyond being human.

When we did the scene it was choreographed, I would throw a punch at him then he was going to do something. I remember I did one-two-three and he was going to hit me, but he put his arm against my chest and I looked at him, and I was wondering why didn't he hit me. And they said, "Cut!" I said, "What's going on?" David Carradine says, "When I touch you, you fly back." So I fly 15 feet away, it was more supernatural stuff.

Q: It must have been one hell of a task to coordinate everything precisely on the final fight scene on the fields in Enter the Dragon. Was it horrendous to film?
John Saxon: Yeah, to me. To tell you the truth it was eight continuous days of fighting, and to be perfectly honest at the end of eight days I was glad it was all over. Bruce choreographed almost everything I did, although once in a while I would make a suggestion and he'd say, "Yes, that's great, let's do that too," other than the scene at the beginning of the movie, when I'm in the park in LA. Along with a Chinese Tai Chi guy I went to the offices where the director was, I asked him, "How do you want to do this?" And he looked at me and said, "I don't know, how do you want to do it?" He didn't have a clue about martial arts - on how to do something like that.

So I spent about an hour in the office explaining and demonstrating. I said, "I could do this," and Jimmy Woo, the Tai Chi guy, said, "We'll try this!" So I was doing this for an hour, then I left the office. So I knew what I was going to do the day after. But I pulled my hamstring on the back of my leg by the time I got home. I was taking a shower and looked at it, it was all black and blue. The next day on the set when I was doing the stuff the director didn't have a clue. He set up on top of a hill where it was difficult, he didn't have much of a clue as far as martial arts.

Q: You enjoyed and spent considerable time with Bruce on a social level. Any amusing anecdotes?
John Saxon: Actually, what I did was after we became acquainted and so on, I suggested having a party with Bruce and his wife, Raymond and his wife, and there was a couple my wife knew, (former world heavyweight champion) Gene Tunney's son, who was living in Hong Kong doing business there. So I called him and asked him if he wanted to come to a dinner party. We all sat down, we were all chatting, finally Bruce understood this guy was Gene Tunney's son, he stopped and said, "I could have taken your father." My shoulders went up to my ears, Oh God! (Laughs). Bruce said Tunney only had two weapons but he had four. Jay Tunney didn't want to talk about whether his father could have been beaten by Bruce or not. It was just a moment where I felt very awkward that I brought a guest at a dinner party and Bruce was talking about having possibly beaten his father, who was the heavyweight champion of the world at one time. Things like that occurred.

Sugar Ray Leonard, for example, was very, very impressed by Bruce. Even Bruce would say when we were making a movie, I think he said one time in a conversation, "It's good you punch him and he falls down - he must fall down because the script says so." Of course, that's the way it is in the movies. In reality fighting of any kind is an unexpected thing.

Q: Bruce Lee was more than a film star who injected a new wave of national interest in the martial arts, he was a real martial artist. What's your opinion?
John Saxon: My advice, going back to the first meeting with him at his home, I felt very comfortable because he had things around like magazines like Ironman, and the Kettlebells, weights and things like that. Very, very quickly we somehow got into a conversation where he said, "I am a martial artist first and an actor second." And I said, "I'm an actor first and a martial artist second." At the time saying I was a martial artist was an awkward thing because the people I worked out with said we were practicing Karate, we didn't call ourselves martial artists. Anyway, that's the way we felt. He thought primarily of being a martial artist.

What I'm getting at is if he had continued, would he be able to play and would he want to play a role where you don't beat up five guys or something like that? That's when he said he was thinking about it. Would he have been a movie star? Possibly, possibly! I mean, outside of being a martial arts actor he had a lot of charm and he was very, very full of energy and had charisma.

The first day, as a matter of fact, when we left his home he said, "I'm going to take you to lunch." I think we picked up Jim Kelly on the way and we were walking. Jim was playing semi-pro tennis, then I heard he became a Minister. But the last time I saw him was at the Gracie's studio, that would have been 1992 maybe, 16 years or so. The producer, Fred Weintraub, I think made him think that I changed the script because Jim said something strange to me once. He died in the movie. Fred may have told him I was the one that was supposed to die but I insisted I wasn't going to die in the movie. That's not true. I think Jim Kelly was told that, because he made a remark once and I couldn't understand. He said, "I'm never going to die in a movie again." He was saying this to me but I didn't realize what he was talking about. My reaction at the time was, "Why? I've died in 15 movies." But I think he felt it was my doings, but it's not true, not true at all.

THE LEGACY

CHAPTER FOUR

THE BOXING LEGACY

Bruce Lee was heavily influenced by Western Boxing and some of the elite prize fighters of his era, which included Jack Dempsey, Rocky Marciano, Edwin Haislet, Jim Driscoll, Sugar Ray Robinson and Joe Louis. The aforementioned all contributed, in some shape or form, to his development as the most innovative martial arts exponent of the century. It's no secret Lee was an avid fan of the greatest heavyweight champion in history, the one and only Muhammad Ali.

The profound impact the flamboyant Ali had on Lee is reasonably well documented. And it's no secret Lee borrowed and analyzed many concepts and movements from Ali's fights. His research lead him to discover and cultivate concepts for his personal art of Jeet Kune Do through countless hours of reading manuals and books written by such legendary fighters as Jack Dempsey, Joe Louis, Edwin Haislet and Jim Driscoll (Welsh featherweight champion in the early 1900s).

According to one source, Ali was a huge fan of Lee and the feeling was mutual. "Bruce purchased video footage of championship fights of Muhammad Ali. He ran these and others through his hand-editing machine, studying combat techniques, constantly thinking of the fight scenes he might use in his films," Linda Lee reveals. In fact, much of the fight action between Chuck Norris and Bruce in Way of the Dragon was choreographed to mirror the second and third rounds of Ali's fight with Cleveland Williams.

Bolo Yeung, co-star of Enter the Dragon and South East Asian bodybuilding champion, remembers Bruce studying an Ali documentary that showed footage from several of his fights when he visited him at the Golden Harvest film studios. Bruce had set up a wide full-length mirror in the room to reflect Ali's image from the screen. He would move to Ali's movements and would try to anticipate the movements beforehand. "Everybody says I must fight Ali someday," Bruce remarked, "I'm studying every move he makes. I'm getting to know how he thinks and moves."

Today, it's not uncommon to hear fans debating if Lee could have beaten Ali. At the end of the day, it's like asking if Mike Tyson could beat Royce Gracie in a Boxing match. Bruce was not a Boxer, and has gone on record professing he could never beat Ali in a Boxing match. But Lee had kicked martial arts tradition into smithereens and pursued his development of the ultimate fighting concept, which within its framework encompassed a composite of elements which reflected all-out street fighting. Lee would have beaten almost anyone in the street.

As much as Lee was intrigued by Boxing champions, and their rigorous training methods - which he eventually absorbed into his system - he had an equal, if not greater, impact on legendary fighters who came after him. One thing that has been established amongst fighters and various sports personalities at their zenith today is that the legendary Bruce Lee inspired them both in their careers and their approach to training. Sugar Ray Leonard - probably the best pound-for-pound Boxer in history - once told Playboy magazine in an interview, "I wanted to do in Boxing what Bruce Lee was able to do in the martial arts. Lee was an artist and like him, I try to get beyond the fundamentals of my sport. I want my fights to be seen as plays." It's not surprising that Leonard's major influence - which has been shared by other elite athletes - was not a Boxer, but Bruce Lee. Even 'Iron' Mike Tyson would study Lee in motion to learn explosiveness.

Ricky 'The Hitman' Hatton has publicly revealed just how much of an impact Lee had on him. "I was heavily into Bruce Lee films as a kid. Don't ask me why but there was something about him which drew me like a moth to a light bulb," he said. "For me, my whole world revolved around Bruce Lee…I had all his movies on video and would watch him morning, noon and night. He was very much my hero, so I started to go to Kickboxing classes at the age of seven." Some of the prominent professional Boxers who professed to me the profound impact Bruce Lee had on them included the four-time heavyweight champion Evander Holyfield, and 'Big' Joe Egan (Mike Tyson's sparring partner and Golden Gloves champion), who Tyson labeled 'The Toughest White Man on the Planet', which is no small label indeed.

> *"Of course, at that time Bruce Lee was the guy who wasn't a big guy but was very quick. I don't know anybody who I'm in contact with who doesn't know Bruce Lee. Bruce Lee was a big thing! Karate (martial arts) was another form of Boxing, you had to learn more things than you would in Boxing (Laughs). In Boxing, you could punch with your hands, but in Karate you had so many different ways of doing things, and you had to be very balanced to do that. I wasn't really into Karate that much because there were too many things you had to learn.*

He influenced a lot of people and showed that size doesn't make a difference. The power is from the knowledge you have. So I think that was the greatest point in his whole thing: power is knowledge if you have it. You have more power than one may not even suspect. He was HEAVY! I don't know anybody who was better. He was very technical."

- Evander Holyfield

"I grew up watching Bruce Lee movies, and everybody wanted to aspire to be an athlete like Bruce Lee. I was into Boxing. I wanted to be as fit as and have the physique of Bruce Lee. He was inspirational to so many people, he was just a fantastic athlete and martial artist. He was just brilliant, absolutely brilliant. And his films were very exciting, even though we were under 18, we used go watch them. He was such a fantastic fighter in his movies and in real life. He was the ultimate martial artist. I suppose anyone involved in Boxing knows it's still full contact, and his martial art was full contact. He was so inspirational to so many people, and no matter what generation, he is still an icon of every generation. He will have a following from the next generation and the generations to come. People will still refer to one of the greatest martial artists of all time, Bruce Lee. His name in martial arts and in films is cast in stone."

- 'Big' Joe Egan

Lee's analytical research methods and revolutionary approach to combat paved the way for future martial arts exponents. And would eventually propagate the necessity of including Western Boxing into their training, which proved to be superior in certain aspects to the various traditional approaches to punching. Dan Inosanto, who was Lee's number one student and training partner and the only person in the world Lee certified to teach his art of Jeet Kune Do, states, "Bruce borrowed something from everybody. He liked Ali's footwork and his outside fighting. He liked Sugar Ray Robinson's moves, his bobs and weaves. He borrowed from all their finer points and adapted their training techniques and devices."

As can clearly be seen in his notes, which were later published as the Tao of Jeet Kune Do after his untimely death, entire passages are quoted from Boxing sources. Notably, the sources were from literature authored by Jack Dempsey, whom Bruce had great respect for and consumed much information on regarding the cultivation of power in his punches. He had assistance from a Boxing manual that was published in the 1940s. His Tao of Jeet Kune Do contains a lot of theories on fighting from this book. "A good Boxer is able to beat his opponent to the punch with lightning-fast leads, draw out his opponent's counter punches with feints in such a way as to make the counter punch miss," Lee wrote. It is imperative for the observer to understand Bruce's mindset, why he researched Boxing and integrated certain elements into his personal repertoire. Lee, standing at 5ft 7 and weighing in at only 135 pounds, was able to hit harder than a man twice his size, because Lee's blow with a heavy force was much faster, which in return cultivated imponderable power.

He was known to have had lightning speed which would just mesmerize the observer. Joey Orbillo, who was a world-class Boxer - ranked fifth in the world at the time - and a Boxing trainer, publicly affirmed that Bruce Lee was the fastest man he had ever seen. He had sparred with Bruce and admits Bruce made him feel like an inept child.

Lee continues in his notes, "Western Boxing is too overdaring because of restrictions on illegal 'unfair' tactics as compared to the overprotectiveness of the Oriental martial arts caused by the no holds barred, full-bodily target." Although Lee absorbed a lot from Western Boxing, implementing concepts and techniques into his personal art's framework, he knew the limits of Boxing in an all-out street fight. Furthermore, if we examine his personal notes, Lee makes a comment that should emphasize the need for adaptability and to 'absorb what is useful', as Lee himself liked to put it. "If you put on a glove, you are dealing in rules. You must know the rules to survive. But in the street, you have more tools in your favor - the kick, the elbow..." wrote Lee.

During the 60s, it was rare to see martial artists employing the training equipment that is commonly seen in today's dojos, such as the heavy bag, speed ball, top and bottom ball and the focus mitts. One of Bruce Lee's fortes was equipment training, which he implemented into his regular workouts to cultivate the devastating power and lightning speed we have all been mesmerized by. In addition to using equipment, Lee would skip, jog, shadowbox and integrate certain Boxing drills and methods, including shadowboxing with very light weights which Boxers use to develop their explosiveness and speed.

He learned one of his favorite heavy bag techniques from a book written by former world heavyweight champion Joe 'The Brown Bomber' Louis. In the book Louis advised that, after hitting the bag whilst stationary, you should give it a slight push to start it slowly swinging and when the bag starts to swing away you should hook sharply with either hand in the direction of the swing of the bag. Lee found this appealing as it would cause him to deal with an oncoming force more than just a stationary target. Lee would always go a step further in his quest for perfection by implementing his own innovative concepts and methods. He would never hesitate to modify ways of performing certain drills or exercises. "Bruce's ability on the speed ball was amazing. He used his head, elbows, shoulders and forearms...then he would move out to long range and work his kicks, heel and hook kicks," recalls Dan Inosanto.

Today, you will rarely find a martial arts gym without focus mitts or pads. Lee got the concept of using focus mitts from the British Boxers. He was using them way back in the early 60s, well before any martial artists started using this versatile piece of equipment. Lee would once again take it to the next level by incorporating kicks, knees, fingers and elbows in addition to hand techniques. Bruce Lee strongly advocated full contact sparring to his students and fellow martial artists alike. Joe Lewis says, "Bruce liked contact and he would put on Kenpo gloves (to spar)." These gloves were similar to those seen in Enter the Dragon's opening fight scene and gave Lee more freedom of movement; he could pull, grab and trap. This further illustrates the point of Lee not limiting himself to a certain method of sparing.

It is clear that Lee did not want to 'serve' Boxing by being molded into a certain type of a fighter, but instead wanted Boxing to 'serve' him. According to Dan Inosanto, Lee would have easily been a top three ranked fighter in the lightweight or junior-lightweight division had he pursued professional Boxing.

Bruce Lee's exposure to Western Boxing did not start in the United States. As a youngster in Hong Kong, Lee was a fervent student of the Wing Chun system of Kung Fu. His first exposure to Western Boxing actually was back in Hong Kong when he entered the Inter-School Boxing Championships. It has been revealed that Lee actually only had three weeks to prepare for this competition, and ironically he had never boxed before. At the final, he met three-time champion Gary Elms and knocked him out in the third round. Before arriving in the final against Elms, Lee had knocked out three Boxers in succession in the first round.

It is imperatively clear that Western Boxing played an integral role in Bruce's own development and elevation of his unique art. Some unique training devices and methods, many hand and evasive techniques, as well as fluid footwork and attributes such as power, speed and endurance would eventually find their way into Lee's core training schedule and regime. He was able to blend these elements to form a cohesive force which worked particularly well for him. Many of the professional and amateur athletes and fighters I've spoken to have one thing in common: they all admire Bruce Lee and have positively been influenced by him in a way which has enriched their lives. Jhoon Rhee, internationally known as the father of American Tae Kwon Do, and one of the few martial arts personalities to have worked with both Bruce Lee and Muhammad Ali, says, "His name is still the biggest in the martial arts. When I went to Russia I met people who didn't know about Muhammad Ali but they all knew Bruce Lee."

In the following exclusive interviews, legendary Boxing champions pay homage to the man who captivated the attention of athletes and fighters of all kinds, inspiring them profoundly.

SUGAR RAY LEONARD

ugar Ray Leonard is no doubt one of the greatest Boxers of all time. Out of all the professional Boxers who were influenced by Bruce Lee, Sugar Ray Leonard is the one who has publicly acknowledged Lee as having an indelible impact on him. In 1997 Leonard was inducted into the International Boxing Hall of Fame. He's also been the co-host and Boxing mentor, alongside Sylvester Stallone, to aspiring fighters on the TV reality Boxing series The Contender.

Q: How did you get involved in Boxing?
Sugar Ray Leonard: I pursued Boxing because I was such a shrimp and a non-athlete. My brother Roger and Kenny were basketball players, football players and track stars. Boxing kind of found me. I was the type of young kid at 14 that was never really athletically inclined; they were real athletes. The same reason my brother Roger encouraged me to come down to the center and get involved with Boxing. So back in 1970, Boxing became part of my life. Muhammad Ali and Bruce Lee were two of my idols, and my dad.

Q: You have openly said Bruce Lee was an inspiration to you. Please expand on this statement.
Sugar Ray Leonard: I've told people all over the world that Bruce Lee was one of my idols. Mainly because of his mental stability, that very few people can reach and maintain to compete at the highest level. His fighting spirit, because it was more mental than just physical, what he called 'emotional content'. And for me, that's what I needed when I had to face major obstacles and opponents like Roberto Duran and Marvin Hagler. Because of my mental stability I was able to beat those guys.

Q: What made Bruce Lee so unique and so appealing?
Sugar Ray Leonard: Bruce Lee had charisma, he had that package, he could fight! He was versatile, he was deadly and he kind of looked like the least guy who could defend himself, but he had such an ability to outperform anyone no matter what size. Bruce Lee always had a way, he had style. I loved that style.

Q: What is the most amazing physical attribute about Bruce which intrigues you?
Sugar Ray Leonard: The most amazing thing about Bruce was that he could generate so much speed and velocity in his punches. Straight punches which he used, he used his body in proper leverage in order to gain this because he understood the mechanics of the body. That was special.

Q: Would you agree he influenced athletes and not just the martial arts fraternity?
Sugar Ray Leonard: Without a question Bruce Lee influenced athletes of all kinds, of every kind, because it's all about having to perform at the highest. It all comes together. I tell these Boxers today on The Contenders show that you must integrate your mind, body and spirit, which is all connected, to get the best results.

Q: What lesson can someone take from Bruce Lee to use as a blueprint in excelling?
Sugar Ray Leonard: Bruce was an example of what hard work is, there were no boundaries, there was no racial barrier, nothing! People saw Bruce Lee as a major force, a positive force, he was special.

Q: What impressed you most about Bruce?
Sugar Ray Leonard: What impressed me most about Bruce was his movement. He would glide and he was not methodical, he was good and spontaneous in his movement. And everything he did was for a reason, he just didn't move for the sake of it. He moved for a reason to get to a specific point, to get into position, to take something, to position himself. Everything was for a reason.

Q: Now that he has gone for more than three-and-a-half decades, can we expect anyone to replicate Bruce Lee's style?
Sugar Ray Leonard: Only Bruce could really perform the type of punches he threw, the power, the speed and the accuracy in his punches. The power he was able to generate was unbelievable. Bruce Lee had the ability to understand the human body and the mechanics and was able to execute powerful punches at such short range with such a velocity, there was

nothing he could not overcome. I've not seen too many other martial artists in the same league. I love Jackie Chan, Jet Li and those guys, they remind me a great deal of Bruce Lee.

Q: Is there anyone big as Bruce Lee - or can be - as far as having a worldwide impact?
Sugar Ray Leonard: I can't think of anyone that can reach that level. Bruce Lee is an icon, he is in the dictionary when you see the word and you say 'THE GREATEST', it's 'Bruce Lee'. That's the way it is. He stands out from the rest. Bruce Lee will never be replaced! Not from this planet.

GEORGE FOREMAN

George Foreman, the two-time world heavyweight champion and Olympic gold medalist, is one of the greats of heavyweight Boxing. He has been named one of the 25 greatest fighters of all time by Ring magazine. At the age of 45, he fought and knocked out 26-year-old Michael Moorer to become the oldest man ever to win a major heavyweight title. Today, he is an entrepreneur and promotes the George Foreman Grilling Machine, which has made him a fortune. Foreman has been heavily influenced by Bruce Lee as can be verified from this rare interview.

Q: Were you ever impressed by Bruce Lee and why?
George Foreman: I think even today, Bruce Lee still holds the intricate part of what an athlete wants to look like. As far as movement, a good Boxer who packs a punch, in his mind he sees himself as Bruce Lee, even if a football player wants to takedown, he wants to stand like Bruce Lee. Bruce Lee has made a great impression on all athletes, especially in America. And the idea of taking his shirt off really shows his appearance, no one is as impressive like Bruce Lee. I think if you look at Bruce Lee and Muhammad Ali, you think about two men who have had the greatest impression on athletes.

Q: What did you think of the power he was able to generate? For a guy who weighed 135 pounds he was known to hit real hard.
George Foreman: I think Bruce Lee's image, once you look at it you will detect so much power, so much dedication, and you look at him (and see) the energy and dedication in what he did - that's what it was. I don't think any athlete can consider himself successful without some impersonation, especially when he competes, from Bruce Lee.

Q: Bruce Lee admired Boxers, including Muhammad Ali, and he took elements from Boxing to integrate into his own personal fighting system. Were you aware of this?

George Foreman: We feel Bruce Lee was pure martial arts and, of course, he integrated a lot of things that we were doing in Boxing into his form of martial arts. So he made it not only accepted into martial arts but it appeared to be beautiful for an audience. And this is what Bruce Lee was able to do better than anyone else: he made it look beautiful.

Q: Why do you think Bruce Lee is still admired after 35 years after his death, and will his enduring legacy continue to last?

George Foreman: Any great athlete, especially a martial artist or a Boxer, all he had to do is see one Bruce Lee movie and he'll say - it doesn't matter how young he is - "That's the way I want to do it! That's the way I want to be!" Bruce Lee still has the impression of how he appeared in the movie and how he carried himself even in interviews. Bruce Lee has had a lasting impression and will still be making an impression 50 years from today on young guys.

Q: Can you recall when he hit the box office with the release of Enter the Dragon in 1973?

George Foreman: I remember, I was in Hawaii in 1973 and I went into see the movie Enter the Dragon. When I walked out after the movie, on all my back I had chills on me! I was the heavyweight champion of the world by the way, all I could think was wow!! I was in shock! He left all the audiences awestruck. Bruce Lee changed everything!

Q: Which is your favorite Bruce Lee movie?

George Foreman: Enter the Dragon was not only my favorite Bruce Lee movie but my favorite all-time action movie, a great movie. Bruce Lee movies were about the good winning, and good had a reason to win. And he was skilful and the camera worked with him like we'd never seen before. Oh, it was just a beautiful thing to remember. Even as I talk to you, I still feel it.

Q: Bruce was facing racial pressures at a time when it was hard in the West for a Chinese guy to be accepted as a major star in Hollywood. Do you feel Bruce Lee broke barriers to lead the way which opened the doors for future stars?

George Foreman: Bruce Lee was very important because not only did he make a great movie but he was a box office 'champion'. He was handsome, nobody could deny that Bruce was handsome. He had everything that makes a top Hollywood movie, he had box office appeal and his action skills. From that point on Hollywood had to pay attention to him.

Q: If Bruce Lee took the professional Boxing route, in your opinion how would he have done?
George Foreman: Bruce Lee was a good athlete and he could've been a good Boxer. He could have been anything; in his weight class he would have been a Boxing champion.

RICKY HATTON

World champion Boxer Ricky 'The Hitman' Hatton was heavily influenced by the late Bruce Lee since he was a young kid. As a youngster, he started attending Kickboxing classes and later made a transition into Boxing. Hatton has fought some of the top Boxers in his weight categories and his popularity can be felt on both sides of the pond. Hatton realizes the profound impact Lee has had not only on the combat sports world but on people from all walks of life.

Q: Before you boxed you trained in martial arts, Kickboxing to be precise, how did you get involved?
Ricky Hatton: I got into Kickboxing really because as a youngster, when I was around eight or nine years old, I used to watch Bruce Lee films. I think he was absolutely brilliant! I used to think this guy is wicked and I'll give Kickboxing a try. From Kickboxing I went to Boxing. When I think about it, if there was no Bruce Lee and his films, I may never have done Kickboxing and maybe I would never have gone into Boxing. So I owe a lot to Bruce Lee really, he was absolutely fantastic.

Q: What fascinates you the most about Bruce Lee?
Ricky Hatton: At a young age I used to like the Kickboxing side of it, and as I got older and little bit of knowledgeable of the sport, conditioning and speed, I think it was his explosiveness, he was so explosive and so passionate. Basically, he was the best. When you first start at a sport you always want to become the best and dream about becoming the best. Bruce Lee was the second to none. We also have good martial artists we've heard of over the years like Chuck Norris and Steven Seagal, who people like, but I think Bruce Lee was

in a class of his own. He was absolutely frighteningly fast and had the whole package really. He wasn't just a martial arts expert, he's an icon now.

Q: Did you know Bruce researched Boxing extensively and researched Muhammad Ali?
Ricky Hatton: I think he's every bit as much of an icon as Muhammad Ali, who wasn't just a great Boxer but a great man. I think Bruce Lee was the same. So I could imagine, when most people are going to look at icons in the sports, in particularly fighting aspects, you would look at Muhammad Ali and Bruce Lee as your hero.

Q: Do you think Bruce Lee is a fine example of someone who was a lightweight but who had the capacity to hit as powerful as a heavyweight? And does this inspire small and light fighters?
Ricky Hatton: It's all about leverages and balance, he could kick and punch from every angle, which is what you really want to be able to do as a Boxer. His technique was fantastic and his unique style, there wasn't anything that he couldn't do. Because he was so small (from) his leverages, angles and his speed he could get more power, which is what basically you have to do in Boxing. All your power comes from your feet from the floor and the timing and angles of which you throw your punches, and that was the same with Bruce Lee. He was able to generate so much power from his angle and timing and speed.

Q: Why do you think Boxers, bodybuilders and athletes of all kinds admire Bruce Lee, what is the key element here?
Ricky Hatton: I just think he was the best. He stood for much more than just martial arts. He was not only a great martial artist but he was a great man. No matter what profession you are in, whether you're a singer, footballer, an actor or whatever you do, you can look at someone like Bruce Lee and you rise to another level because he was so exceptional.

Q: What was the first Bruce Lee movie you saw?
Ricky Hatton: I was only about seven, I've seen them all, of course, over the years and in fact I still watch them every now and again. One of the most which sticks out in my mind is Enter the Dragon, absolutely fantastic, great film. I've got it on tape and I still watch it every now and again. The Big Boss and the others I still watch, I'm just a huge fan. At that time for a Chinese guy to become a Hollywood star must have been damn hard for him compared to white actors, it just shows you what type of a man he was.

Q: Bruce Lee died at a relatively young age and his legacy lives on, just how much of an impact has he had on the world?
Ricky Hatton: Massive, massive. Strange one really, I find it absolutely fascinating, obviously his death was a bit of a mystery, and the same thing happened to his son many years later. I find it incredible, unbelievable story. Nobody will ever get to the bottom of exactly what happened and it was really tragic, but you find for most superstars there always seems to be a tragic ending - Muhammad Ali with his Parkinson's syndrome, Bruce Lee with his sudden death.

I'm sure Bruce Lee wanted it to be different but stuff like that helps his legacy go even further. He's not just remembered for his excellence in martial arts but also the sad way of the mystery of his death, a kind of an Elvis Presley syndrome. I'm a massive, massive Bruce Lee fan. I still watch his films to this day, and I think in 50 years in time people will still be watching Bruce Lee's films because he was that good.

★ ★ ★ CHAPTER FIVE ★ ★ ★

THE BODYBUILDING LEGACY

Bruce Lee was a paragon of health and fitness and a true proponent of physical conditioning. He was a pioneer in his approach to combining weight training and cardiovascular training with his martial arts practice. To this effect, he spent an inordinate time researching bodybuilding, fitness and exercise physiology. As new and different approaches came out, he would physically try them out and he would incorporate these into his regime if he felt they would aid him and accelerate his performance in his martial arts. Above all, it had to be functional, and the strength which was developed through training able to be utilized in excelling in combat skills. He was constantly changing and refining his workout techniques. For Lee, this meant constantly trying new exercises and retooling his programs.

Lee's 5ft 7, 135-pound frame was covered with rippling muscles. With his lean, muscular and striated physique, he was an envy of even the bodybuilders. Bruce Lee's impact and influence on bodybuilders, both professional and amateur, is evident. His feats of strength and lean, shredded physique have been marveled at by some of the elite bodybuilding luminaries and IFBB champions, which include Dorian Yates, Lenda Murray, Flex Wheeler, Franco Columbu, Shawn Ray, Lou Ferrigno and Lee Haney to name a few. Bodybuilding magnate and trainer to the champions Joe Weider described Lee's physique as 'the most defined body I've ever seen'.

According to some of Lee's early students, he had used various form of resistance training methods when he was in Seattle. However, it wasn't until he moved to Oakland, Southern California, that he developed a deep interest in bodybuilding. Lee discovered his best friend, James Lee, had a lifelong interest in bodybuilding and was a weightlifting champion. As soon as Lee moved to the Los Angeles area to carve out a career in Hollywood, persistent weight training became an integral component of his overall training schedule. Allen Joe, who was one of Lee's devoted students and close friends in Oakland, recalls, "I remember visiting him at his house in Bel Air years later, and I could see the development of his body was incredible. He went from this skinny kid to this incredible Adonis." Joe was a champion bodybuilder himself. Lee had started to assimilate as much information as possibly he could relating to bodybuilding and exercise physiology. He also delved into proper nutrition and supplements. He eventually amassed a collection of hundreds of books and periodicals. He read and even subscribed to bodybuilding magazines including Strength and Health, the predecessor to Muscle & Fitness.

By now, Lee had dedicated himself to a seemingly impossible pursuit, that of building his naturally frail-looking frame into an awesomely effective and well-conditioned fighting machine. His passion for cultivating a strong, healthy and powerful body bordered fanaticism. Bruce Lee's training regime, unlike those of most of his contemporaries, consisted of all the imperatives of 'total' fitness: strength, endurance, coordination, flexibility and so on. Adapting a cross-training methodology, he believed that fitness training should have three key elements: stretching for flexibility, weight training for strength and cardiovascular for endurance. He was cognizant that strength and power were not exactly synonymous. His interest lay in functional strength. He believed strength needed to be translated into accelerated velocity to produce power, an attribute which was much more important than strength. Lee's garage housed unique training devices, which he would implement to train various parts of his body and martial arts, which included specially made hand grip machines, a squat stand, barbell set and a basic bench.

Lee heavily concentrated on two body parts: the forearms and the stomach. His rectus abdominis is so prominent that to this day it is marveled by all those in pursuit of developing washboard abs. Athletes from diverse disciplines are sometimes tempted to emulate training programs of their idols and champions. In the martial arts, the overwhelming tendency appears to reside in duplicating the unique methods of training utilized by the Little Dragon. Many believe Lee might have been the best pound-for-pound athlete in history. Although one may not - professional or amateur - be able to rise to the standard and heights that of Lee, one can certainly be inspired to reach one's own genetic potential by absorbing Lee's methods and integrating them into one's own regime.

The legendary bodybuilding champion Bill Pearl was the first professional bodybuilder to author bodybuilding training course manuals and booklets. The former Mr. Universe had the opportunity to meet Bruce Lee in the mid-60s on Muscle Beach, California. Another legend from the 50s and 60s that Lee admired was Larry Scott, the first ever bodybuilder to win the Mr. Olympia title. Lee would collect and analyze the champion bodybuilder's routines and experiment to see what would work for him. Lee's impact went beyond the legendary iron-pumpers of the 60s decade.

"He (Bruce Lee) was involved with weight training. I had also written some training courses on big arms, big chests and big forearms and so on. And Bruce Lee was interested in getting my booklets because he wanted to improve his hand strength for martial arts. So I was happy to give them to him. And he used some of our training courses to improve his martial arts. I gave them to him. It was the only time I met him, and we corresponded a few times, and then he died. I think he was as impressed with me as I was impressed with him. It was obvious he knew I was a weight trainer and who I was. When he saw me, he walked up to me because he knew who I was. He was very muscular, he was extremely agile and a tremendous athlete, and I admire him. He was very lean and muscular, and he had a physique which could be 'used'. I had a physique which had to be 'shown'. There was a difference between the two of us - he could 'use' his physique, I had to 'show' mine. There's no question Bruce Lee was the forefront of the whole weight training-martial arts combination."

- Bill Pearl

"Well, Bruce Lee...I hate to say this but he wasn't the focus of my attention, but I was very impressed by his muscularity, it was fantastic. And his stage presence was very good and he certainly was a fantastic athlete. There's no way you could not be impressed by that. I never knew what his training program was, and I had no idea that he knew I was even alive. I heard about that recently, that he happened to follow some of our training ideas. But as far as Bruce Lee, there's no way you could look at his physique and not be impressed. He had a great physique, really muscular. It wasn't just muscular but he had beautiful proportions as well. He had a physique that would have done well in bodybuilding, had he chosen to pursue (the sport) wisely. It was something he was good at, and could make a name for himself in. It's interesting and very flattering to know he found what I had of being a benefit to him, it's nice to hear that. I don't think I've ever seen a martial artist to have the degree of muscularity that Bruce Lee had, and looking as impressive as he did. Obviously he was using something (training methods) normal martial artists weren't -

291

he looked terrific. He knew something those before and those after him learned like he did."

- Larry Scott

The greatest bodybuilder of all time (turned politician) Arnold Schwarzenegger was clearly impressed by Lee. The Governor of California revealed this to former FLEX writer and Bruce Lee historian John Little in an interview.

"Bruce Lee had a very - I mean a very - defined physique. He had very little body fat. I mean, he probably had one of the lowest body fat counts of any athlete around. And I think that's why he looked so believable. There's a lot of people that do all these moves and they do have the skill, but they don't look visually as believable or as impressive as Bruce Lee did. He was one of a kind. He was an idol for so many. The greatest thing about Bruce Lee is that he inspires so many millions of kids out there who want to follow in his footsteps. They want to become martial artists, they want to go and be in movies... someone like Bruce Lee provides a tremendous inspiration, which helps so many kids around the world. He had a profound and tremendous impact worldwide, and I think that he will be therefore admired for a long time."

- Arnold Schwarzenegger

Bruce Lee's sheer athleticism allowed him to build the perfect body, which not only helped him in his objective but gave him a physique that looked finely tuned. Lee defied attempts to separate his dazzling public persona from his athletic brilliance. His trademark physique was a marvel ahead of its time and still fascinates people all over the world. Lee's well-muscled and balanced frame has become the criterion by which so many others are measured. His conditioning, mental focus, commitment, training and approach is what today's physique competitors and bodybuilders aspire to.

Today, there are athletes, actors and individuals engaged in the pursuit of replicating the physique Lee had. In the following exclusive interviews with some of the great physique champions, you will discover just how much of an impact Bruce Lee had on these IFBB bodybuilding champions. One thing is for sure, they are all cognizant of the dedication which went into developing one of the most lethal physiques of the century.

DORIAN YATES

Dorian Yates is considered by many to be the greatest bodybuilder of modern times, and the most popular and inspirational bodybuilder on the planet. He won the Mr. Olympia title six consecutive times and dominated bodybuilding in the 90s in the manner Arnold Schwarzenegger did in the 70s. Inspired by Bruce Lee, Yates started training in the martial arts as a teenager before pursuing bodybuilding. To this day, Bruce Lee continues to have a positive influence on Yates, who has admired Lee's feats of strength since he was a kid.

Q: Dorian, how did you get into bodybuilding?
Dorian Yates: Actually, I was involved in martial arts first, through the Bruce Lee movies as many people were in the early 70s. Initially Kung Fu wasn't available to me so I was doing Karate in this gym, Temple Gym, which is mine now.

Q: You were, of course, influenced by the late great Bruce Lee...
Dorian Yates: I think Bruce Lee is more than a martial artist, he's an icon. And he brought martial arts to the mainstream. Even the average guy in the street is going to know who Bruce Lee is. That's where Bruce Lee is different, he transcended his genre and made martial arts mainstream.

Q: Being a professional bodybuilder, did his physique appeal to you in anyway?
Dorian Yates: When I first studied his physique I found it to be very impressive, because he was very lean and also very symmetrical. I'm sure he would have made a very good bodybuilder had he pursued this.

Q: He was persistent in his quest to fully reach his potential as a martial artist and athlete. He has been acknowledged as being the first person to combine weight training with the martial arts...

Dorian Yates: If you look back at his training manuals you could see he was bodybuilding and weight training back in the 60s. This was 40 years ago. Back then people were saying if you do weight training it's going to slow you down, make you inflexible and muscle-bound. Now people know it's going to make you more powerful and give you more advantage. Bruce Lee knew that back then.

Q: Why are a lot of the top professional and amateur bodybuilders mesmerized by his physique?

Dorian Yates: I think a lot of guys around my age have been influenced by Bruce Lee since they were teenagers. This was the first exposure to somebody who was really developed. He wasn't huge, but very lean, ripped and symmetrical. I think a lot of the guys have been influenced by him since then.

Q: As a professional athlete, how would you assess Bruce Lee's physical attributes or what would be the most fascinating element about Bruce Lee?

Dorian Yates: I think he's an outstanding individual, and almost obsessed at what he was doing and obsessed with perfecting what he was doing. His mental focus and dedication and thinking, that's what makes him stand out. His whole goal was pursuing that goal, that's why he got to be the best in the world.

Q: Can you recall the 70s Kung Fu boom?

Dorian Yates: Yeah. I was actually too young to get into the theaters. I think Big Boss was the first film I saw. Enter the Dragon, which is the one everyone knows about, was an American and Hollywood production. Everybody was impressed by it and talking about it.

Q: Which professional bodybuilders did you admire?

Dorian Yates: Of course, Arnold was a big name, he brought the sport to the mainstream, although he had retired and was in the movies when I started. Also Mike Mentzer, I followed his training philosophy, and Tom Platz came to the UK doing seminars when I first started.

Q: Now you are retired from competition, you also spend some time training in martial arts I believe?

Dorian Yates: I've always had an interest in martial arts, but I had to focus on one whole thing so I couldn't really train much in the martial arts, because in bodybuilding you have to focus on what you're doing and avoid risking injury. I do some training with guys and they teach me some martial arts and I help them out with weight training and nutrition. So it works out fine.

Q: Will we ever see Bruce Lee replaced?
Dorian Yates: He'll never be replaced. Bruce Lee was a pioneer, he was ahead of his time, he was mixing martial arts with weight training and mixing different martial arts. Especially guys in the UFC and MMA who are fighting now realize Bruce was ahead of his time.

Q: You're the only person outside of the United States to win the Olympia. This must have been an obstacle to overcome, just like Bruce Lee had to overcome certain obstacles to achieve success in his craft?
Dorian Yates: When I started people were saying, "You're not going to be able to get to the top, and you're not going to win titles because you come from England," and that it's an American sport, and also there's better equipment there, etc. The thing is, it doesn't matter where you come from, if you have the potential and determination you can do it. So I think it's a good inspiration for people.

Q: Had Bruce Lee lived what path do you think he would have pursued?
Dorian Yates: I think Bruce would probably be involved with films, and I'm sure he would have big influence on the mixed martial arts scene as it is now, maybe it may have happened earlier had he been alive.

LENDA MURRAY

L enda Murray is the most successful female bodybuilder in the
world to date. She is the greatest female bodybuilder ever!
She has won the Ms. Olympia title a staggering eight times,
the highest achievement in professional female bodybuilding.
Murray's physique became the standard against which
professional female bodybuilders are now judged. This wonderful woman
and great athlete is just one of many professional IFBB bodybuilding
champions influenced by Bruce Lee.

**Q: Lenda, when did you start bodybuilding and how hard is it for a
woman bodybuilder in far as acceptance?**
Lenda Murray: I formed an interest in bodybuilding back in 1984. This
was my first introduction to weight training. As far as being hard for a
female bodybuilder, it is very difficult. First of all, it's not the norm that a
female has that much muscle or the appearance of that much muscle. It
was very tough in the beginning, my father wasn't happy with it and my
mom wasn't either, but because I was an athlete I had the love for sports.
I participated in sports through high school and college. When I was first
introduced to bodybuilding in 1984, I immediately fell in line with it. But
it is difficult and the diet is the hardest part of it.

**Q: Bruce Lee had a remarkable influence on so many of today's
physique champions. What makes Bruce Lee so admired by the
bodybuilding fraternity?**
Lenda Murray: The thing about Bruce Lee which was so amazing was his
conditioning, as an athlete he was just in great condition. When I think of
'abdominals' I think of Bruce Lee. That may not be what he was
necessarily striving for, but through his hard work it was very clear he was
what I call a 'top-notch' athlete. I think the key about Bruce Lee is he was

truly so complete in all areas. Even if you look at people who aren't necessarily martial artists or are not into athletics, there is a piece of what he does and part of his movies that just attracts people. There's a part of him that women looking may say, "Oh my God, he's handsome." Even in the martial arts today, he's so awesome that he's still remembered.

Q: Do you think Bruce Lee was the first to combine weight training with the martial arts?
Lenda Murray: I definitely believe that he was the pioneer in the martial arts and combining this with weight training. What was really unique about that was, during his time, even other athletes in other sports and disciplines had difficulty understanding how weight training could truly benefit what they did. That's what I would say what really makes Bruce Lee such a remarkable person who, very early in the 70s, knew the importance of weight training.

Q: What is the most fascinating attribute that captured your attention? Was it his physique?
Lenda Murray: The first thing when I think about him I think about abdominals, but also his power and charisma. He had the complete package from head to toe, he was extremely handsome, he was just great. Actually, he was probably one of the first men I had a crush on. Bruce Lee was very well-rounded in his physique. Coming from a point of view of bodybuilding we are so extreme, in particular we have a very critical eye looking at his physique. I can tell you that he had big shoulders, down to his small waist and then he had legs, everything was complete. He was what we would call in bodybuilding a 'top-heavy' athlete and he was excellent.

Q: Do you think Bruce Lee paved the way for action film stars of today who seem to strip down to their waist on film to display their chiseled frames?
Lenda Murray: Bruce Lee definitely paved the way. I mean, his package in what he presented he was so entertaining, and his movements of martial arts was a really beautiful art form. He really combined everything, he was a great actor. He had the complete package and I know that the athletes of today know that he's definitely paved the way for them to be as accepted as they are today.

Q: Do you remember your first Bruce Lee movie?
Lenda Murray: For me, the first movie I ever saw was a Bruce Lee movie. I think it was Enter the Dragon, and it was huge, it was a big thing. And my mom - I will never forget because it was a popular thing at that time -

let me go on my own. This is the first movie I saw and she let me go on my own because I made such a fuss about seeing it.

Q: Would you agree when you repeatedly watch other movies you get bored, but Bruce Lee movies you can watch them over again without getting bored?
Lenda Murray: Oh, yeah, you definitely don't get bored with Bruce Lee movies. And I think that's a real sign of a great movie, actually I've seen it at least seven times.

Q: Pound-for-pound Bruce Lee was one of the fastest and most dedicated athletes the world has ever seen. Do you think he will ever be replaced?
Lenda Murray: I really believe Bruce Lee is one of a kind and he's so unique. You have different athletes come along, and some are such great at their art but when you're so well-rounded as Bruce Lee was, it's amazing. I think Bruce Lee is one of a kind and I don't think we'll see that again. There's no question that if Bruce Lee was alive today the things he would have accomplished would have been unbelievable. He had that personality, drive, charisma. He had so much he could have offered or given to us that's missed.

Q: How has Bruce Lee inspired you in your life and work?
Lenda Murray: Bruce Lee has inspired me in many ways, for one, his conditioning. To win the Ms. Olympia I had to always remember to be strong, using my diet - which was to last 15 weeks prior to the show. And with monitoring your calories and training consistently, when you look at an athlete such as Bruce Lee you know he trained hard, you know that he watched his diet and at the same time he was totally prepared to know all the other areas. One thing I can really say is that he so inspired me throughout my career. He is truly, truly missed and is one of a kind.

FRANCO COLUMBU

Dr. Franco Columbu, born in Sardinia, is a legend in the world of professional bodybuilding. Starting out his athletic career as a Boxer, Columbu progressed into the sport of Olympic weightlifting, powerlifting and eventually bodybuilding. He won the prestigious Mr. Olympia title in 1976 and 1981. From the time he arrived in America in 1969, Columbu was considered one of the strongest men in the world. He is a legend in the bodybuilding world, and has trained in Brazilian Jiu Jitsu.

Q: I believe you boxed before you got involved in bodybuilding?
Franco Columbu: Yes, I boxed then I went into bodybuilding, which helped me to be better than I could be. Boxing and martial arts make the body defined. I knew it would make me so defined with the martial arts and it helped me with Mr. Olympia. I won Mr. Olympia two times, in 1976 and 1981.

Q: You are, of course, Arnold Schwarzenegger's best friend and both of you were training partners, what was it like training with Arnold?
Franco Columbu: When you are doing bodybuilding or martial arts you need a training partner, not a trainer. He can compete with you and he can help you with some exercises.

Q: Can you tell me the degree of influence Bruce Lee had on you as a professional bodybuilder and on a personal level?
Franco Columbu: Bruce Lee to me was so incredible! The story in the film wasn't the greatest, but his films were like classics. One of the things that appealed to me was in Enter The Dragon, with Bruce Lee and John Saxon, who was also a bodybuilder and he was my friend, you were looking at a body moving, a good body moving, a body with the best proportion and

the best technique. And every time he did a move you saw muscle movement. Everybody in bodybuilding, Boxing and martial arts have a lot in common - muscle movement. He had the best body where you could move the anatomy and the muscle tissue.

Q: It's no small accomplishment considering Bruce Lee never entered a physique contest that so many bodybuilders - professional and amateur - are inspired by Bruce Lee. What is the appeal?
Franco Columbu: It's like this: he trained and he obviously practiced movements of the martial arts, and he was perfect at that. But in his training he incorporated elements to get in the best shape for every part of his body. It didn't matter if you looked at the front, back, the sides, legs, the upper body, his body had every muscle. All 500 muscles in the body you could see in his body.

Q: How do you think he was able to generate so much power for a 135-pounder?
Franco Columbu: Number one: he understood leverage, and with leverage he could create explosive power. He had so much practice that his accuracy and his way of hitting was so perfect that created the power.

Q: It's clear that Bruce Lee epitomized the athletic ideals of hard work and diligence. What sets Bruce Lee apart from all the other martial artists and athletes?
Franco Columbu: I can tell you in three words: he meant it! Bruce Lee believed in his martial arts so much that the minute you turned the camera on, or in the gym, and you said, "Now you do martial arts," and from a normal relaxed position he could start martial arts movement and transition into the spiritual side.

Q: You are involved in the movie industry yourself, how did Bruce Lee changed the action films genre?
Franco Columbu: He obviously changed the world of action films, but the main thing wasn't that. The main thing was he was conditioning in athletics, and athletes then became actors because his movement was admired. For me, an actor was above - head and no body - because the actor uses the face which is above the body. When he went in there he didn't do anything with his face without using his body. Everything from his upper body, the face and the legs were like a robot. And it was his physical movements and physique, whilst (regular) acting was just using the expression of the face.

Q: In your opinion, just how big and popular is Bruce Lee on a

worldwide scale?

Franco Columbu: I compare him to James Dean. He died young as an actor but is someone we still hear about. Bruce Lee was in his prime when he died and he would only have improved and would be in his 60s now.

Q: With Bruce Lee movies people don't seem to get bored no matter how many times they watch them. Do you feel he left some kind of a trademark which cannot be emulated?

Franco Columbu: Bruce Lee films have one thing in common, and that was everything you saw on film created a desire that you wanted to look at it again and again. I probably saw Enter the Dragon ten or 15 times. Why? Because his body movement and the way he developed incredible movement. Then when you see the martial arts moves you could see his ability performing them perfectly, and see the power from inside to out. He wasn't doing martial arts in the movies for make-believe, he meant it! He was spiritual in that sense. You can see that Bruce Lee films are seen by all kinds of people. Finally, in our time we will never have another Bruce Lee. In a thousand years time there will be another Bruce Lee.

Q: Anything you would like to add?

Franco Columbu: I would like to add that Bruce Lee inspired the world of all the athletes from different sports, not just martial artists, to train. Because they associate him with 'vision muscles' which inspires you, and it's a big inspiration. For kids, he was the best. His pictures and posters could be seen in dojos, and thousands of thousands of kids who admire him and train. He's a legend. Bruce Lee is the legend of all the legends.

SHAWN RAY

Shawn Ray is one of the top professional bodybuilders, and although he never won the Olympia he was voted unanimously in 2003 as the 'Best Bodybuilder Never to Win the Mr. Olympia' by his peers, magazine editors and industry insiders. Ray has appeared on more FLEX magazine covers than any bodybuilder in history. His awesome physique is matched by very few and his dedication and hard work made him the 'people's champion'. Ray has been profoundly influenced by Bruce Lee and the training philosophy Lee used to make himself into the specimen he was.

Q: Shawn, when did you start bodybuilding?
Shawn Ray: I got involved in bodybuilding in1983. I was training from eight to18 years old as a football player, and always wanted to be an American football star playing in a big major college as a running back. That was my childhood dream all the way up to high school. Sometime in my junior year, I started to lift weights and put on some size and strength. I had some 'dead time' and joined the gym where I met a bodybuilder by the name of John Brown, who was a two-time Mr. Universe and three-time Mr. World.

I knew nothing about bodybuilding and I knew nothing about Arnold Schwarzenegger. The guy in front of me was 6ft 2, 260 pounds, and I thought, "This isn't humanly possible for me. I want nothing to do with bodybuilding." But I took him on as a training partner and he showed me the ropes. Five months later I competed in my first show and placed second place. And a week later I won my first contest and became hooked on bodybuilding at the age of 17.

Q: You never won the Olympia but were always close?
Shawn Ray: Yeah, in all my years of training for Mr. Olympia, 14 to be

exact, I competed in 13 of them but I never won. But throughout that run, 12 straight years I'd been in the top five and first runner-up for two of the years. Not winning that show didn't leave a bad taste in my mouth, because I came up in an era where there was Lee Haney 5ft 10, 250 pounds, Dorian Yates 5ft 10, 260 pounds, and now Ronnie Coleman, 5ft 10, 280 pounds. I was totally on the other end of the spectrum. And by not winning that show, and competing with those three champions for more than a decade who had 22 Mr. Olympia's between them, I was in very good company. For that very reason I became the 'people's champion' because I represented the very thing about bodybuilding that those three guys didn't. So I count the satisfaction of being the 'people's champion', but it would've been nice to get one of those Sandow trophies.

Q: You were inspired by Bruce Lee, what was so appealing about this martial arts icon?
Shawn Ray: Bruce Lee, and maybe one or two other individuals in my lifetime coming up as a kid, represented what an athlete is to me, what a superstar is to me. Very few people I know, in any profession, have risen to such heights at such a young age as Bruce Lee. And what he did no one else in the world was doing in his time. His time actually crosses over because what he did back then people are still not able to do today, as far as acting and martial arts persona. Very few personalities have what he had. Muhammad Ali had a little bit of Bruce Lee, I think Michael Jordan had a little bit of Bruce Lee and even now Tiger Woods, as far as being an icon, people who do just amazing things and they sustain it over a period of time.

What he did as a man, martial arts person and an actor, I always dreamed about doing as a professional bodybuilder. I wanted to be different, and to be different I had to be better than everybody else. I knew I was 5ft 7, 210 pounds - I can be one of the guys or I could be 'the guy'- and for what I did on the bodybuilding stage, without winning that Sandow trophy, by training for that bodybuilding contest I was like Bruce Lee in the martial arts movies. I wanted to be 'the man'. Bruce Lee to me represented everything that a professional is in every sense of the word.

Q: Why are so many professional bodybuilders mesmerized by his trademark physique?
Shawn Ray: They are inspired and mesmerized by Bruce Lee's physique as small it was, because of the completeness of it. I mean, Bruce Lee didn't have an ounce of fat on him, you could see every fibre and literally every muscle. I think Bruce Lee when he was in shape could've barely been 140 or 135 pounds dripping wet, but on the big screen he was a giant. I mean, he was bigger than Kareem Abdul-Jabbar, he was bigger than life on the

screen because he was in shape. I think any bodybuilder who trains to be in shape knows and respects how hard it is to be in shape, let alone have a full six pack of abs, to be able to flex from the shoulders and separate the bicep and the tricep. And to master the body and take control of it, Bruce Lee knew that it was a work of art. Bodybuilders train for that, they diet for that, and for him to be in that physical condition in that time period, he was ahead of his time. This is why he still gets respect from bodybuilders competing even to this day.

Q: Why do you think Bruce Lee made weight training an integral part of his training regime when no other martial artists made this a focal point of their training?
Shawn Ray: I think Bruce Lee, as an athlete and an actor, was smart to incorporate weight training to be a part of his regime. He not only saw the importance of nutrition and good health, but he saw the importance of physical exercise and weight training. And by doing that he developed his body to the fullest, while other people weren't lifting weights because they thought they'd get muscle-bound and inflexible. Bruce Lee was like an artist using a paint brush to create an image of himself that was larger than life.

Bruce Lee was not a big man but on screen he looked massive. All it was that he was in shape. Very few actors - even athletes - can grasp the total concept of good health, good training and nutrition the way Bruce Lee mastered it in his time. There's only one word to describe Bruce Lee, and that would be 'master'. He was a master actor at his craft and a master technician when he came to holding his physique, because people didn't only come to watch him do his martial arts but they also came to gaze at this work of art. He created that physique which transcends martial arts now into bodybuilding 20, 30 years later.

A guy like myself coming up as a kid, not knowing anything about bodybuilding, when I got into bodybuilding I had appreciation as a teenager what Bruce Lee did back in the 70s. Even now, in my 40s I can appreciate him, that's what I mean when I say master, he's timeless. What he did back then still resonates today.

Q: He bridged the gap between martial arts and bodybuilding and is the foremost pioneer in this respect. Today, martial artists incorporate weights into their training...
Shawn Ray: If you are going to be a pioneer in anything, you're going to have your copycats. Bruce Lee coming up the way he did, as fast as he did, created a slew of copycat martial artists who now workout with weights and who now pay attention to their diet. There would have never been Jean Claude Van Damme or Bolo, or even Dolph Lundgren, even Sylvester

Stallone; these guys knew the importance of getting in shape before getting in front of the camera. Even beyond your skill as an athlete, the physique speaks volume to a body.

Bruce Lee took a lot of time and effort not only following the routine of a training schedule but his eating schedule. Because he knew what he put into his body is what his fans watching out there in his movies would see. We've got to give Bruce Lee credit for that. You can't get in that kind of shape without using a proper healthy nutritional diet. And from that, copycat actors and martial artists came out. Not even just martial artists, but the big Boxers and football players, they kind of look at a guy like Bruce Lee because they get it now. He did bridge the gap between athletics, entertainment and health and fitness.

Q: Bruce Lee proved to the world what a small man could achieve in terms of supreme physical attributes, power and speed. Do you feel this ignited a passion in physically smaller individuals to succeed?

Shawn Ray: Yes. If it wasn't for someone like Bruce Lee coming along like he did, and the way he did, his style and manner, supremely confident in what he did, because he knew he mastered what he did...and it came across the way he performed on stage in front of the camera. You didn't recognize how smart he was. But other smaller people thought, "If he could do it, I can do it too."

Me being 5ft 7, 210 pounds, I was by no means the biggest guy, but certainly harking back to Bruce Lee's movies when I was training the competition was bigger than it can be. It was like: If he could do it, so can I. It's amazing how that transcends from martial arts all the way to bodybuilding. How many other small actors and athletes use Bruce Lee as a yardstick for something, that at one time was impossible, but now they believe that it is possible because they saw Bruce Lee do it?

Q: What is it about Bruce Lee that seems to appeal to people from all walks of life?

Shawn Ray: I think Bruce Lee has a crossover appeal that all cultures, ethnic groups or religions can relate to. Like I said, he's a supremely confident individual, and in that kind of confidence you've got to be a very different kind of individual. Here's a guy from China, doesn't speak English, learns the language, comes to the States and walks into Hollywood and says, "I'm going to be a big star one day." There's only one other person I know who did that, and that person is the Governor of the State of California, Arnold Schwarzenegger himself, seven-time Mr. Olympia.

Very few individuals can do what Bruce Lee did. And I think that the fact he set out to accomplish all of the things he did speaks volumes of the man's character and the discipline. As tragic it was, he came so fast and left so soon which puts him alongside the likes of Elvis Presley and the Beatles. As far as what he could've become had he lived to a ripe old age…but there's something to be said for him coming for the time he did to fulfill his purpose in this life. What he did in front of the camera allowed people like myself to have somebody to believe in and be elevated to a higher level as well.

Q: Do you think Bruce Lee got his message out via the medium of film?
Shawn Ray: I think Bruce Lee movies were Bruce Lee telling his stories and the way he could tell them. I don't think Bruce Lee was a guy who needed direction in his movies, if anything he would tell the director, "This is how it's going to be." Fist of Fury and Game Of Death, and his adversaries like Kareem Abdul-Jabbar and John Saxon, Bolo and the fight scenes he had with 50 guys where he's motoring through was always this big menacing force. I think Bruce Lee continued to set out to deal with obstacles in his way, and in the end Bruce Lee comes out triumphant. What he wanted to do in his movies was to be a hero, and he was a hero, in front of the camera and off the camera. The thing I like most about Bruce Lee is that off-camera he was able to recognize his abilities, he wasn't afraid to venture out by becoming a father, being in a foreign land and pursuing a career. He was the embodiment of the American dream.

Q: Bruce's body was not only a thing of immense grace and beauty to watch in action, but it was supremely well balanced in terms of proportion. As a bodybuilder, what went through your mind when he put his physique on display in Way of the Dragon?
Shawn Ray: I think that for an actor and an artist, there comes a pivotal moment where you've got to highlight your passion. And while we know he was a martial arts master, probably one of the best actors in the world because of the type of acting he did, one thing he had control over is how he appeared. I think when he decided to 'speak' in the form of a physique artist, he knew he had to get that up to notch. The Way of the Dragon was his coming out party, as far as look at me, this is me, this is what my passion is beside the martial arts. Look at my body.

And everybody knows that feeling, and wants to get in front of the camera and be put on the stage, have a packed audience where they're looking at your body. They're looking beyond the eyes and emotions on the screen, and they're looking at your body. There's something to be said for having respect for somebody who can achieve such physical perfection and, Bruce Lee for his height, weight and size, there's nothing you could have done more to his physique. I mean, if he had to train for bodybuilding there's no doubt in my mind he would have been a bodybuilding world champion.

Q: Bruce Lee's influence continues to be felt and reaches all four corners of the globe. Would he have gone on to achieve a lot more had he lived?

Shawn Ray: Had Bruce Lee lived to ripe old age, his movie career would have certainly grown. I believe he would have been much like Arnold Schwarzenegger, Arnold embodies that a person's vision can become reality. I think he would probably have done the Hollywood thing, then he may have become an ambassador for China or ambassador for the States, the way Arnold is the Governor of California. If there's anyone who has that crossover appeal because they had such a wide fan base, it's Bruce Lee. Like I said, he crossed color lines, cultural and age differences.

It would have been nice to see Bruce Lee at 75 years old looking back at the body of work over a period of time. I think a lot of things about Bruce Lee we will never get to see, all we have is what he left for us. How many times we watch them (movies) over, over and over again, and we read the books and watch the movies, and we slow it down in slow motion. We get remastered versions of them, and you look for the lost Bruce Lee tapes, anything we can get our hands on. It shows the fascination for Bruce Lee is still there. He was only here for a short time, and there's very few people in the world who come along like he did, and their legacy lives on. And I think he wouldn't have written it a different way.

★ ★ ★ CHAPTER SIX ★ ★ ★

THE MMA LEGACY

Bruce Lee was the pinnacle of what mixed martial arts is all about. Widely recognized today as the pioneer and godfather of MMA, Lee epitomized the athletic ideals of diligence, pushing oneself to the extreme and refusing to settle for second best. It is evident that his unique concepts were the basis of MMA today. Lee had realistic notions on fighting. His Jeet Kune Do is seen as the genesis of the modern spate of hybrid martial arts developed through devoted, extensive and thoughtful research. A lot of UFC and MMA fighters credit Bruce Lee as their inspiration for getting involved in the martial arts.

"I watched a movie called Enter the Dragon, and in the very first scene he's fighting some big dude. He gets the guy on the ground and jumps into an armbar. That's when I first saw an actual submission mixed in with the stand up fighting. Bruce Lee did it! Bruce Lee was actually one of the first guys who ever did the cross-training, where two combatants would fight on the ground and also standing up. Back in those Karate days, people didn't go to the ground and fight, but Bruce Lee knew this was an important part of being a complete fighter."

- Ken Shamrock

"I think Bruce Lee is a great inspiration and a great fighter, and was ahead of his time. Now people are starting to realize what his message was. Was it not for mixed martial arts, people would just say, 'Bruce Lee said this', or what not. I think they would (still) have appreciation for him, but not like now. Now they understand just how truly great he was,

because he was there from the beginning experimenting with MMA. He didn't believe one single style was the best; he was mixing all different styles to make a complete fighting style. He was saying it back then, and people thought this dude's crazy. He was preaching it in his day. And now people can see mixed martial arts, they can see that you need to have all these elements to become a great fighter and flow quickly into all of them."

- Rashad Evans

"I love Bruce Lee! When I was young, kids were playing baseball but I was watching Kung Fu Theater with my old man. I love Bruce Lee and his movies: Enter the Dragon, Game of Death, Return of the Dragon (aka Way of the Dragon). He was one of the first mixed martial artists if you ask me. He was doing armlocks in there, everything. I think it was awesome."

- Matt Serra

"The guy used to practice a lot...Bruce Lee was already trying to incorporate grappling in his game, that's good. Of course, he left his mark, that's why he's very well known all over the world. What he did nobody's going to repeat that. I don't believe he had to compete in order to be a good fighter or a good instructor."

- Royce Gracie

Bruce Lee was cognizant of being well-skilled in all ranges of combat and was probably the first martial artist to emphatically state just how imperative this was. Lee had a great thirst for knowledge in everything he pursued. He was a true innovator and a revolutionary in bringing the fighting arts into the spotlight on a grand scale. Few can forget the opening fight scene from Enter the Dragon. In what more or less resembled an MMA fight, a young Sammo Hung is seen sparring full contact with Lee. He was able to exemplify the true nature of MMA via the medium of film, as well as in his personal martial arts training.

His entire martial art was built around reality, functionality and totality. His method of researching and absorbing principles and concepts was more than just accumulating various techniques. Lee started from the principles and concepts as the bottom line, and then developed something that could exemplify those principles. His extraordinary skill and understanding was derived from countless hours of painstaking research into all aspects of combat arts, which included grappling methods of Jiu

Jitsu, Wrestling, Judo and the Chinese form of joint-locking known as Chin Na. As he endeavored to become a versatile and more complete fighter, he sought out various grappling experts with whom he exchanged ideas and philosophies. Lee's influential personal notes, later published as Tao of Jeet Kune Do, highlighted his views and concepts. Evidently, Lee became aware of the integral link between the traditional martial arts and the unpredictability of street combat. His principles were the most advanced at the time. He preached a philosophy which emphasized absorbing what was useful for the individual and rejecting what is useless, and what worked for the individual's physical capabilities.

Lee believed learning was not mere imitation, nor the ability to accumulate knowledge and conform to fixed knowledge. And he refused to be bound by tradition. He felt martial arts were too riddled with tradition to be of any use in a real all-out street fight. "Most of the traditional martial arts instructors are so doggone stubborn, I mean (their attitude is), 'Well, 200 years ago it was taught this way, therefore...' you know? To still maintain that type of attitude, you've had it. I mean, you will never grow because learning is a discovery thing," he said.

Lee believed Judo was the most practical of all martial arts next to Jeet Kune Do. According to Lee, although it lacked certain techniques like striking, at least it had plenty of body contact. When you throw or wrestle a person down, you know it is working. To this effect, he worked with two prominent Judo champions from the Los Angeles area, Hayward Nishioka and Gene LeBell. "We worked out on a one-on-one basis and we both learned a great deal from each other. Bruce could do everything, he was that bit of a jock and an athlete, very sharp. He was an innovator and the best at what he did," recalls LeBell, who also worked as a stuntman on Green Hornet with Lee.

Lee, a voracious reader, would pay hundreds of dollars for rare and out-of-print books. The late Larry Hartsell, world-renowned Jeet Kune Do grappling authority, recalls, "He had one guy he had a book on called Gama, who was a world champion then. He died in the 1920s. He was one of Maharashi's champion grapplers, huge guy. And they used to fight in the dirt pits, and Bruce admired that style of Wrestling." Lee had amassed well over 60 tomes on Wrestling alone in addition an extensive collection of books pertaining to grappling arts Judo, Jiu Jitsu and Aikido.

"I think Bruce was the first person to tell people to look within themselves and in what they needed - cross-train. And a lot of different classical martial artists today are cross-training in different arts to supplement their training, going from Boxing and Kickboxing to add to their own styles, going into grappling systems to add to their styles. But I think Bruce at that time was way ahead of his time on cross-training, utilizing different methods. He borrowed from different systems and put them together to develop his system, his concept of fighting," Hartsell revealed in an interview once. "What people don't know is that Bruce actually, before he passed away, had plans to take Jeet Kune Do to sort of like the UFC-type rules, into Kickboxing range, takedowns to submission. That never came about."

Furthermore, many seasoned grappling champions and experts agree that his ground game would have been equal to that of everything else in his art. UFC legend Royce Gracie says, "I heard he was learning some grappling and I firmly believe if he was alive today he would be doing grappling." Had he lived, no doubt he would have gleaned much knowledge and experience, and modified many of the grappling techniques which would be much more suited for the street environment. One can clearly see the rudimentary takedowns he was investigating from leafing through Tao of Jeet Kune Do. Lee was known to have heavily practiced brutal techniques such as eye gouging and groin kicks, both of which rightly had their place in a street environment where all rules are thrown out.

Lee believed if you wanted to be on top you need a proven, effective, efficient system and think outside of the box. Dan Inosanto, Lee's premier student and training partner, states, "When Bruce Lee advocated cross-training, it was ridiculed, it was violently opposed. Now if you read any magazine, the thing to do is cross-training. Now it is accepted as being always true, the thing you should have done."

Lee's revolutionary approach to training by looking beyond the confines of traditional methods and techniques has inspired many martial artists and MMA athletes. Ultimately, his approach would propagate an amalgamation of both Eastern and Western philosophy behind unarmed combat.

One of the toughest of the toughest fighters the MMA world has ever seen, Rickson Gracie, earned himself a reputation and almost mythical status in the martial arts world. Gracie himself acknowledged Bruce Lee as the greatest fighter of all time. In the following exclusive interviews, MMA legends pay homage to and express their opinions on the original godfather of MMA.

RANDY COUTURE

Randy 'The Natural' Couture is considered by many to be the most popular UFC fighter in history. A member of the UFC Hall of Fame, Couture was a successful amateur Wrestler and a three-time Olympic team alternate before making his UFC debut in May 1997. He has gained acclaim as one of the prime reasons for MMA's recent growth in popularity. He was voted 'The Greatest Fighter of All Time' by viewers' choice. He made a transition into Hollywood and will always be remembered as a legend in combat sports.

Q: You were influenced by Bruce Lee?
Randy Couture: Who wasn't? I don't know a kid who didn't watch Bruce Lee movies and afterwards got a pair of nunchaku and started twirling them around. I thought Bruce Lee was 'the man' when I was a kid. He was studying in the University of Washington. I heard about him as a kid and read some of his writings, he's definitely somebody I admired.

Q: What do you think of the caliber of technical skills which he possessed as a martial arts exponent?
Randy Couture: I think he was an innovator in a lot of ways. First, he started different forms of styles of martial arts and tried to pull the best and analyze what was effective from a lot of different styles and developed his style of fighting.

Q: Dana White, and a lot of the UFC fighters, have gone on record saying Bruce Lee is the godfather of MMA. Bruce Lee can be seen propagating MMA in the fight with Sammo Hung in Enter the Dragon...
Randy Couture: It didn't exist back then (MMA). Basically, the style he

came up with was to create a more effective system than the more traditional martial arts in that he took from a lot of different martial arts styles and wrote about different styles, and came up with a hybrid style of martial art. It was his way of doing things. The gloves were innovative and the precursor of what we use today.

Q: Do you feel Bruce Lee would have evolved as far as grappling and groundwork is concerned?
Randy Couture: He definitely would have, I thing he would have been all-rounded. He did some Wrestling and in the University of Washington he worked out with Wrestlers and analyzed the technique and the things they were doing. So he definitely would be interested in this. He realized when the fights go to the ground, Jiu Jitsu and ground fighting techniques would come into play. Had he been around he probably would have focused on some of that stuff for sure.

Q: We know Bruce was not a competitor but his focus leaned towards street fighting with no rules. Do you think he would have modified sports grappling moves to best suit his goal?
Randy Couture: Ending up on your back in a street fight is one thing, and putting yourself there is another. No one in a street fight is going to put themselves on their back, because you have to know when you get knocked down or end up on your back, having the posture and the way to survive is technique, this is the difference. So I think he would have understood the difference.

Q: Do you think Bruce's ability and mystique places him on an elevated level who is unlikely to be replaced? We had John Wayne, Clint Eastwood, Muhammad Ali, Mike Tyson...
Randy Couture: I think a lot of these people are individuals in their own way, none of them participated in the same endeavor as Bruce Lee. John Wayne and Clint Eastwood were both great actors and Muhammad Ali and Mike Tyson were certainly great Boxers. Another individual like Bruce Lee, I don't think anybody could replace him.

Q: You're an advocate of conditioning, do you feel Bruce Lee was the first to integrate conditioning and building the body, which almost every martial arts fighter integrates into their training now?
Randy Couture: Of course. If you're in a sport and the shape you're in walking into a fight then you have to. I think Bruce Lee always was like that as far as martial arts. I think it was the mind, discipline and the body. Bruce Lee was the kind of guy who would integrate some of the things that

he did, conditioning the muscles, which were pretty new and innovative at the time in martial arts circles.

Q: The ultimate question! How would Bruce Lee do in the UFC if he competed in a lightweight division - he was 135 pounds?
Randy Couture: Well, I think he could have competed in the 145-pound weight class. Sure, he could have got himself in that weight class and done well, there's no doubt about it.

Q: How has Bruce Lee inspired you?
Randy Couture: As a martial artist, he stressed keeping an open mind and allowing for individual style, and not getting caught up in traditional trappings, which limits some of the traditional styles. The way his thinking was: everybody can learn from him, not just martial artists.

TITO ORTIZ

Tito Ortiz emerged as one of the sport's biggest stars at a time when UFC was on the verge of breaking through into the mainstream. Ortiz, who had a rough childhood, started fighting in the UFC in 1997 and fought some of the biggest names in the game, winning the light-heavyweight title in the process. Like many elite MMA fighters, Ortiz was influenced by Bruce Lee and acknowledges him as the godfather of MMA. He is widely known as 'The Huntington Beach Bad Boy'.

Q: A lot of MMA fighters were influenced by Bruce Lee, tell me about the impact he had on you.
Tito Ortiz: I guess as a really young kid watching Kung Fu films and watching Fist of Fury when I was growing up, Bruce Lee was the first guy to know what mixed martial arts was about. He would go with a Wrestler, and he would go with a Karate guy, he would go with a Jiu Jitsu guy; he would try to learn all the stuff. I've read a lot of his books and watched a lot of the series on him. It's too bad to see him pass away quick as he did, but I still look up to him as an athlete and as a mixed martial artist. Hopefully, I can follow in his footsteps one day with people knowing that I'm a full-blown martial artist myself.

Q: I would be interested in your comments on the opening scene of Enter the Dragon, which clearly seems to be propagating MMA.
Tito Ortiz: He was way ahead of his time, he was doing things back then what we're doing now. He had ideas! It's one of the things we saw. Bruce Lee was the first fighter of mixed martial arts, and it's truly nice to see this.

Q: What did you think of his supreme conditioning and unique state-of-the-art training methods?

Tito Ortiz: As much as I knew, I think conditioning was very big for him. Myself, I'm huge on conditioning. There's nothing worse in a match when you're getting tired and gassing out. I've done that once and I'll never do it again. But we're athletes, you have to train hard enough where cardio is never a factor, you should never be out of shape or gassed or tired in a match.

Q: Do you feel Bruce Lee was one of the first martial artists to implement specialized training devices and methods in his quest for pushing the human body to the limits?
Tito Ortiz: I think so, in the long run it really showed outside of the box and not just Karate or Tae Kwon Do. I think it was knowing everything, and he showed us the need to integrate Boxing, Wrestling, Jiu Jitsu, Karate, Tae Kwon Do, etc. I think he was the first person to make that happen. The guys in the UFC such as Frank Shamrock, Royce or myself later put it into use. It wasn't TV or movies, it was where we competed as athletes, and if Bruce Lee had a chance the way we did - it's a big difference because he was 135 pound - he was a great martial artist in his own right. If you compare him to guys like us now there's no difference. I mean, the biggest difference is the weight difference. He understood all the martial arts and put them together, but we're just doing it at an athletic level as athletes and competitiveness.

Q: Had Bruce Lee lived, do you think he may have pursued avenues which would be parallel to investigating and integrating the ground game, which has become a necessity these days?
Tito Ortiz: Of course, because he was the first person to do this thing, Wrestling and Jiu Jitsu. He would have evolved in the martial arts side and he would have got better, of course.

Q: Bruce Lee had a street fighting style which was geared towards sound martial arts techniques and street-proven tactics. Can we compare this with the sport of MMA and differentiate between the two?
Tito Ortiz: It's hard to compare what he did and what we're doing now, just because it (his) was more of a street fighting method. What we do now is reality fighting, there's a big difference, someone kicks you in the head, who is trying to stay out of range and trying to punch you. You've got to put the whole thing together.

Q: What would you say is your favorite Bruce Lee movie?
Tito Ortiz: Enter The Dragon was the best. They had the same type of fighting thing that we did. They're on the island where they all fought. He

just showed the different type of fights. I think it was really intriguing when I watched it as a kid, and I never thought I'd be doing all that stuff. Look at me now!

Q: What inspiration do you take from Bruce Lee - from the athletic, philosophical or the fighting component?
Tito Ortiz: A little bit of everything. The philosophy of training, knowing that there's always a better opponent out there, knowing you have to train for the worse, always be in shape and never take a shortcut. A lot of stuff I experienced on my own, the challenges of hard work pays back. All athletes do the same thing too, you've always got to work hard.

Q: Can you please tell me what sets Bruce apart from other icons and the impact he's had on the world?
Tito Ortiz: I think it was that the different nationalities were intrigued by the type of athlete he was, and in the movies the things he did. For his time, I think he lived a short life and he never got a chance to use his full potential, that's too bad. Compared to other people, he's a reality fighter. People are known for their voice, or their beauty, the only person that compares to him is Muhammad Ali. I think Muhammad Ali did a lot more than Bruce Lee did because he's had a longer life. He had so many different avenues and so many different things, because Bruce Lee never got a chance to compete the way Ali did.

Q: Will anyone ever replace Bruce and be able to duplicate him in every sense of the word, and had he lived what avenues could he have pursued?
Tito Ortiz: Never! Because in his time no one knew what martial arts was, and mixed martial arts. He was the first person that did it. I don't think there will be anybody to show us the things the way he did. On TV it showed a lot of different things than what we're doing. I think he would have stuck with the movies, movies were big money. I thing he would have shown movies on a different level, it's too bad he passed away.

FRANK SHAMROCK

Bruce Lee influenced legendary UFC and MMA pioneer Frank Shamrock profoundly. Shamrock, who was catapulted to fame by fighting in the UFC, was heavily influenced by Lee's art, training methods and philosophy which he continues to abide by to develop himself as a fighter and athlete. A five-time UFC middleweight champion, Shamrock is recognized as one of the earlier pioneers of the sport of mixed martial arts. He's one of the most dedicated MMA athletes.

Q: Bruce Lee influenced you profoundly!
Frank Shamrock: When I was a kid he was the guy who really sparked interest in martial arts for me, because he looked cool, he was different and there was always some lesson to be learned or story to take in (from his movies). So that was the first of martial arts I latched on to. When I got older, in my teens, I started reading about him, his philosophy and stuff. He was the first person, in my opinion, to be looking at a very old art form in a very modern spiritual way, and that just made a lot of sense to me - have some way to live your life and have a goal and a path.

Q: So you were fascinated by both the physical and philosophical expressions of his art?
Frank Shamrock: Yes, it was really different and it was eye-catching the way he trained. He was so passionate about what he did and he was able to translate those ideas onto screen, and that just made my interest grow.

Q: Looking at the opening scene of Enter the Dragon we can see it was parallel to what we can call mixed martial arts. Do you feel he was the pioneer of MMA?
Frank Shamrock: He was the first guy to 'get it', I think. Me being a

mixed martial artist, I understand that for him it was trial and error. He was learning arts, practicing and drilling, nothing happened as it was supposed to happen, everything had its flaws but things changed. You had to be able to adapt to the situation at hand. You could see in his movies and everything he talked about, he was forward-thinking on developing techniques to survive or be successful in any situation. And that scene describes it all. He does proper distance, he closes in for strikes, takes him down and throws, and goes right into a submission hold. At that time in the film genre the guys were just breaking the guys arms off or stomping on the head, or something like that, but his opponent had to tap and then there was a show of respect. I thought it was a huge explanation of what mixed martial arts supposed to be. Yeah, he's the godfather of all this.

Q: From the perspective of a top professional MMA fighter, what did you think of Bruce Lee, weighing in at 135 pounds with a rather small stature, being able to hit hard as a heavyweight?
Frank Shamrock: Yes, I think he was probably one of the most adapted people for this, and at the time to have that extraordinary strength, leverage and balance. I think he was 5ft 7 but he worked on his striking, movement, distance and timing. Chuck Norris was (also) probably one of the top two guys at the time.

Q: I believe you took inspiration from his physique and conditioning methods.
Frank Shamrock: Oh, yeah, absolutely! His build was so amazing and inspirational for anyone who wants to get into sports or athletics. He understood the basics of fighting, he was a trained dancer so he understood conditioning and having good footwork. Who wouldn't want to have a build like that? Even his bodybuilding movements and mechanics were incredible, so that's kind of what I do.

Q: Personally, do you feel Bruce Lee would have evolved and become a top grappler had he lived?
Frank Shamrock: Oh, yeah. He would have 100 percent. He would have adapted, he was again, an incredible student who was always studying and focusing, unlike any other martial artists at the time. He was always practicing and trying to see if something was effective or not.

Q: The philosophy behind his personal art of combat or martial art was to exist outside of parameters and limitations. Some people say Bruce Lee never competed but was into street fighting. What are your opinions on this matter?

Frank Shamrock: Most definitely (into street fighting). I think not for sports competition, I think his would have been a (street) fight art.

Q: What is your favorite Bruce Lee movie and why?
Frank Shamrock: It has to be Enter the Dragon. That was a perfect example of a journey, a goal and a mission, and how to carry that outwards with honor and respect. His journey had the 'life' to chase victory and to experience loss, it had everything that you'd go through in your journey of life. I think that was his goal from reading his memoirs. His short presence in this world had such an impact. I mean, we're still talking about it 40 years later.

Q: How would Bruce Lee do in the UFC in his weight division?
Frank Shamrock: He's an artist and a world trained athlete. Most people are fighters not artists. Somebody who is able to combine their body and their mind and turn that into an art form has huge advantage over anybody who's bigger, stronger or even technical. I think Bruce was that man.

Q: Some people can't differentiate between real and movie actors and anyone with an ounce of intelligence will no doubt know Bruce Lee was first and foremost a martial artist.
Frank Shamrock: Well, I had the same experience, people believe what they see on TV, there's nothing you can do about it unfortunately. But those people are missing a huge side of it, an actor reads his lines and goes away. But a guy like Bruce Lee, he's actually a real martial artist and so much more.

Q: How has Bruce Lee affected your life on a whole?
Frank Shamrock: For me, he's been someone to model not only my art but my life on. For him to translate forms of martial arts, it's amazing because so many people think it should be only a certain way. So for him to have the strength and the ideas saying that there's a better way, and bring it out on the big screen was great. It's molded me into who I am.

Q: Will we ever get another Bruce Lee?
Frank Shamrock: I think that he won't ever be duplicated or have other person like him, for a lot of reasons. At the time martial arts in the United States was very immature, and media in our country was just turning and there was a war on. I think it was a time, especially in our country, the world was looking for somebody and he just happened to be the guy through the wall. I don't think he will ever be replicated.

RORION GRACIE

Rorion Gracie is the famous Gracie family patriarch who was responsible for creating the UFC. Many will agree the Gracies were responsible for revolutionizing the world of combat, and Rorion and Royce Gracie were the two single most important individuals who helped propel Gracie Jiu Jitsu onto the world stage. Rorion himself took part in no holds barred fights to prove the effectiveness of Gracie Jiu Jitsu. Mr. Gracie lives in the Los Angeles area and is the owner of the famous Gracie Academy.

Q: What are your impressions of Bruce Lee?
Rorion Gracie: He was a very interesting individual because he was the one who made the martial arts very acceptable in the media and the movies so on. And he was a talented martial artist himself. People had recognized Bruce Lee, the whole thing about Bruce Lee was just starting in America. I didn't follow much of Bruce Lee's growth in Brazil, that was pretty much the time when I was moving from Brazil to America to make things happen there with Gracie Jiu Jitsu.

Q: Bruce Lee was researching grappling, as can be seen in the Tao of Jeet Kune Do and his research notes. Do you think sooner or later he would have pursued this avenue to the extent where this would be a core part of his repertoire?
Rorion Gracie: I think had he lived he would have trained Jiu Jitsu here at the Gracie Academy for sure. He's a smart guy and he was researching grappling, and any smart researcher eventually gets to Gracie Jiu Jitsu.

Q: Would you say Bruce Lee's biggest asset was his desire to be the best?
Rorion Gracie: I never met Bruce Lee but I heard he was a very dedicated martial artist. And the fact he was researching on grappling, beyond his

fighting ability, shows that he was a very talented individual and has a great following. He was the first person to combine traditional punching and kicking styles going into grappling, he was a smart individual.

Q: Do you think he proved that a smaller guy can overcome a bigger adversary in a fight?
Rorion Gracie: I think not only Bruce Lee proved that, but my father also proved that.

Q: Why do you think Bruce Lee is so popular to this date?
Rorion Gracie: Bruce Lee reached the point of becoming very popular because he was able to place the martial arts in the movies, and that created a certain special image. And he was ahead of his time. He's going to be remembered by many people for many years to come.

CHAPTER SEVEN

THE MOVIE LEGACY

Since Bruce Lee's untimely death, his influence has filtered into the upper echelons of the filmmaking elite. One of the most significant contributions Bruce Lee made is that he opened the door for other Asians in the entertainment industry. And there is no doubt Bruce Lee's maverick, pioneering drive opened the doors for other action stars of our time: Jackie Chan, Jean Claude Van Damme, Steven Seagal, Dolph Lundgren, Sylvester Stallone. These stars no doubt share a commonality with Lee parallel to being exciting action film stars the public enjoys watching. With great respect, Bruce Lee transcends them all because of his chemistry, charisma and unique image which has never been replicated on screen since. It's amusing when someone starts to compare any other action star with Bruce Lee. Lee is clearly in another league; a league in which only iconic legends deserve to be in, who are unlikely to be duplicated.

"Somebody always comes along with a different style, a different idea…there was John Wayne then Clint Eastwood, and that's the way it works. But you don't replace somebody like Bruce Lee," states Enter the Dragon producer Fred Weintraub. The profound influence Lee had on world cinema and the martial arts genre is unparalleled.Today, Lee's impact in Hollywood is readily apparent. Some of the elite personalities in the Hollywood community who have been influenced positively by him include award-winning directors like Quentin Tarantino, John Woo, Brett Rattner (Rush Hour) and actors such as Nicolas Cage and John Travolta.

In his 32 years, Bruce Lee lived a fuller life than many who live twice as long. It's extraordinary that, in the space of only two years, someone could have such a huge effect on millions of people around the world, and continue to do so more than 35 years after his death. His movies are still loved and enjoyed by millions of old and new generations, and have been dubbed as 'electrifying' and 'exceptional' by critics.

Had it not been for Bruce Lee's movies in the early 1970s, it is arguable whether or not the martial arts film genre would have ever penetrated and influenced mainstream Western cinema and audiences the way it has. More than 30 years after his death, controversial Hollywood director Quentin Tarantino's Kill Bill made a 20th century statement about the enduring legacy of Bruce Lee and the martial arts action genre. This proved to be a landmark film in mainstream martial arts action, which once again catapulted Lee's legacy to the forefront of mainstream moviegoers across the world.

Most importantly, we are left with his films and the magic he was able to create in his movies, which will most probably never be surpassed and which will forever mesmerize audiences and keep startling the generations to come. In this section, you will be treated to exclusive interviews with some major action stars and directors from the motion picture industry, paying homage to the one and only Bruce Lee.

DOLPH LUNDGREN

Dolph Lundgren belongs to a generation of film actors who epitomize the movie action hero including Arnold Schwarzenegger, Sylvester Stallone, Steven Seagal and Jean Claude Van Damme. He grew up in Stockholm, Sweden, and his idols included the late action movie star and martial arts legend Bruce Lee. A keen martial artist and iron-pumper, he is known for being one of top Hollywood action heroes. He has appeared in more than 40 films and continues to act and direct movies.

Q: Were you influenced by Bruce Lee?
Dolph Lundgren: Yeah, he did influence me. I started getting more into martial arts when I was younger, as a teenager. I saw couple of Bruce Lee movies. Like everybody else, I bought all the magazines and I read about him and his fighting art. Then I got involved in Kyushinkai Karate, which is Japanese. It emphasizes more physical force and it has a lot to do with weight training, full contact and breaking. So I got attracted to that, but Bruce Lee's definitely somebody I was influenced by.

Q: What made Bruce Lee stand out from his peers?
Dolph Lundgren: He was much shorter than everybody…I'm just kidding! He was somebody who I think had charisma as an actor. I didn't realize it at the time, but he had natural charisma. On screen he didn't do that much, he was very minimalistic and he relied on his expression and eyes, he didn't act a lot. He was very relaxed. So that's one thing. Secondly, he moved very well, he had good choreography for his fight scenes. And also I suppose because he died young, which added to the mystique of his character. He lives forever as a young man. Something that happened to James Dean and a few other people like Elvis.

Q: Do you feel Bruce Lee represented the American dream and lead the way for today's action movie stars?
Dolph Lundgren: He represented martial arts driven action stars. There were a lot of action stars before him like Robert Mitchum and Kirk Douglas - Spartacus and Ben Hur - Humphrey Bogart, but he was the first Oriental martial arts superstar. I guess to some extent I'm martial arts driven but not as much as some other actors such as Steven Seagal and Jean Claude Van Damme, who are more martial arts driven than I have been. I've done martial arts in films but not a whole lot.

Q: You read about him when growing up. How do you view Bruce Lee's martial arts skills outside the scope of movies?
Dolph Lundgren: Yes, I did read about it, it was interesting to me because he did all styles and he wanted to mix up all styles, which nowadays people do 40 years later. They mix Boxing, Wrestling, Karate, Kickboxing. Everything's mixed martial arts and he started that 40 years ago in the 60s and early 70s. In those days you were strict; I only did KyushinKai Karate which was sort of a very regimental Japanese style. So he was different, a lot different to me but I still read about him a lot.

Q: Can you differentiate the fight choreography in his movies and compare it to today's martial arts action sequences?
Dolph Lundgren: I think his choreography was new. When he made those films in Hong Kong, he brought some of the Hong Kong fight choreography to Hollywood before Hong Kong movies became in fashion, which was 20 years later with John Woo and all the others. His choreography was very flashy and spectacular. There were a lot of techniques thrown, a lot of kicks and a lot of punches, whereas traditional fight choreography in those days leaned more towards the Westerns, a couple of punches and maybe a kick to the head or something. He did a lot of flashy stuff, charismatic flashy moves. I think everybody was influenced by Bruce Lee.

Q: Tell me of your experience of working with Brandon Lee.
Dolph Lundgren: Yeah. It was a good experience, he was a nice kid, very talented and very dedicated. He was going to be a big star had he lived. We got along very well. He did mention he was training with a sword when he was a kid. I believe his father died when Brandon was really young. I worked with Brandon in 1992, so he was only eight years old when his father died. Obviously, Brandon idolized his father, I mean, who wouldn't have? Obviously, he was following in his father's footsteps and he did. Then, of course, it was really sad of what happened, very sad.

Q: What is your favorite Bruce Lee movie and why?
Dolph Lundgren: (Pause) Enter the Dragon I think is the best one I like, the classy one on the island.

Q: Bruce Lee died at the pinnacle of his success. Had he lived where do you think his career would have taken him?
Dolph Lundgren: He was born in 1940, so he would have been 68 years old now. I don't know what he would have been doing but he would have been a big star, huge star probably! God knows where his career would have gone, you know. He did a lot for the Orientals.

JOHN WOO

John Woo is the critically acclaimed action movie director whose masterpieces include Face/Off, Broken Arrow, Mission Impossible II and Van Damme's Hard Target. Mr. Woo started working in the film industry in 1969, and later made his directorial debut in 1974 with The Young Dragons. He proudly states how much of an impact Bruce Lee had on him and his work and calls Bruce Lee his hero. He continues to work out of Hollywood and South East Asia.

Q: You were working in Hong Kong in the early years, when the Bruce Lee phenomenon was happening. How did Bruce Lee influence you?

John Woo: Bruce Lee in my time was a hero. I mean, he still is my hero. We admire him so much, he was so amazing in what he had done for the movies. His image is so strong and so fresh and so convincing, he was like James Dean and Elvis Presley. He had changed the whole Chinese movie look. Whatever he did on the screen, he did it for us and he spoke for us, and let the whole world know we not weak anymore, we are strong.

We also like his philosophy, and his performance really had made a change and also had given us a lot of inspiration. Before him the action in Chinese movies was so different and so tender. Then after his movies everybody changed and we all started to go for the powerful action. I'm sure you can see a lot of imitations where a lot of people tried to imitate the way he kicked, punched and the way he acted. For myself, the day he died was when I was directing my first movie in 1973. My first movie The Young Dragon was also a Kung Fu movie, and the stunt coordinator was Jackie Chan and Corey Yuen. We also had imitated Bruce Lee's actions in my film, like the turning and the side kick - a little bit like Bruce Lee. He was a very influential filmmaker. He gave us something which told us to be brave and to make a change. I would say he was an inspirational power and we were so proud to have him in our movie world.

Q: Do you feel Bruce Lee opened the doors for Asian actors and directors, who later broke into Hollywood?
John Woo: Yes, I believe in that. After Bruce Lee we were able to have such a great opportunity to draw so much attention, especially from Hollywood. He did open the door. The people around the world really started to pay attention on the Chinese action movies, and the talent.

Q: How popular was Bruce Lee in South East Asia?
John Woo: He was extremely popular in all of Asia, not only in Hong Kong and Chinese areas but he was extremely popular in Japan, even though in some of the Bruce Lee movies he beats up the Japanese fighters; but they really admire him and love him. He became a huge, huge star in Japan, Korea and everywhere in Asia. And after he died, he also became so much popular in the United States and Europe. I think he was the first one to really make it as an international Chinese star at the time.

Q: Why do you think Bruce Lee movies are so popular to this day?
John Woo: Because we couldn't find another Bruce Lee, even though we have Jackie Chan and Jet Li, who are doing some great things, but Bruce Lee was different. I think no one can do the things that Bruce Lee did and the way he did them. And he had charisma. Some of the popular action stars have to go a long way - throw so many punches and kicks - to create great action, but Bruce could use only one punch and one kick, that was enough to accomplish this. We could believe what he did and the power he had, he was so powerful. Also, he had screen presence and a lot of charisma. It doesn't happen with the other stars. He is like James Dean. There's only one James Dean in the world, it's hard to find someone who could compare with him.

Q: Bruce Lee changed the production values in Chinese films and transformed it. Did Bruce Lee take it to another level with a frame of mind, determination and style never seen before?
John Woo: Yes, before Bruce Lee, even though we had a popular action star and director it was very hard to open the international market, the movies were only watched in Asian counties. So when Bruce Lee appeared he appealed to so much audience on an international level and was able to break into the market. A lot of people started to notice Hong Kong Chinese movies, he was really the one to open up the Hong Kong film market.

Q: From a director's perspective, what are your views on Bruce Lee the director and his directorial debut Way of the Dragon?
John Woo: I think that was really Bruce Lee's movie. Some people think Bruce Lee was only a very powerful action star and so charming, but actually he was also a very funny guy. He had a very good sense of humor. I mean, a lot of the times he was so serious, but in Way of the Dragon he really had proved himself. He was a very interesting and funny guy on screen, and this made his character more likeable and the audience could have fun with him. In some of the scenes he acted a little bit like Jerry Lewis (Laughs), which was very rare in Hong Kong action movies because they were pretty serious. But Bruce Lee placed a sense of humor in his film.

I really enjoyed watching the final fight, Bruce Lee fighting with Chuck Norris in the Roman stadium. In other action movies when the good guy and the bad guy fight there's no atmosphere, or how you are feeling and expressing your emotions. But in Way of the Dragon there was so much warrior spirit and excitement, you could feel it was the real deal. They looked so calm and eloquent, and really had shown another great attention. When they fight, even though the fight was so beautiful, so intense and so brilliant, they both also respect each other and that was very unusual in the action movies. After Bruce Lee beat Chuck Norris, he also gave a lot of great respect to him.

Q: You have worked with many action stars in Hong Kong and Hollywood, what sets Bruce Lee apart?
John Woo: I've worked with Jackie Chan, Chow Yun Fat, also Van Damme, John Travolta and even Tom Cruise. I think every actor I worked with all have a different kind of charisma, unlike Bruce Lee. Bruce Lee had such a power, not only in action but also in performance. Some actors don't have both elements. When I worked with Chow Yun Fat and Tom Cruise, I also wanted to get some of the best choreography on screen. And also make it tremendous and skilful.

When working on Mission Impossible II, I found out Tom Cruise was very interested in Bruce Lee - you can see in the final scene - he also asked to do some of Bruce Lee's actions. So I decided to use some of Bruce Lee's side kick and Kung Fu movements for Tom Cruise. For me, that shows what kind of inspiration Bruce Lee was to actors; they all remember and love Bruce Lee. Nicolas Cage and Tom Cruise both love Bruce Lee. Originally in M-II for the final battle we decided to film an eloquent scene. I heard John Travolta also likes Bruce Lee movies, and he also admires him as a great actor. When we talked about Bruce Lee we didn't usually say he was a great action star, but he was such a great actor. So we admire him as a great actor.

JEAN CLAUDE VAN DAMME

Jean Claude Van Damme was one of the biggest box office draws of the early and mid-90s. Born in Brussels, Belgium, the young Van Damme moved to Southern California in 1981 in pursuit of becoming a movie star. Van Damme thrilled movie audiences with his trademark helicopter kicks and quickly secured himself as one of the biggest action stars in the world. In this very rare and exclusive interview Van Damme explains the profound influence Bruce Lee had on him.

Q: Did Bruce Lee inspire you when you were growing up? Please tell me what your first impression was the first time you saw him on screen.

Jean Claude Van Damme: Bruce Lee is a one of a kind true legion!! He played a major role in my growing up years. His will and determination motivated me in such a tremendous way to a point that I knew if I wanted to be the next action hero I had to follow his path of wisdom, mental power and strength, and his wonderful side of sense of humor and charm. So every time I knew there was going to be a Bruce Lee Week on TV, I was ready and waiting anxiously in front of my small TV set.

Q: Did you try to model yourself on him in any way when your movie career kicked off?

Jean Claude Van Damme: I tried to do my best in the way Van Damme could be. No one is ever perfect. But I do hope that many of my fans that have stayed loyal will and can understand this. This (entertainment) is a very high demanding business. But I love it!

Q: Do you feel Bruce Lee opened the doors for future action stars and set some kind of a benchmark?

Jean Claude Van Damme: Yes. Look at the list: Chuck Norris, Arnold Schwarzenegger, Sylvester Stallone, Bruce Willis, Steven Seagal, Brandon Lee...and the list will still go on...

Q: How would you describe Bruce Lee as a martial artist and athlete?
Jean Claude Van Damme: Bruce Lee! There will only be one Bruce Lee - The King of Martial Arts and a true athlete.

Q: You became well known for an admirable physique. Did his physique have any influence on you?
Jean Claude Van Damme: Bruce Lee's physique is amazing and, yes, looking at him always to this day motivates me to continue at my age to feel great and young at heart.

Q: How would you differentiate between Bruce Lee's fight choreography compared to the modern day?
Jean Claude Van Damme: Bruce Lee's technique will always be 'his' no matter what. I have been motivated by him, but I have my own and many others as well.

Q: Your thoughts on the greatest martial arts movie Enter the Dragon?
Jean Claude Van Damme: I love Enter the Dragon !! Full of action and, of course, love. Bruce had a way with women.

APPENDIX
THE TED THOMAS INTERVIEW

Bruce Lee was known to be a charming, thoughtful and very articulate interviewee. Hong Kong-based British journalist Ted Thomas was one of the first Westerners to interview the Little Dragon just after he smashed the box office with his first Chinese-language movie Big Boss. This interview was conducted in 1971 for a radio station.

Q: Bruce, as a screen tough guy you are going to have to suffer what all movie heroes suffered: challenges from exhibitionists and nuts asking you to fight, challenging you to fight. It's already happened, hasn't it?
Bruce Lee: Yes, it has.

Q: How do you deal with it?
Bruce Lee: When I first learned martial arts, I too challenged many established instructors and, of course, some others challenged me also. What I have learned is challenging means one thing: what is your reaction to it? How does it get to you? Now, if you are secure within yourself, you treat it very, very lightly because you ask yourself: am I really afraid of this man, or do I have any doubt this man's really going to get me? I do not have such doubt. And if I have no such feeling, I would certainly treat it very lightly. Just as today the rain is going on strong, tomorrow, baby, the sun's going to come out again. It's that kind of a thing.

Q: Of course, they can't lose by challenging you. Even if they lose they get the publicity of being the guy who actually challenged you!
Bruce Lee: Let's face it, in Hong Kong can you have a fight? I mean, no holds barred fight. Is it a legal thing? It isn't, is it? To me, you see, a lot of things like challenging, I'm the last to know. I am always the last to know. I always find out from newspapers and reporters before I personally realize what the hell is happening.

Q: Bruce, you were teaching martial arts in the States, and two of your students were Steve McQueen and James Coburn. Did you find

them (to be) tough people the way they are portrayed on the screen?
Bruce Lee: First of all, James Coburn definitely is not a fighter, lover yes.
I mean, he's really a super nice guy. Not only that, he's a very peaceful
man. He learned martial art because he finds that it is a very...it is like a
mirror to reflect himself. I personally believe that all type of knowledge -
I don't care what it is - ultimately means self-knowledge, and that's what
it means. And that's what he is. Steve is very uptight. Steve is very high-
strung. Steve could be a very good martial artist. But I hope that martial
arts would cool him a little bit and make him a bit mellower and be more
peaceful like Jim (Laughs).

**Q: Did he achieve that this time with you? Did you feel that perhaps
he learned something from you?**
Bruce Lee: Definitely not yet. But because of his shooting schedule, he
cannot have it on a regular basis. And secondly, he is still on the level
where he's enjoying it, as an excitement like his motorcycles and sports
cars, sort of a release of his anger, whatever you want to name it.

**Q: Bruce, how much of your screen personality is really you? I mean,
you teach martial arts and you're good at it, but teachers are not
always the best exponents or practitioners. Are you able to take care
of yourself, would you say?**
Bruce Lee: I will answer this first of all with a joke, if you don't mind.
All the time people come up to me and say, "Hey, Bruce, are you really
that good?" I say, "Well, if I say I'm good, probably you'll think I'm
boasting. If I tell you I'm no good you'll know I'm lying." Going back
to be truthful to you, let's just put it this way: I have no fear of an
opponent in front of me. I'm very self-sufficient, they do not bother
me. And that should I fight or do anything, I have made up my mind,
that's it, baby, you better kill me before...

**Q: Bruce, in Big Boss you play a man who is very slow to anger; he's
shy, diffident and you even stay out of the fights in the early scenes
because of the promise you made to your mother. Is that a little bit like
you or is it a screen personality?**
Bruce Lee: This is definitely a screen personality. Because as a person, one
thing I have definitely learned in my life is a life of self-examination and
self-appealing, bit by bit, day by day. I do have a bad temper, a violent
temper in fact (Laughs). So that is definitely some person that I'm
portraying, not Bruce Lee as he is.

**Q: As well as being an exceptionally successful film in terms of
finance, it grossed more than any other pictures done in Hong Kong,**

Big Boss does show some very explicit sex scenes, doesn't it? What's your reaction to being in bed with a lovely young movie star in front of the whole studio crew? Does it intimidate you, does it worry you?

Bruce Lee: It certainly would not intimidate me, I can tell you that (Laughs). Well, it's all right as long as the script justifies it. But I definitely do not agree to put something just for the heck of it because it is an exploitation. First instance, when I first started shooting Big Boss the first question asked was, "Hey, man, how many thousands of feet...of film...my English is getting terrible now (Laughs).

Q: (Laughs).

Bruce Lee: ...is it going to be. My reaction first of all was: why do I start fighting? You see what I'm saying now?

Q: Motivation!

Bruce Lee: Oh, definitely! I mean, it seems to be the thing now where they (producers) go for blood and sex, just for the sake of sex and blood.

Q: May I ask you a question, which has been puzzling me since I saw the film? At the stage where you decide you're going to get revenge, and obviously leading up to the fight you suddenly decide to go and make love to your girlfriend at the bordello, what's the motivation for that?

Bruce Lee: The way I look at that is this was the suggestion of the director, and I accepted. In such a way that is (the character) being a very simple man, when all of a sudden he's made up his mind that he's going to go and either die, either kill or be killed, right? So, he walks past and it's a kind of a sudden thing for human beings. A thought just occurs; such is a basic need of a human being. I might as well enjoy it before I kick the bucket. That kind of an attitude. I mean, it's just an occurrence.

Q: I think you probably agree, Bruce, that the thing that's limited the appeal of the Chinese films to Western audiences is that it's very unusual to find a Chinese actor who can act, and when I say this, I mean act in a Western style, a manner in that would make non-Chinese to pay money to see the film. You seem to have crossed that barrier. How do you think you've achieved it? You think it has to do with your time in the United States, you studied there?

Bruce Lee: Yes, it definitely has. Because when I first arrived I did the Green Hornet television series, back in 66. As I looked around I saw a lot of human beings (Laughs), as I looked at myself I was the only robot there. Because I was not being myself. And I'm trying to accumulate external security, external techniques, the way I move my arm...but never to ask and say what Bruce Lee would have done, if such anything happened to me. When I look around I always learn something, and that is to always be yourself and to express yourself, to have faith in yourself. Do not go out and look for a successful personality and duplicate him. Now it seems to me that is the prevalent thing happening in Hong Kong. Like they always copy mannerism. But they never start from the very root of his being, that is: how can I be me?

You see, I never believed the word star, that's an illusion, man. I mean, that's something the public calls you. And when you become successful, when you become famous, it is very, very easily to be blinded by all these happenings. Everybody comes up to you (saying), "Mr. Lee!" When you have long hair, they will say, "Hey, that's 'in', man, that's the 'in' thing." But if you have no 'name' they will say, "Look at him, what a disgusting juvenile delinquent." I mean, too many people say yes, yes, yes to you all the time. So unless you've done a lot and understand what life's about, and right now some 'game's' happening and (you) realize such thing is a game, then that is all right. But most people tend to be blinded by it. I mean, if things are repeated too many times you believe in them and it becomes habit.

Q: The danger is believing the public impression of you. Your father warned you about the bad things in show business, have you met them too? Apart from the illusion, you seem to have come through it remarkably well.
Bruce Lee: Well, let me put it this way, to be honest and all that, I'm not as bad as some of them. But I'm definitely not saying I am a saint (Laughs).

Q: Could we go back to the fighting, because like it or not, it's the thing that you're mainly identified with at this moment? There's a number of styles of fighting, Karate, Judo, Chinese Boxing and a question you may have been asked hundreds of times before: which do you think is the most effective?
Bruce Lee: You see, my answer to this, there is no such thing as an effective segment of a totality. By that I mean, I personally don't believe in the word style. Unless human beings have three arms and four legs, unless we have other group of beings on earth that are structurally different from us, then there might be a different style of fighting. Now, why is that? We have two hands and two legs, the important thing is how can we use it to the maximum in terms of path: straight line, curved line, round lines. They might be slow, depending on the circumstances, sometimes fat might not be slow. And in terms of legs, you can kick up straight, same thing.

Physically, how can I be so well coordinated? That means you have to be an athlete, you've got to do jogging, and all these basic ingredients. And after all that, you ask yourself how can you honestly express yourself at that moment and be yourself? When you punch, you want to punch and not because you want to avoid getting hit, but really be with it and express yourself. Now, that to me is the thing...how can I in the process of learning how to use my body understand myself?

The unfortunate thing is now there's Boxing that uses hands, Judo uses throwing. I'm not putting them down but I'm saying one thing, which is the bad thing, because of styles people are separated, they are not united together because styles became law. But the original founder of the style...now it has become the gospel truth. People who go into them become the proud owner. It doesn't matter how you are, who you are, how you are structured, how you are built, how you are made - it doesn't matter. You just go in there and be the product and that, to me, isn't right.

APPENDIX
THE DAN LEE CONVERSATION

Dan Lee was one of Bruce Lee's top students from the Los Angeles Chinatown period. In this phone conversation - which took place in April 1972 - Bruce and Dan talk about martial arts and movies, Bruce updating his friend and disciple on his first two movies. Bruce would always try to keep in touch with his close friends and disciples after he left for Hong Kong. Although he did this through the medium of the written word, he would occasionally call them informing of his progress.

Bruce Lee: You saw the Tai Chi Self Defense?

Dan Lee: Yeah.

Bruce: Well, Dan, I hate to tell you this. If you were there you would have seen all the foreign trend, sitting next to us watching all that fake. Jesus, you will be so embarrassed.

Dan: Yeah, it's a free brawl.

Bruce: No, it's not even a free brawl. To be a free brawl, it would at least be like that Joe Frazier. Now, there's a man who is capable of using his tools and who is very determined in a savage legless attack. When those sons of a bitches are cowards, turning their heads when they swing their punch, and after the second round they are out of breath. They're really pathetic looking, very, very amateurish. I mean, even Boxers, they concentrate on two hands, regardless of how amateurish they are they do their thing. But whereas most guys go out there and haven't decided what the hell they're going to use. Before they contact each other, they do all the fancy stance and fancy movements, but the minute they contact they just don't know what the hell to do. I mean, that's it. They're stiff and fall on their ass, and they hug, hold and grapple. In Hong Kong, even those guys see it that way. I mean, what do you think of the appreciation of the people here? So what I'm hoping to do with film is to be just that, man, to raise the level.

Dan: A real mission there?

Bruce: It is, really.

Dan: Yeah, I mean, it upgrades the respect from the Western world.

Bruce: That's what I hope to do, man. The reason I'm coming back is

Warner Brothers wants me to do a television series, but I don't think I'll do it now. I'm going to concentrate on Hong Kong and do it.

Dan: Yeah.

Bruce: And naturally, I might be able to expand it to here, like the Italian picture A Fistful of Dollars and things like that, if the quality can be uplifted. More and more it's becoming more simple as a human being, and the more I search myself. More and more the questions are more lifted and more and more I see clearly, you know?

Dan: It's really the simplicity.

Bruce: It is. It really is, man. You see, what man has to get over is the consciousness of self.

Dan: I always remember that you used to say that you have to sharpen up your tools in order to make them work properly.

Bruce: That's it, you see. If you can move with your tools from any angle then you can adapt to whatever the object is in front of you.

Dan: That's right.

Bruce: And the clumsier, the more limited the object is the easier for you to punch on it. That's what it amounts to. What it is…it utilizes the body to come to some sort of a realization in regard of whatever your pursuit happens to be. In my case, it's the pursuit of becoming moment to moment, whatever that thing is and constantly questioning myself, you know? "What is it, Bruce? Is it true or is it not true? Do you really mean it or not mean it?" Once I find out, that's it. My coming back to refuse the television series is one of the main conversations (Laughs).

Dan: That's right. You come to the point where it's quite philosophical where you can see the ultimate goal.

Bruce: I haven't as yet been able to control my anger (Laughs). I have a violent anger.

Dan: This comes with age (Laughs).

Bruce: Well, it's not only that. If I just give myself the time to just stop for a few minutes - I will be able to control it. But unfortunately, like someone does me instead of going to a newspaper or walks up to me and slaps me. That's the end of him (Laughs). I have yet been able to turn the other cheek, man (Laughs).

Dan: Even years ago you used to say pick the time.

Bruce: Pick the time, pick the time. I wouldn't even say anything. I would just show up right in front of his door waiting for him. That's all there is to it. I have yet to refuse a challenge ever since I was in the United States. Wong Jack Man and all these bullshit artists, all of them. I just accept it, you know.

Dan: Yeah.

Bruce: First question I ask myself is: do I have any fear or any doubt about this man? I don't. Do I know what his intention is? Yes, I do. So what the hell are you going to do about it? Nothing (Laughs). That's it. It takes a hell of a lot for me not to do anything than to do something.

Dan: It's actually a process of maturity.

Bruce: Not maturity. There is no such word as maturity. Maturing.

Dan: Maturing?

Bruce: Damn right, man. Because when there is maturity, there is a conclusion, that's the end, that's when the coffin is closed (Laughs). You might be deteriorating physically in the long process of aging but your discovery daily is still the very same every day. Where there is a way, there lies the limitation, a circumference, a trap that rots. When it rots it's lifeless.

Dan: It has made a great impact though in my training. In my thinking of martial arts as a whole. I mean, once you've talked and worked with you, you would never go back to Kenpo. Do you reach another level of understanding?

Bruce: It's like man, you know, he's constantly growing. And when he is bound by a set pattern of ideas or way of doing things, that's when he's stopped growing.

Dan: That's right.

Bruce: Well, I'm lucky. That's about it.

Dan: Well, you have influenced many people in terms of freedom from their original boundaries.

Bruce: Well, I hope so.

Dan: Danny (Inosanto) was all excited all over yesterday.

Bruce: Yeah, he was at my house the night before.

Dan: He was really turned on (Laughs). He doesn't want us to do any more heavy bag kicking, he wants us to kick at something light.

Bruce: When you use your leg it's much better to kick at the foam pad or something like that.

Dan: Yeah.

Bruce: Watch out for the side kick on air kicking too much because it's bad for the knee.

Dan: It's kind of dangerous, yeah?

Bruce: Well, if you snap it too much without contact at the end you know you can get hurt. Well, just think of economical moves.

Dan: Yeah. There's the Kickboxing Association right on Hollywood Boulevard. You have to go and see it.

Bruce: They have Kickboxing. I saw it in Thailand personally. The bantamweight champion was one of the stuntmen.

Dan: Yeah.

Bruce: Well, the problem with them is that they are John L. Sullivan with their legs (Laughs). I mean, they have no finesse. Nothing.

Dan: No. They hurt the thigh and they try and make the other to

completely give up.
Bruce: Well, not all of them do that. You can do that when you are stationary, but not when you're constantly moving.
Dan: I hear the Japanese have incorporated the sweeping kick on the Thailand high kick. The moment they high kick, the Japanese move in and sweep the foot away. Thai have real trouble with their balance because they kick too high.
Bruce: That's right, and because they're too obvious. That's the whole deal, you see. There is no suddenness, no economy.
Dan: No broken rhythm either, you can see it coming.
Bruce: That's right - John L. Sullivan. That's why 80 percent of the knockouts are done by hand.
Dan: ...that Chandler? Guy..
Bruce: No, you put him in the ring, the Boxer would just hit on him.
Dan: Right.
Bruce: OK, Dan, I'm packing right now.
Dan: Yeah, I know that you're busy. I just wanted to get the chance to say hello to you.
Bruce: Thank you. I'm glad to hear your voice again. I'm selling my house, you know?
Dan: Yeah, Danny told me. Anything you want me to help with, clean...let me know?
Bruce: Thank you. Well, this time I'm getting in the men. Too much trouble, I'll just let them do it. Right now I'm just sorting out what I need. I'm going to bring some of my books, some of my clothes, that's about it.
Dan: Yeah. Are you going to store things?
Bruce: Yeah.
Dan: And when are you coming back?
Bruce: Well, depending on how the film situation is. If it is good then I'm going to be buying another house.
Dan: Actually, I think whatever you do over there will have a tremendous impact on your work over here.
Bruce: Well, depending on how the quality is going to be. I mean, I'm not talking about myself alone, but directing, budget wise, cinematographer wise, a lot of things, lighting, everything.
Dan: Do you think the Hong Kong films are up to standard?
Bruce: Not really, but they can be.
Dan: Considering the manpower and the films.
Bruce: It's the Hollywood of China, you see.
Dan: They make more films sometimes in a year than in Hollywood over here.
Bruce: That's about it, you know.
Dan: In Big Boss you speak Cantonese, right?

Bruce: Yep.

Dan: Then what do they do?

Bruce: They just dub it all for the Mandarin picture. All of them.

Dan: Will they be coming over here sometime?

Bruce: They will be but I don't know when, because like I told you of the tremendous success, they are really holding it back. Trying to get the best deal they can and are trying to distribute it. Rank in England are trying to distribute it all over England. I don't know how the deal came about. I opened a film company recently called Concord. My partner (Raymond Chow) is coming over next week so I'll find out more about it then.

Dan: I see, good. Well, we're eagerly awaiting for these films to be here.

Bruce: I think you will like it. (some words spoken in Cantonese)...I died afterwards.

Dan: That's the historical figure?

Bruce: No, I'm FOK Kap's student not FOK Kap himself. That is more interesting because FOK Kap is sort of limited, because you know, we gotta follow how the history goes. So I'm actually portraying his student.

Dan: His student?

Bruce: Yeah. There are some things, I fought with the Japanese and the Russian and all that, just like FOK Kap. The fight scenes are really tremendous. I mean, I like them myself. I enjoyed them so the regular people should really take to them.

Dan: Do they all fight in their own style like the Russian Wrestler?

Bruce: The Russian fights like Karate and all these things - Boxing, Wrestling, everything all together. I bite him and everything (Laughs). The Chinese are not allowed in the park and all that - remember?

Dan: Yeah, I know the history.

Bruce: Well, exactly. At the end I died under the gunfire. But it's a very worthwhile death because it's a big moment - for the Chinese and all that. I walk out and say fuck you man! Here I come! I leap up into the air and they stop the frame - 'bang, bang'! Like in Butch Cassidy and the Sundance Kid.

Dan: Yeah.

Bruce: Except they stop the frame so I'm in the middle of the air.

Dan: Yeah, it's a very honorable end.

Bruce: Yeah, according to the Chinese people (Laughs), and the audience do eat it up. Boy, you should see the filmgoers in Hong Kong. They are very, very…they're too much (Laughs). When they don't like it, they will say (Bruce talks in Cantonese). When they do like it, they clap their hands.

Dan: They clap their hands?

Bruce: Yeah, that's what it is.

Dan: Well, I think you're going to have more and more films coming

up in that theme idea and more higher...?

Bruce: In fact, for the third film I am going to Europe to film it. It's about a Chinese, you know, who doesn't know how to speak English, somewhere in a Western country. Where he carries ancient weapons and darts and all that. The fourth one is going to be very much like The Silent Flute except it's not, you know, where it shows how man started off, you know? You will see it in the future. I mean, it's very beautiful and entertaining as well.

Dan: I heard there's a film being done over here about Chinese Kung Fu and all that?

Bruce: Yeah, but it's a television deal.

Dan: Television deal - Kung Fu?

Bruce: Yeah, it's called Kung Fu and I was supposed to do it. But the network decided against it and Warners wants me to be in another television series. I'm glad they decided against it (Laughs), because if not, I would have been tied up this year (1972).

Dan: They're shooting it?

Bruce: Yeah.

Dan: Well, when you come back and do another good series.

Bruce: Television is really, I mean, ah…

Dan: A one-shot job.

Bruce: Yeah, you look at all the television series, right. I mean, all of them are gimmicks and shallowly treated. You look at Ironside. It's all fast money, not like a film where you can put a few months into it and work on it. But not television, man, it's gotta finish in one week and how can you keep up the quality every week?

Dan: Yeah.

Bruce: And people get tired of it. It's not that bad, you know what I mean, Dan - It's my personality.

Dan: You want to actually get deeply into it and the quality - make it right?

Bruce: That's right. You know, money comes second.

Dan: That's right.

Bruce: That's why I did ban all the schools of JKD because it is very easy for a member to come in and take the agenda as the truth and...as 'the way', you know what I mean?

Dan: I think you have to pick a few ones so that our true diehard followers that don't go out and teach JKD.

Bruce: That's why I tell Dan to be careful in selecting more students. You should help him in that area.

Dan: Yeah, you can rest on me. I've been working with Dan a lot.

Bruce: Great.

Dan: We're really close together.

Bruce: Great. Dan…I told him last time that he's becoming very stylized. All the preparation before kicking and it seems like his consciousness is really bothering him. Something is bugging him, you know what I mean?

Dan: Yeah. Well, I think his heavy bag kicking, too much heavy bag kicking has affected him. It's got too much body twisting instead of just going right through. Instead of 'boom'!

Bruce: Yeah, and then get the power and momentum and the preparation right out, because you can kick a heavy bag that way but you cannot kick an opponent that way.

Dan: Yeah. The instep...he was checking it because his toe was touching first instead of flat. But he's working on it real hard and he sort of had a taste of it. We're trying not too much heavy bag, rather get the suddenness of movement and just feel and work on it.

Bruce: Yeah...so…

Dan: Well, before you leave. Have you got any training session or something?

Bruce: Training! How? Because I'm so goddamn busy (Laughs).Well, anyway…

Dan: I wanna see you personally too (Laughs).

Bruce: OK, man...let's see now…

Dan: It'll be another year until you come back.

Bruce: Yeah, anyway I have your phone number. So if anything should happen I'll give you a call.

Dan: OK, if you come over for just a few minutes it'll be satisfying.

Bruce: OK, Dan. Great!

Dan: Good talking to you, Bruce.

Bruce: Same to you, Dan.

Dan: Well, take care now.

Bruce: Thanks for calling.

Dan: You're welcome, Bruce.

Bruce: Thank you.

Dan: Bye-bye

ABOUT THE AUTHOR

Fiaz Rafiq is a major columnist for the bestselling martial arts magazine *Martial Arts Illustrated* and a major contributor to *Impact: The Global Action Movie Magazine*. He is a biographer of two of the most influential and popular icons of the century Bruce Lee and Muhammad Ali; author of the critically acclaimed biographies *Bruce Lee: Conversations* and *Muhammad Ali: Conversations*.

His work as a journalist has appeared in magazines in the United States, United Kingdom, France, Germany and Australia. Rafiq has also written for major mainstream magazine *Men's Fitness* and contributed to *The Sun's* UFC coverage. He is also the author of *Ultimate Conversations*. A passionate Bruce Lee historian, he contributed to the official Bruce Lee documentary *How Bruce Lee Changed the World*.

Author on Bruce Lee's Hollywood Walk of Fame star.

Rafiq is the founder and director of HNL Media Group and publisher of HNL Publishing, a company dedicated to publishing sports-related books for the international market. HNL has published a *New York Times* Bestseller and various books have received mainstream coverage. He was one of the co-executive producers of *Sensei*, the movie directed by Bruce Lee's goddaughter Diana Lee Inosanto. Rafiq's diverse career has also seen him appear as a background artist in TV shows and movies. His qualification in Close Protection also lead to work in security.

Having had a lifelong passion for the martial arts and being profoundly influenced by the late Bruce Lee since the tender age of ten, he pursued his passion by making several trips to Los Angeles to train with three of Bruce Lee's personal students, and also privately with UFC legend Royce Gracie. A publisher, acclaimed author and magazine columnist, Rafiq has interviewed some of the greatest Boxers, UFC fighters and professional bodybuilders in the world as well as numerous Hollywood actors.

NEW YORK TIMES BESTSELLER

RANDY COUTURE
with Loretta Hunt

MY LIFE
IN AND
OUT
OF THE
CAGE

BECOMING THE NATURAL

AVAILABLE FROM BOOKSTORES EVERYWHERE

EVERY WARRIOR MUST LEARN THE FINAL LESSON...

"A film that will change hearts and minds"

YOU HAVE A RIGHT TO DEFEND YOURSELF AGAINST HATRED

THE SENSEI

WWW.THESENSEI MOVIE.COM